POWER PARENTING
IN THE LDS HOME

AVOID THE **25** MOST COMMON **MISTAKES**

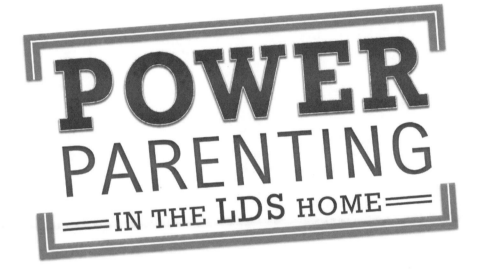

POWER
PARENTING
IN THE LDS HOME

RANDAL A. WRIGHT

CFI
An Imprint of Cedar Fort, Inc.
Springville, Utah

ISBN 13: 978-1-4621-1379-8

Published by CFI, an imprint of Cedar Fort, Inc., 2373 W. 700 S., Springville, UT 84663
Distributed by Cedar Fort, Inc., www.cedarfort.com

LIBRARY OF CONGRESS CATALOGING-IN-PUBLICATION DATA

Wright, Randal A., author.
Power parenting in the LDS home : avoid the 25 most common mistakes / Randal A. Wright.
   pages cm
ISBN 978-1-4621-1379-8
1. Mormon families. 2. Parenting--Religious aspects--Church of Jesus Christ of Latter-day Saints. I. Title.

BX8643.F3W75 2014
248.8'45088289332--dc23

2013033441

Cover design by Shawnda T. Craig
Cover design © 2014 Lyle Mortimer
Edited and typeset by Emily S. Chambers

Printed in the United States of America

10 9 8 7 6 5 4 3 2 1

Printed on acid-free paper

CONTENTS

INTRODUCTION
WHAT? ME, MAKE A MISTAKE?

A few years ago as a member of a bishopric, I was asked to accompany a group of scouts on a river rafting trip in the Texas hill country. We were to camp on a Friday night and then spend all day Saturday on the river. Upon arrival, three other adult leaders and I started setting up the tent we had borrowed. No instructions were included, but since our group consisted of two men holding master's degrees, one with a dental degree, and one with a PhD, we weren't worried. We soon discovered that the tent we had borrowed was undoubtedly defective. After all, if we couldn't figure out how to put it together, something must be wrong with it. We were somewhat puzzled, however, since all the pieces appeared to be included, and the tent looked almost new.

For the next two hours we tried everything possible to get that tent set up—without success. Finally, in total frustration, one of the leaders got out ropes and tied the tent off to several nearby trees. However, it hardly even resembled a tent. When the scouts came back from a short hike, they laughed and laughed at the mangled-looking thing draped between two trees. It was a very embarrassing situation for the leaders. While most of the boys slept out under the stars that night, the leaders decided to appear united and sleep in their makeshift tent. During the middle of the night, one side of the tent collapsed—on top of me. After crawling out, I attempted to sleep in my car the rest of the night. It was then that I saw another leader sleeping in the back of a pick-up truck. When morning dawned, we found ourselves miserable with aching backs and necks because of lack of sleep.

As we prepared to put the raft into the river, two college-aged girls drove up to a camping spot directly beside ours and unloaded several items from their car. I watched as they brought a fairly large tent out of the trunk. What a coincidence! The tent appeared to be exactly like the one we had borrowed. Shortly before they drove up, we had untied our tent from the trees and put it back in the van. I couldn't help but laugh to myself as we watched the girls prepare to assemble their tent—I knew something they didn't. Instead of telling the girls that the tent was defective and that they undoubtedly would not be able to assemble it, I decided to let them learn the hard way. I watched as they pulled out what looked like a little book of instructions. They studied it for a moment, then quickly organized the different pieces into groups. Clearly they had never put the tent up before, because they constantly looked back and forth at the instructions. Once the pieces were in place, they spread the tent out and within fifteen minutes had it completely put together and their camping gear moved in.

It was then that I realized there were no defective or missing parts in our borrowed tent. I was hoping we could leave before our scouts noticed the girls' identical tent, but it was too late. We took their taunts and teasing like men; however, because we were miserable from lack of sleep, we couldn't really enjoy the river trip. I found myself wishing that the girls had arrived prior to our tent problem so that we could have borrowed their instruction book. I have found over time that life goes a lot smoother when we have an instruction book to follow. I have also noticed over the years that it is the nature and disposition of most men to *not read* the instruction manual even when it is available.

Imagine for a moment that you arrive at a campsite with a borrowed tent and have been struggling for hours to figure out how to put it together without instructions. Then, two college-age girls camping next to your site see that you are struggling to put up your tent. They have an identical tent and have come over with the needed instructions in hand. They ask if you would like help putting up your tent. Which of the following would most closely reflect your response?

"No thank you, I want the experience of figuring this out on my own."

"Who do you girls think you are, interfering in my business?"

"You girls think you are so smart, don't you, with your college degrees, coming over here and telling me what I'm doing wrong?"

"Look, girls, this tent is my stewardship, not yours. You worry about your tent, and I'll worry about my tent!"

"Thank you so much. I would appreciate the help."

There are some definite advantages to listening to someone who has experience and a set of instructions to follow. Isn't it interesting that most are willing to listen to instructions from others as long as it is in regard to trivial things? For example, we would have no problem with help assembling tents or power point presentations or holding a tennis racket correctly. However, if suggestions come to us in the area of personal behavior or mistakes we made with our families, we usually act like the person has just declared war on us. Imagine, for example, that a member of your ward comes up to you and says:

- "I've noticed you have really put on a lot of weight lately. You do not look nearly as good as you once did. Did you know that too much weight can lead to heart disease? You are obviously making some serious mistakes. I feel inspired to share with you a proven diet and workout plan that I think will help with your problem."

- "I have noticed that you have been letting your fourteen-year-old daughter date. Did you realize that the prophets have spoken out against underage dating, and when youth date that young that they are much more likely to be immoral? I feel inspired to share several statements by the brethren on appropriate dating rules with you."

- "As I watch you deal with your young daughter, I notice that you never follow through with what you tell her you are going to do. Did you know that she is going to be spoiled rotten if you keep this up, and she won't believe a word you say? I just felt inspired to tell you that."

If someone approached us with any of the above examples, they'd be using fighting words. Many hold lifelong grudges against people who say anything that even resembles correction of our individual behavior or comments regarding our parenting. Yet, it may be that we really do need help with a healthier diet or information for better parenting. And it may be that our friend from the ward truly was inspired to share the message and is only trying to help.

Over the centuries, prophets have been given the unenviable assignment to point out mistakes that people are making and to teach them correct principles. Their role is similar to the ward member who tells us we're getting a little flabby and need to go on a diet. In your opinion, how have their teachings been received over time? Think, for example, of the reaction of King Noah's people when Abinadi came in and told them they were not living correctly and that they obeyed a wicked leader. Historically, very few people have listened to the prophet's counsel. Often people have reacted violently. What a lonely world the prophets have endured. And yet, these courageous men are not trying to win a popularity contest. President Ezra Taft Benson said, "A revealing characteristic of a true prophet is that he declares a message from God. He makes no apology for the message, nor does he fear for any social repercussions which may lead to derision and persecution."[1]

The scriptures and teachings of modern prophets are the instructions that are preserved to point out the errors we make while teaching us correct principles that will help us put up our family tents successfully. "And now, it has hitherto been wisdom in God that these things should be preserved; for behold they have enlarged the memory of this people, yea, and convinced many of the error of their ways, and brought them to the knowledge of their God unto the salvation of their souls" (Alma 37:8). Many, however, fail to follow the inspired counsel of the prophet's instruction books and have a terrible struggle trying to put together their individual and family tents.

Traditionally, very few people have been willing to follow prophets after they have been chastened. Most are furious and seek to cast them out of their lives or even kill them. There are some notable exceptions. What common trait or characteristic made men like King Lamoni, Zeezrom, Alma the Younger, the four sons of Mosiah, Corianton, Paul, Enos, and Joseph and Hyrum Smith humble and great? Each of them shared one thing in common. When they were rebuked, they admitted their mistakes and quickly turned their lives around afterward. Now think of characteristics that men like Oliver Cowdery, Sidney Rigdon, Lyman Wight, King Noah, Nehor, and Amalickiah have in common. I think it is safe to say that none of these men were willing to take correction from the prophets of their day. Maybe our lesson from them is that humble men and women accept inspired correction, while prideful men reject it.

I have always been completely impressed with Hyrum and Joseph Smith's humility in being rebuked and proceeding to change for the better. Joseph was rebuked on multiple occasions. "And now, verily I say unto Joseph Smith, Jun.—You have not kept the commandments, and must needs stand rebuked before the Lord" (D&C 93:47). How did Joseph respond to this chastisement? He corrected the mistakes he was making.

In Section 95 of the Doctrine and Covenants, the Lord rebuked the Saints for not building the temple. Consider the fact that in the year this revelation was given, only a handful of extremely poor members had received the assignment from the Lord a few months earlier. Many had walked away from their own comfortable homes and didn't even have a place to live at that time. How did the Saints take this reprimand? As history shows, some were offended, some ignored it, and some were humbled and accepted the reproof. As you read the following quote from Joseph Fielding Smith, remember that this revelation from the Lord was given on June 1, 1833: "My grandfather Hyrum Smith and Reynolds Cahoon commenced the digging of the trench for the foundation of the Kirtland Temple on the fifth day of June 1833."[2]

If the Lord were to give us a personal rebuke, what would be the reason? Would we then reject it, ignore it, or be like Hyrum and get our shovels out? What if the rebuke came from a member of the ward or one of our own children?

Our day is like no other in the history of the world. Think of the great changes in technology that have taken place. How much has changed from 1937 when President Thomas S. Monson was born until now? When I wrote my first book it was on an IBM typewriter. Now, I can sit on my couch and work on a notebook computer hooked up to a whole world of instant information on the Internet. How did we achieve this much progress during such a short period of time? It is obvious that researchers and engineers learned from past mistakes and studied better ways of doing things. In the world of technology, there is no place for a scientist who looks to the outmoded Commodore 64 as the end of the line for computers.

Consider now the progress made with the modern family during this same time period. We have universities with entire departments of brilliant professors devoted to the study of families and how to make them more successful. We have modern prophets who counsel us and teach us step-by-step how to put up a successful family tent. What is the result of all this research and inspired counsel? Not only are we not going forward as our technology is, but we are actually moving in the opposite direction. Gordon B. Hinckley said, "Perhaps our greatest concern is with families. The family is falling apart all over the world. The old ties that bound together father and mother and children are breaking everywhere. We must face this in our own midst. There are too many broken homes among our own. The love that led to marriage somehow evaporates, and hatred fills its place. Hearts are broken, children weep. Can we not do better? Of course, we can. It is selfishness that brings about most of these tragedies."[3]

And so our society is making tremendous progress when it comes to technology while the most important unit in society is falling apart. What is the problem? I believe it is the failure to accept correction of our mistakes!

For those parents willing to admit that they make mistakes, accept the counsel given by prophets, and teach the prophet's words to their children, great promises are given. Consider the following two promises from the past:

- Wilford Woodruff: "Ninety-nine out of every hundred children who are *taught by their parents* the principles of *honesty* and *integrity*, *truth* and *virtue*, will observe them through life."[4]
- Joseph F. Smith: "Not one child in a hundred would go astray, if *the home environment, example* and *training*, were *in harmony with the truth in the gospel of Christ*, as revealed and taught to the Latter-day Saints."[5]

Perhaps some will say that these statements were made so long ago that they no longer apply in our day. On the other hand, maybe we as a people have not followed their inspired counsel to see if the promises are true. It is certain, however, as our families fall apart, we are losing our youth by the hundreds of thousands to the world. Assume for a moment, as an experiment, that the words of these prophets *are true*, and that by following their counsel, we would not lose our children to the world. The counsel simply requires us to be in total harmony with the gospel of Christ in three areas:

Our home environment

Our own examples

Our teachings

This book is about the most common mistakes made by parents that directly relate to going against one of these three requirements mentioned by President Joseph F. Smith. If the prophets are to help us with our families, we will have to first admit we are making mistakes and need the offered help. It is not easy for most of us to do. In addition to this challenge, we usually can point out the mistakes that others make, but we generally have a blind spot or a quandary about our own. With this in mind, I asked approximately five hundred active LDS members nationwide to answer two questions about how their parents raised them:

What things do you feel your parents did right when you were growing up in their home?

What mistakes do you feel your parents made when you were growing up in their home?

The first question of this survey will be discussed in a future book. I want to focus on the responses to the second question regarding the mistakes parents make. Since there were no multiple-choice answers for the respondents to choose from, every individual could say anything they wanted about the positive or negative aspects of how they were raised. Some listed a page full of mistakes they felt their parents had made, and some listed only a few. All participants thought their parents made mistakes, including my own children who participated in the survey.

It didn't take long to see certain patterns developing among the answers. Similar mistakes began to show up on the list of various respondents from around the nation. In the end, I grouped the perceived errors parents made into twenty-five different categories. These are the mistakes that are either listed most frequently or that seem to be doing the most damage to our families. Each of these errors makes up the chapters of this book. I have used statements by the brethren to teach correct principles about families and have also backed up their teachings with modern research where possible.

I realize how unpleasant it is for many of us to have our faults pointed out. It may be especially hard to have our children point them out. However, we need to face the fact that we may be making mistakes in our family that will damage our children and spouses if we fail to change. These *are* the last days. Satan is pulling out every trick in his huge bag to destroy our families. We must recognize Satan's deceit, admit we are falling for it, and then stand up to him through change or action. Bishop Victor L. Brown said, "Satan's ultimate goal is to destroy the family, because if he would destroy the family, he will not just have won the battle; he will have won the war."[6]

To stop Satan from succeeding, we must work as brilliant scientists have in developing technology. We must learn from our mistakes and work to improve. It is critical that we realize the importance of the family unit if we are to win this battle. Spencer W. Kimball stated, "The time will come when only those who believe deeply and actively in the family will be able to preserve their families in the midst of the gathering evil around us."[7]

Special Note:

1. At the beginning of each chapter, you will see an actual response from one of those who participated in the survey. These responses are italicized. Remember that these individuals are sharing their feelings about the mistakes they feel their parents made raising them.

2. There are many statistics given throughout the book on a teenager's willingness to have premarital sex that are not referenced. This information comes from research conducted for the author's doctoral dissertation ("Family, Religious, Peer and Media Influence on Adolescence Willingness to Have Premarital Sex," Brigham Young University, 1995) and in follow-up research in the same high schools in several states. The follow-up study is called the *American Youth Survey* and was conducted in 2001.

Notes

1   Ezra Taft Benson, "Joseph Smith: Prophet to Our Generation," *Ensign*, November 1981, 61.

2   Joseph Fielding Smith, *Answers to Gospel Questions* (Salt Lake City, UT: Deseret Book, 1963), Vol. 4, 191.

3   Gordon B. Hinckley, "Look to the Future," *Ensign*, November 1997, 67.

4   G. Homer Durham, *Discourses of Wilford Woodruff* (Salt Lake City, UT: Bookcraft, 1946), 266–68; emphasis added.

5   Joseph F. Smith, *Gospel Doctrine* (Salt Lake City: Deseret Book, 1975), 302; emphasis added.

6   Victor L. Brown, "Our Youth: Modern Sons of Helaman," *Ensign*, January 1974, 108.

7   Spencer W. Kimball, "Families Can Be Eternal," *Ensign*, November 1980, 4.

HOME
ENVIRONMENT

MISTAKE: Failure to establish a home environment that reflects the gospel.

"Our home environment did not seem to reflect what my parents professed to believe in. For example, there were no pictures of Christ or temples on the walls of any of the rooms in our home. There were a few religious books, but they were in my parents' bedroom so no one ever really saw them. I guess the only focus we had in our home was the television since it was at the center of the living room with all the chairs facing toward it."

Several years ago, our eight-year-old son came into the house carrying a huge potted plant. He excitedly presented it to his mother as a gift. After thanking him for his thoughtfulness, we asked where he got this special gift. He told us he'd found it in a clearing behind our home. The plant was about five feet tall and extremely green and healthy. This just didn't make sense to me. It was obvious that someone had taken good care of the plant. It was even in a nice container. After further questioning, we had our son show us exactly where he found the plant. We couldn't imagine how the plant got there and didn't know who had taken such good care of it, but we were convinced that our son really found it behind *our* house.

We decided to put the plant in our living room next to the sofa, where it looked very nice. We have frequent visitors to our home, and several people (including our home teachers and several ward and stake leaders) commented on how nice the plant looked. But something about the plant never seemed right. Maybe it was the strange smell that was always apparent when you sat near it or the feeling we got as we looked closely at it. It looked more like a healthy weed than anything else. Finally, after about a month, I pulled down a book from the bookshelf to see if I could identify what kind of plant we were tending. I flipped through the pages until I finally spotted a plant that looked exactly like ours. I checked closely to be sure. I even pulled off one of the leaves and put it on the kitchen-stove burner. There was no question about it. We had in our living room a healthy, five-foot-tall marijuana plant. We were so naïve! We not only harbored the plant in our living room, but we invited friends and family to sit in its shade! I believe that it is possible to have inappropriate things in our home environment that influence family members and not even recognize the danger.

We live in a frightening world in many ways. There is hardly an extended family, even in the church, that has not lost a family member to the world, if only temporarily. And yet there are those who seem to make it through unaffected by the storm of evil surrounding them. How can this be? Are these families just lucky, or are they are doing something that increases their chances of success?

In the introduction to this book, I quoted a remarkable promise that President Joseph F. Smith gave concerning our children. President Ezra Taft Benson reemphasized that promise in our day. Again, the statement is "Not one child in a hundred would go astray, if the home environment, example and training, were in harmony with . . . the gospel of Christ."[1]

Notice that three conditions must be met for the promise to be in effect. Let's talk more about the first item: the home environment must be in harmony with the gospel. As an institute director, I have often had young single adults in our home. I remember Monica, a recent convert, who came to visit our family shortly after her baptism. When she sat down, I noticed that she was looking very intently around our home. I was wondering what she was looking at when she said, "You know, this is the first LDS home that I have ever been in." That statement made me think deeply about our home environment. I too began to look around at what I saw and what my children were surrounded with every day. What do visitors see (or not see, for that matter) when they come into our homes?

Strong Political Families

The environment we choose to expose ourselves to on a daily basis will affect the way we see things and possibly influence our behavior. Our home environment usually reflects what we feel strongly about. Let's consider for a moment the two strong political parties that we have in this nation and then compare this to our home environments. This two-party tradition has existed for many generations, and almost every family in the United States has chosen a side. Some highly visible families are strongly connected with each of these political parties. For example, when we hear of the Kennedy family from Massachusetts, we may think of the Democratic party. On the other hand, when we hear of the Bush family from Texas, we would most likely think of the Republican party. The loyalty that these families have to their political parties is insurmountable. What chance do you think you would have of converting a Kennedy to the Republican party, or a Bush to the Democratic party? Would money influence them to make the change? Would logic or peer pressure? Their families have indoctrinated them for so many years that it has become a way of life.

I have often wondered how political parties have had such a strong hold on these specific families through the generations. It is remarkable that this could happen when the party's platform is constantly changing. This way of life obviously goes far beyond the ever-changing political platforms. Think of this important question: When political parties lose so few to the other side, how do we as Latter-day Saints, with the gospel of Jesus Christ, lose so many of our children to the world?

Maybe we can learn something from these strong political families that will help us hold onto our families. Let's consider a hypothetical situation for a moment. A Kennedy family lost one of their children to the Republican party (which would definitely be considered a loss if that happened). Upset, they call you to come to their home to help them determine what could have happened. You go over, with a pencil and paper, to take notes and to discover any apparent clues. As you walk into their home, you see no evidence whatsoever in the living room that this family is Democratic. You ask if you can visit the children's bedrooms to look for clues. In the first bedroom, you notice a huge poster of Gerald Ford in his University of Michigan football uniform. In the next bedroom, one of the Kennedy teenagers has a large poster of George Bush in his Yale baseball uniform. In the game room, one of the children and a friend are playing with Mitt Romney action figures. In the media room, another child is watching an old Ronald Reagan movie on television. In the kitchen, the radio is on the *Rush Limbaugh Show*. Can you imagine any of this happening in a Kennedy home? Of course not! A die-hard member of the Democratic party would never allow any of these Republican influences in their homes. Maybe we need to take a few lessons from our politicians.

If what we just imagined, however, were real, would you be surprised if one of their children joined the Republican party? Of course not! In fact, you probably would almost expect it. Perhaps we should be more concerned about the home environment that our children are immersed in daily.

Religious Pictures

Over the years, I have had the opportunity to stay with many LDS families across the United States and Canada while on speaking assignments. I have often been very surprised at how many of these homes have no outward signs to indicate that they are members of the Church. President Ezra Taft Benson said, "Enter the homes of those who have been born again, and the pictures on their walls, the books on their shelves, the music in the air, their words and acts reveal them as Christians."[2] When we say we are committed to the gospel but have no outward displays of that commitment in our homes, we may produce confusion in our children.

Often on speaking assignments, I sleep in a displaced teenager's room. I believe you can tell a lot about children by the things on their walls and in their rooms. In some of these bedrooms, I see strong evidence of the gospel, such as pictures of Christ and temples. In other bedrooms, no evidence is found that the teenager is even a member of the Church. Often I have seen posters with scantily clad models, tattooed rock stars, and other unseemly role models. Is it possible that these images of their role models in their bedrooms are affecting the children?

In contrast, several years ago, I spoke at a youth conference in a southern state. The stake leader had me sleep in his teenage daughter's bedroom while she stayed at a friend's home. Before going to bed that night, I looked around her room. She had a beautifully framed picture of Christ, a temple picture, and a series of Mormon Ad posters hanging on her walls. She also had a list of goals typed and framed, hanging above her bed. On a small table by her bed were a journal and the scriptures. She had no television, no computer, and no stereo system in her bedroom. I remember saying to myself, "I hope my boys are worthy of a girl like this one day." The next day, when I met this young teenager, I discovered that she matched her room. She was outstanding. I heard later that she went to BYU and has married a fine returned missionary in the temple. But Chelsea is definitely not the typical teenager in America.

A home with visual displays that reflect our beliefs will help family members remember what is most important in life. Sister Marjorie Hinckley had a mother who helped her remember who she was and her relation to Christ. She ended up married to a prophet. From a biography of her life, we read,

> When we were very young, my mother used to read to us a lot. She read to us all kinds of books—from the classics to the stories of Jesus. There was a large picture that she had hung in our bedroom where my sisters and I slept. It was a picture that I know you are familiar with—the one of Jesus when He was twelve in the temple with the wise men. Every morning when I opened my eyes, the first thing I saw was the face of the young boy Jesus. I am grateful to my mother for many things that she did for us in a very subtle way. She didn't preach to us about Jesus, she just hung His picture where we could see it. I think that I was grown and long gone from the home before I realized what an impact that had on my life.[3]

Sister Hinckley's mother took deliberate steps to help her remember who she was and who Jesus is by placing a visual reminder in her bedroom. We have all been counseled to do the same.

Media

Most homes in America are completely focused around some type of electronic media. High school students have access to an incredible amount of media in their home environments. In recent years, many teenagers' bedrooms include televisions, stereo systems, DVD players, game systems, cable access, and computers hooked up to the Internet. In my experience, the youth with media or inappropriate posters in their bedrooms seem to be struggling spiritually. That is of real concern.

Over the years we have seen an increased availability of electronic media to children. The Pew Research Center shows to what extent American teenagers have access to social media.

Teen Social Media Stats

• 78 percent of teens now have a cell phone, and almost half (47 percent) of them own smartphones. That translates into 37 percent of all teens who have smartphones, up from just 23 percent in 2011.

• 95 percent of teens use the Internet.

• 93 percent of teens have a computer or have access to one at home.

• The volume of texting among teens has risen from 50 texts a day in 2009 to 60 texts for the median teen text user. [4]

• Today's teens spend more than 7½ hours a day consuming media: watching TV, listening to music, surfing the Web, social networking, and playing video games.[5]

When inappropriate media is blasting into the homes and bedrooms of our children, helping them to remember they are children of God with a divine mission may prove to be a difficult task. Now families have far more media availability than even a few years ago with the widespread availability of smartphones. These small handheld devices house almost every major technological invention in modern times. These "phones" allow individuals to call friends, watch movies, play music, access the Internet, play games, send instant messages and pictures, and unfortunately, access the most vulgar images in history with a single click. With access to smartphones, electronic media is no longer confined to the home or bedroom but is instantly available 24 hours a day, 365 days a year no matter where an individual may be.

Our goal should be to help family members remember who they really are. I believe President Spencer W. Kimball was speaking of this when he said, "Remember is the most important word in the English language."[6] Although difficult to obtain, a home free of worldly environment will help us concentrate on the important things in life.

The Solution

A few years ago, my wife and I made a goal to visit every temple in the United States. Even though we still have a few to go, it has been a remarkable experience for us to view these beautiful buildings. By visiting the Lord's house, we have learned a lot that we can also apply to our own home. Although our home will never be exactly like the Lord's house, one of the reasons for temples is for us to learn what our own home environments should look like. They are our divine examples. All of the temples we have visited have beautiful grounds. The lawns are green and mowed, and there are always beautiful flowers and shrubs. They are always very well maintained. Once you walk inside, there is a feeling of peace. Pictures of Christ, prophets, and beautiful landscapes adorn the walls. Everywhere there is order and a peaceful atmosphere. I have never once heard yelling or put downs in these buildings. The workers treat each other and the patrons with respect and kindness. There are movies shown in the temple, but they have a G rating. You would never think of seeing something in the temple with profanity, violence, or sexual content. The most peaceful room is the celestial room. It is a gathering place, and no media is shown in that room. I believe the equivalent in our homes should be our living rooms. Of course, our homes can't be exactly like the temple. However, they should closely resemble them since "Only the home can compare to the temple in sacredness."[7]

The Benefits

I met Summer while speaking at a priest/laurel activity in eastern Canada. During one of our class breaks, she shared an experience she had during the school year. While reading the *New Era,* she came across an article about a girl who hung a small picture of Christ on the inside of her locker door to remind her to be more Christlike. Summer was so impressed by that idea, she decided to do the same thing. She shared a locker with a non-LDS friend and thought it best to get her permission before putting up the picture. Her locker mate told her that she had no problem with the idea and encouraged her to put it up. When Summer opened her locker on the first day the picture was up, she heard several people laugh and make derogatory comments about the picture, as well as its owner, as they passed. The next day, several people gathered around her locker when she opened it and made comments. She heard one boy say, "I told you this girl had a picture of Christ in her locker." Several laughed at her. For the next few days, crowds gathered every time she went to her locker, and rude comments continued. Summer thought it strange that others had pornographic pictures in their lockers and no one seemed to say anything about it. But when she hung a picture of Christ in her locker, it caused a huge commotion. After days of mockery and crowds around her locker, Summer decided to take the picture down. It was not because she was embarrassed to have it there but because she felt it wrong to have the Savior ridiculed. She opened her locker and started taking the picture down, when her locker partner walked up and asked what she was doing. Summer explained her feelings. Her friend agreed that it had become crowded around their locker since the picture went up. Then she said, "Please don't take the picture down. I don't know why, but ever since you put that picture up, I have wanted to be a better person. Every time I am tempted to do something wrong, I think about looking at the picture of Christ, and I am able to resist." Summer left the picture up as a constant reminder to her and her locker mate to be more Christlike.

I shared that experience during an Education Week talk and challenged the participants to think about the influence our home environment can have on family members. After arriving home, I received the following letter from a sister who attended my class:

> I've been feeling for a long time that I would like a picture of Christ in my home, but being married to a nonmember, I was afraid that he wouldn't understand how the picture fit in with my decorating scheme. Thinking on it now, I also realize that I was afraid that when visitors came into my home they would think that I was some sort of religious fanatic. After Education Week, I felt humbled and truly ashamed that

I was actually afraid to put Christ in the center of my home. I cried because I thought that I loved my Heavenly Father and Jesus so much and yet I was still scared of what people would think.

I came out with a new resolve to do better. I now have pictures of Christ in my home and when I look at them, *I feel the warmth.* . . . I'm now proud of the testimony that I have about Jesus as my Savior. If he loved me enough to die for me, then I can at least show the love I feel for him by not being afraid or ashamed to have outward signs of him in my home.[8]

Visual reminders help us remember to keep His gospel foremost in our lives. The things we choose to display in our homes and bedrooms tell a lot about the direction in which we are headed. If we want our children to marry in the temple, then we should put pictures of their favorite temple in their rooms at an early age. President Boyd K. Packer said, "President Kimball has continually recommended that there be a picture of a temple in the children's room. From their earliest day they should look forward to the temple."[9]

One of our human tendencies is to become desensitized to our surroundings, or in other words, insensitive or less sensitive. For example, if we live close to railroad tracks, with time the trains don't seem to bother us any more. If we live by the airport, with time the planes are no longer consciously heard. If we put a list of goals on our mirror, with time it becomes part of the mirror and we no longer notice our goals. However, just because we become less sensitive to our surroundings does not mean that we are not being affected by them in positive or negative ways. Have we become desensitized to our home environment? Are there things in our homes that are like the marijuana plant that we do not consciously notice but are having an impact? Sit down in your most used furniture and look straight ahead.

Whatever is at the center of your most-used room is obviously important to you. If it happens to be a television, we tell our families that it is very important to us. Take a tour of each bedroom in your home and take notes of what you see. You can tell how your children are doing by checking their bedrooms. Look closely at posters or pictures on their walls, along with CDs, DVDs, Facebook pages, books, magazines, clothes, and shoes. All tell a story of how children are doing. If you see no evidence of Christ and abundant evidence of the world, there is reason to be concerned. After taking inventory of your home environment, take the necessary steps to make it match your beliefs.

Notes

1   Ezra Taft Benson, "Fundamentals of Enduring Family Relationships," *Ensign*, November 1982, 61.
2   Ezra Taft Benson, in Conference Report, October 1985, 6.
3   Virginia H. Pearce, *Glimpses into the Life and Heart of Marjorie Pay Hinckley* (Salt Lake City, UT: Deseret Book 1999), 214.
4   Amanda Lenhart, "Teens, Smartphones & Texting," Pew Research Center, March 19, 2012.
5   "Generation M2: Media in the Lives of 8- to 18-Year-Olds," The Kaiser Family Foundation News Release, January 20, 2010.
6   Spencer W. Kimball, "Charge to Religious Educators," June 28, 1968.
7   LDS Bible Dictionary, 781.
8   Personal correspondence in author's possession.
9   Boyd K. Packer, *The Holy Temple* (Salt Lake City, UT: Bookcraft, 1980), 268.

QUALITY TIME

MISTAKE: Failure to spend enough quality and quantity time with family.

"My parents were very detached emotionally, and we seldom spent quality time together as a family. Both of them were workaholics. I don't ever remember playing games together or going on a picnic or just sitting around talking with each other. They just never seemed interested in doing those things or were too busy with their projects. Once we were old enough, we spent most of our time with friends, which I think, was a relief to my parents. That way they didn't have to be bothered."

A few years ago, my wife, Wendy, and I had two very busy weeks in a row. Wendy was serving as stake Relief Society president and had several extra assignments because of the visiting Apostle attending our stake conference. The next weekend, we were in charge of a marriage seminar with guest speakers from out of town. After the Friday night meeting and adult dance, we stayed to help with cleanup and setup for the next morning's classes. We got home around 2:00 a.m. and had church meetings at 8:00 a.m. When I got home Saturday evening, one of our young teenage daughters was sitting alone on the couch looking very sad. I asked her what was wrong, but she had little to say. I then asked where her older sister was, and she told me that she was in her bedroom with a friend. I asked why she wasn't with them. She said, "They don't want me in there." I started to say, "Of course they do," but then remembered that older teenagers usually don't want their younger siblings around with their friends over. Then without warning, she began to sob. Between tears, she let me know that her sister "is always too busy for me. She is either with friends, sleeping, or on the phone. And Mom is always doing Relief Society work. And you are always gone." I thought what she was saying was not exactly true, but from her perspective at that moment, it was. Then she said something that really had an impact on me. She said, "I guess I'm just lonely, Dad."

Her comment made me think a lot about quality family time. A statement made by President Howard W. Hunter seems to apply when he said, "We reiterate what was stated by President David O. McKay: 'No other success [in life] can compensate for failure in the home.' In similar counsel President Harold B. Lee said, 'The most important of the Lord's work you and I will ever do will be within the walls of our own homes. Effective family leadership, brethren, requires both quantity and quality time.'"[1]

Less Family Time

While living in Utah, I heard a public service announcement on the radio that said, "The average American family spends 40 percent less time together than they did just 20 years ago." This statistic shocked me. I have no idea whether the information is correct or not. Nonetheless, researchers feel that families are spending less time together than they did in the past. I remember asking myself how we could be spending less time together as families when we have more time-saving devices than in any previous generation. For instance, we now have indoor running water and bathroom facilities. Dishwashers automatically do the job that would have taken several hours a week to do in the past. We have fast food, pre-packed dinners, stoves, and microwaves, allowing family members to have food available in a fraction of the time that it would have taken our ancestors to prepare. Indoor washers and dryers, as well as vacuum cleaners, now save huge amounts of time. We have cars, planes, trains, and buses to cut down travel time. There are no more trips to "town" to buy supplies, since almost everyone in America has supermarkets, gas stations, department stores, cleaners, and hardware stores within minutes of their homes. To communicate with each other, we have telephones, faxes, cell phones, email, text messaging, instant messaging, and so on. All of these marvelous inventions allow us to communicate quickly with others, no matter how far the distance. How is it possible that American families spend less time together than even our parents did?

After hearing this public service message, I asked that question to a group of students I was teaching at BYU. A coed answered by saying, "All these time-saving devices are the reason that families spend less time together now than in the past." At first, I was puzzled by her comment. After all, how is it possible that time-saving inventions could be the reason for less family time? She went on to say, "In the past, cooking, washing clothes, and doing dishes was a family affair that involved many hours of working together to accomplish. That time has now been basically eliminated by these modern 'time-saving' conveniences. Plus, almost every family has multiple cars, allowing family members to go in all different directions at the same time." I interrupted her and asked the class how many cars their parents owned when they graduated from high school. No one came from a family with one car. Most said that their families had two or three cars, while several said their families had four or more. I then asked the young woman to continue. She offered more examples of how time-saving devices like computers, television, stereos, and game consoles separate family members from each other, even though they are all together in the same house. Someone else pointed out that houses are bigger than ever before, allowing family members to be more isolated from each other. Finally, one student concluded with this thought-provoking statement: "And who pays for all these modern conveniences? Many of our mothers, even with small children in the home, now work out of the home to pay for these time-saving devices, leaving less time for family activities. But it is not just the mothers leaving the home. Fathers are working more hours than ever, and even teenagers have left the home in droves pursuing jobs to pay for the latest fashions and gadgets."

Extra Time?

A story is told about a gentleman who visited the home of a prosperous friend. He was shown many laborsaving devices and was informed of the great savings in time made possible through the miracle of modern science. As the guest neared the end of the tour, he asked his host, "What do you do with all the time you save?" Perhaps we should all ask ourselves that question.

As I reflected on these students' insights, I must confess that I didn't feel a strong desire to go back to the good ol' days and try to live without modern conveniences. However, I did feel a strong desire to use my time wisely and not use the extra time in an endless pursuit of pleasure or materialism. With proper planning, we should have far more time available to spend with our families than any preceding generation. Many are not using the extra time offered by time-saving devices in a positive way.

It takes time to nurture children properly. It takes time to teach our children the principles of the gospel. It takes time to bond together through family activities. We should all remember that we have one chance to get it right with our children. There is no going back and repeating the past. As stated earlier, Bishop Victor L. Brown said, "Satan's ultimate goal is to destroy the family, because if he would destroy the family, he will not just have won the battle; he will have won the war."[2] If we do not spend quality time together, then he has definitely won a battle.

Several years ago, when Elder David A. Bednar was a professor at the University of Arkansas, the *Church News* interviewed him about his family. He shared an experience he had while a student at BYU. He said,

> I went to about 12 very prominent and financially successful people, and asked them if they could do anything over again, what they would do differently. All of them said they would spend more time with their children when they were little. They talked about how fast time passes. Some of them told me they had been so busy establishing themselves in their careers that they felt they didn't have time to play with their children, and then, when they finally became secure in their careers, they discovered their children had grown older and weren't interested in being with them any longer.[3]

One day, I took several items out of a storage closet and put them on a table at the front of my institute class. These items had been sitting untouched for many years. There was a 16 mm film projector, a record player, a reel-to-reel recorder, a filmstrip projector, a monochrome computer monitor, a cassette player, and a VCR player. Each of the items had a price on them, which I'm sure to the students seemed ridiculous. For example, the computer monitor was listed at $495.00.

As the students entered the classroom, I told them that the institute was having a fund raiser, and we were trying to sell some of our high tech items. Several laughed as they looked at the items on the table. One young man commented, "I wouldn't give you five dollars for everything on the table. It is all out of date and worthless. The only thing these items would be good for are boat anchors." I then told them to look very closely at the items on the table because the price tags on them were the approximate prices that were actually paid for them. It got very quiet in the room as we contemplated the tremendous decrease in the price of these items over a relatively short time. One student said, "You can now buy a very powerful computer with a monitor and printer for what the monochrome monitor cost alone in the past." I then said, "Now look very closely because these items are one of the reasons that fathers in America started working more hours on the job. The items on the table are also one of the major factors leading to many mothers and teenagers leaving their homes to seek employment."

The items on the table now look a little different. Now it is 3D smart TVs, smartphones, iPads, MP3 players, 20 MP digital cameras, touch screen computers, and so on. But the point is the same. In a few months or years, all of these things will be worthless junk, just like the items on the table at that institute class.

Quality or Quantity

Many have heard the trite little saying that it is quality time and not quantity time that matters. Let's suppose that we go to a fine restaurant for our twenty-fifth wedding anniversary and order a twelve-ounce rib eye steak for twenty-four dollars. You have been told this restaurant has the best steaks in town. You have saved your money for this special event. You are very hungry and sit in anticipation as your food is prepared. When your food finally arrives at your table, you see a one-inch by one-inch square steak. Shocked, you ask your waiter what is going on. He explains that this is the top-rated steak in the city. "But it is tiny," you reply. He says, "Look, it's the quality not the quantity that counts!" What would you say to that argument? I don't know about you, but I think we need both quality and quantity.

Sometimes in the name of doing good things, we lose the opportunity to do great things with our family. For example, my wife has taught piano lessons for many years in our home. One day a nine-year-old boy named Austin, dressed in his soccer uniform, was attempting to play a song he had been assigned to practice. Suddenly, he burst into tears. My wife had no idea what was wrong with him. He finally blurted out, "I just can't do everything my parents want me to do." What was this third-grade student involved in? He went between piano, soccer, Tae Kwon Do, basketball, science league, homework, and a church youth organization during the week. I'm sure his parents were only trying to expose him to a variety of opportunities. As parents, we must be careful not to involve our children in so many activities that we never really have a chance to spend quality time with them. Some may feel they are depriving their children if they don't involve them in everything available. In reality, we may be putting tremendous pressure on our children, leaving no time for leisure or involvement with even more important things.

Most parents have good intentions for their children, but it could be that some are trying to relive unrealized dreams themselves. Recently, I was talking to one of my former students about his family. During the conversation, he said that his son Craig was playing on an all-star baseball road team that traveled around the state playing in tournaments. I was interested, but a little shocked, that he had a son that old. He went on to tell me that it was a huge time commitment and that the team had traveled almost every weekend for the previous five months. I asked him how old his son was, and he said he was seven years old. He then told me, with a smile on his face, that his son went to sleep with a baseball game playing on his bedroom TV. I couldn't help but wonder if the father was living a little through his son. In the name of building character and self-esteem, I wondered if family time was suffering and if his son was acquiring unrealistic goals for the future.

Many argue that children need to be involved in multiple activities like sports to build character and help them become well rounded. Someone has said, "Sports don't build character, they reveal character." If sports built character, then our professional athletes should be the most character-based people in the world. I hope no one misunderstands what is being said. It is not that children do not need to be involved in some activities. It is just that we probably need to help them pick a few things to be involved in. Then they can become proficient in a few areas instead of being mediocre in many. One of the ways the adversary gets families to spend less time with each other is to get them to spend all their free time outside the home pursuing good things. If a kid is an eight-sport athlete, when does he have time to learn gospel principles?

One mother told me that she seldom saw her high school children because they were involved in so many extracurricular activities. One daughter, for example, was involved in a private singing group, two school choirs, multiple drama productions, several clubs, the school band, and ballet dancing. Of course, she had a hard time making her mid-week Young Women activities and even sometimes missed seminary and church. One night, I attended a school talent show where this young woman performed a ballet dance routine. As I watched her, I wondered what she was doing up there. She was involved in so many things that she just wasn't really very good at any of them. In the meantime, she was spending large amounts of time away from home and family.

Sometimes we may feel that we don't have enough time to spend with our family. I find that we usually have more time than we think we do. My brother has eleven children and owns his own business. He often worked long hours while serving in Church leadership callings. While he served as a bishop, one of his young sons called him at work and asked if he would take him to play miniature golf. He carefully explained that he was working and would not be able to take him right then. The son was very persistent and pleaded his cause, but to no avail. When my brother told my mother what happened, she said, "I'll bet if a ward member needed your help, you would find the time to go." He found that he did have a little extra time after that comment was made, and he and his son took off to play miniature golf.

In addition to quantity time, when we fail to spend quality family time, our children may seek it elsewhere. One of my friends was home teaching when a little six-year-old boy brought him a crude drawing of what looked like a man with a fishing pole. My friend asked what it meant. The little boy said, "Will you take me fishing? My dad won't take me." The dad of course was very embarrassed at his son's request. If parents don't spend enough quality time with their children, they will seek that time with others.

In the Dyer and Kunz study of effective LDS families, they found, "The family is characterized by love and unity. The parents put their children above work, recreation, and friends. Siblings are more important than friends. Family time is more important than time spent on anything else."[4]

Set Aside Time

A friend once made a suggestion to help me gain more family time. I had been speaking at multiple stake firesides on consecutive weekends. He asked if I had a hard time saying "no" if there was no conflict on the calendar. He said, "Why don't you circle some dates on your calendar that you are available for speaking. On the rest of the dates, simply write in 'family fireside.' That way, when someone calls you to speak on your non-available dates, you can say, 'I'm sorry I have a conflict on that day.'" That simple suggestion has helped our family spend more time together.

Eat Together

In our fast paced society, few families have mealtimes together. With everyone going different directions, it is now unusual to have all of the family home at dinnertime. Yet the benefits of this ritual are inestimable. For example, researchers at Columbia University's National Center on Addiction and Substance Abuse found that: "Eating family dinner at least five times a week drastically lowers a teens' chances of smoking, drinking, and using drugs. Teens who have fewer than three family dinners a week are 3.5 times more likely to have abused prescription drugs and illegal drugs other than marijuana, three times more likely to have used marijuana, more than 2.5 times more likely to have smoked cigarettes, and 1.5 times more likely to have tried alcohol.[5]

President Ezra Taft Benson said, "Mealtime provides a wonderful time to review the activities of the day and to not only feed the body, but to feed the spirit as well with members of the family taking turns reading the scriptures, particularly, the Book of Mormon."[6]

Pause before Entering

Before entering our homes, we should pause and reflect upon what we need to do while we are at home. Sometimes we forget how little quality time we spend with our families. Have you ever paused and asked yourself how much time you spend with each family member during a typical day? Often fathers are tempted to bring work home and forget the needs of their children. Elder Gene R. Cook said, "Leave your briefcase at work. Parents who bring their work home almost always rob their children of 'family time.' If you do bring work home, perhaps it ought to be done early in the morning or late at night when the children are in bed."[7]

Family Is Most Important

Imagine that at some point in the future, you call your family together to talk to them for one last time. You say, "Guys, I've made some mistakes as a parent that I don't want any of you to make. I'm really sorry that I haven't spent more time aimlessly searching the Internet, reading the newspaper, and flipping through the channels on our big screen television. I certainly hope you will spend more time doing this. Oh, and by the way, will you please make sure that you spend more time at work?" Can you imagine saying those things at your last meeting together? No! Those on their deathbeds usually regret not spending more time with the family, not with the media or work.

Elder L. Tom Perry said,

I've often thought of the happy times we had when our family was young and our children were at home. I have made a mental review of those days and considered the changes I would make in our family organization and administration, if we had the opportunity to live that period over again. There are two areas I would determine to improve if that privilege were granted to me to have young children in our home once again.

The first would be to spend more time as husband and wife in a family executive committee meeting learning, communicating, planning, and organizing to better fulfill our roles as parents.

The second wish I would like, if I could have those years over, would be to spend more family time.[8]

A sister shared the following experience from her journal:

Last evening I attended a meeting where a medical doctor was talking about "tucking" his young son in bed. He said that the son had accomplished something very good, and they were discussing it. The son said something like, "Dad, I wish you could have helped me with the project, but you're never at home." Whereupon the father said he launched into his "I have to be the provider in the family, provide food, cars, clothing, and even a roof over our heads." The son was quiet for a minute, and then he said, "Dad, I wish we didn't have such a big house."[9]

Let's remember the television and radio announcements sponsored by the Church that remind us of what is really important in families. The message is simply: "Give your children everything. Give them your time!"

Notes

1 Howard W. Hunter, "Being a Righteous Husband and Father," *Ensign*, November 1994, 49.
2 Victor L. Brown, in Conference Report, April 1975, 103.
3 "Getting Serious about Family Fun," *Church News*, September 30, 1989.
4 William G. Dyer and Phillip R. Kunz, *Effective Mormon Families* (Salt Lake City, UT: Deseret Book, 1986), 9.
5 "The Importance of Family Dinners II," The National Center on Addiction and Substance Abuse at Columbia University, September 2011.
6 Ezra Taft Benson, in Conference Report, October 1970, 25.
7 Gene R. Cook, *Raising Up a Family to the Lord* (Salt Lake City, UT: Deseret Book, 1993), 272.
8 L. Tom Perry, in Conference Report, April 1994, 49.
9 Personal correspondence in author's possession.

THE
CROSSROADS

MISTAKE: Failure to be at the crossroads of their children's lives.

"During my teenage years, I don't ever remember a time when either of my parents were at home when I came home from school. Nor were they ever up waiting for me when I came home from a date or being out with friends. I believe that not having to account for my time and actions led me to make many mistakes that I may not have made otherwise."

I have gained a new appreciation for a statement made by President Ezra Taft Benson. He said, "Take time to always be at the crossroads when your children are either coming or going—when they leave and return from dates—when they bring friends home. Be there at the crossroads whether your children are six or sixteen."[1] Though this statement was made many years ago, it appears to have even more meaning today than when given.

Critical Time 1: In the Afternoon When Children Come Home from School

Being interested in the subject matter for the night, I watched *ABC Nightline*. The program covered the same material that I studied in my graduate degree programs: teen sexuality and teen pregnancy. I was very intrigued by a statement made by a university researcher who was a guest on the program. She said, "75 percent of first-time sexual experience is in the home of one of the partners."[2]

31

When I first heard this statistic, I was shocked. How could this possibly be? If this research is true, then there has been a dramatic change in our society from years past. President Spencer W. Kimball said, "In interviewing repenting young folks, as well as some older ones, I am frequently told that the couple met their defeat in the dark, at late hours, in secluded areas. Troubles, like photographs, are developed in the dark. The car was most often the confessed seat of the difficulty. It became their brothel."[3] Apparently, this is no longer the case. How could the home of one of the partners be the place where most first sexual experiences occur? There is one obvious answer—the alarming number of children who are coming home after school to empty houses. According to *Parents Magazine*, "More than a million grade-schoolers have nobody to take care of them once class lets out . . . Overall, the number of self-supervised children has jumped to 15.1 million nationwide."[4]

The term we use in America for children who come home to empty homes is "latchkey kids." This almost always happens because both parents work outside the home. Many dangers are associated with this phenomenon. With no supervision, the chances of the children being involved in inappropriate behavior rise dramatically. President Ezra Taft Benson also said, "In Proverbs we read, 'A child left to himself bringeth his mother to shame' (Prov 29:15.) Among the greatest concerns in our society are the millions of latchkey children who come home daily to empty houses, unsupervised by working parents."[5]

Researchers studying latchkey kids have found multiple correlations to delinquent behaviors. Those who come home to empty homes are more likely to be involved in drugs, alcohol, smoking, and spend more time with the electronic media (television, movies, pop music, Internet, video games, and so on). Of even more concern is this fact shown in early studies: females whose mothers were employed outside the home had a greater tendency to engage in sexual relations than those whose mothers were not working. This was attributed to their greater independence and lack of supervision.

We revisited that association twenty years later and found that the tendency toward permissive premarital sexual attitudes and lack of supervision still holds true. High school students were asked if their mothers worked outside the home, and then the information was correlated to whether the students would engage in sexual relations before marriage.

When children are left at home alone, they are placed in a very dangerous situation. Frances Kemper Alston said,

> Most teachers believe that being alone at home is the number one cause of school failure. The afternoon hours are the peak time for juvenile crime. In the last 11 years, juvenile crime has increased 48 percent. The Carnegie Council on Adolescent Development found that 8th graders who are alone 11 hours a week are twice as likely to abuse drugs as adolescents who are busy after school. The Council also found that teens who have sexual intercourse do it in the afternoon in the home of boys whose parents work. Unsupervised children are more likely to become depressed, smoke cigarettes and marijuana, and drink alcohol. They are also more likely to be the victims of crimes. When home alone, latchkey children generally watch television, eat snacks, play with pets and fight with siblings.[6]

The American School Board also reported the following:
- "Alone at home, children are at high risk of injury and poor nutrition. And unsupervised preteens and adolescents are often tempted to try risky behaviors such as experimental drug use and sexual activity."
- "3 to 6 p.m. are the hours when young children and teens are most likely to get into trouble. During these hours, unsupervised kids without constructive activities are more likely to commit crimes, be crime victims, be in or cause car crashes, and smoke, drink, and use drugs."
- "Violent juvenile crimes—murder, rape, robbery, and aggravated assault—soar during the hours immediately after school . . . About 5 percent of violent juvenile crimes occur at noon, and 6 percent occur at 9 p.m. At 3 p.m., the crime rate peaks at 13 percent."
- "Unsupervised homebound children suffer high degrees of stress. Older kids who fend for themselves—as well as look after younger brothers and sisters—often feel "lonely, fearful, and worried."[7]

It is obvious that children need supervision. Of course, some parents, for reasons beyond their control, cannot be at the crossroads even though they desperately want to be. In these cases, it will take careful planning and inspiration to provide proper supervision. President Gordon B. Hinckley spoke on the critical role that mothers play in the lives of their children. He realized, however, that some mothers must be employed outside the home for basic needs and cannot always be at the crossroads. For those who are in this situation, his message is to simply do the best you can. He said,

> Some years ago President Benson delivered a message to the women of the Church. He encouraged them to leave their employment and give their individual time to their children. I sustain the position which he took.
>
> Nevertheless, I recognize, as he recognized, that there are some women (it has become very many in fact) who have to work to provide for the needs of their families. To you I say, do the very best you can. I hope that if you are employed full-time you are doing it to ensure that basic needs are met and not simply to indulge a taste for an elaborate home, fancy cars, and other luxuries. The greatest job that any mother will ever do will be in nurturing, teaching, lifting, encouraging, and rearing her children in righteousness and truth. None other can adequately take her place.[8]

Critical Time 2: At Night, When Children Come Home from Dates or Being Out with Friends

There is another category of latchkey kids in our society that many parents seem totally oblivious to. This phenomenon seems to particularly apply to Latter-day Saint parents. Many of these parents would be shocked if someone referred to their children as latchkey kids. After all, they believe they try to be at the crossroads of their children's lives. They're at home, but in reality, when their children come home after being with friends or on dates, these parents are literally sound asleep. This creates a latchkey effect because the youth come home unsupervised, and therefore unaccountable for the night's activities.

Recently, I was talking to an LDS father who I hadn't seen in a while. During the conversation, I asked him about his family. After discussing things in general, he told me how much his son, Tyler, had struggled before turning his life around. This young man was a very good-looking star athlete. He was popular in his school where there were very few Latter-day Saints. This father explained he and his wife had learned the summer after his senior year he had been drinking almost every weekend with his school friends. These parents were totally unaware of this problem and had only found out because a younger son informed them of it. Both parents were shocked at the news. Of course, there were also other more serious sins involved. Should they have been so surprised? After all, he was hanging out with cheerleaders and members of the school's football team every weekend.

How was this young man able to get away with drinking almost every weekend of his senior year, without his parents realizing it? Isn't it because he was a latchkey kid? There is no way that he could come in from a night of drinking, look his parents in the eyes, and carry on a normal conversation if they would have waited up for him. Even though his mom was a stay-at-home mom, these parents never waited up for their son when he was out at night. Is there a difference between parents working when the kids come home from school and parents sound asleep in their bedrooms when their children come home from nighttime activities?

How could Tyler possibly have gotten away with drinking regularly if his parents had followed the counsel of Elder Larry Lawrence? He said, "There is a great deal of wisdom displayed when parents stay up and wait for their children to return home. Young men and women make far better choices when they know their parents are waiting up to hear about their evening and to kiss them good night."[9]

When this young man began to break the Word of Wisdom, he placed himself in extreme danger of breaking other commandments. For example, President Heber J. Grant pointed out that "Nearly always those who lose their chastity first partake of those things that excite passions within them or lower their resistance and becloud their minds. Partaking of tobacco and liquor is calculated to make them a prey to those things, which if indulged in, are worse than death itself."[10]

Modern research now backs up what President Grant taught and explains why parents should be at the crossroads. In a survey of fourteen-year-old girls who were virgins, researchers found that 4 percent of those who had never used alcohol or drugs lost their virtue during the next twelve months. However, 23 percent of fourteen-year-old girls who had used marijuana and alcohol lost their virtue in the next twelve months.[11] The lesson is unmistakable. In this study, the girls had a 575 percent greater chance of losing their virtue in the 12 months following their fourteenth birthday if they had used alcohol or drugs first.

Waiting up for your children will be a huge factor in keeping children from sin, yet far too few parents take advantage of this great protection plan. We asked high school students how many of their parents waited up for them when they were out on dates or with friends and found the following:

Parents Who Wait Up for Children

16% Parents always wait up
20% Parents often wait up
32% Seldom wait up
31% Never wait up[12]

If this research is a true reflection, then only *16 percent of teenagers* have parents who always welcome them home at night. That makes the other 84 percent latchkey kids to some degree. We then asked if they would be willing to have premarital sex, based on whether their parents wait up on them.

Willingness to Have Premarital Sex Based On Whether Parents Wait Up

49% Always wait up
53% Often wait up
73% Seldom wait up
79% Never wait up[13]

From the biography of Camilla Kimball, we read of this family tradition, "As the children started dating they had rules and regulations to follow. . . . Camilla always stayed awake, reading, no matter how late, until the children were all home."[14] We live in a society where breaking the Word of Wisdom and the law of chastity is rampant. One solution to this problem is very simple: Never go to bed when your children are out. Be there to talk to them about the night, look them in the eye to make sure there is nothing wrong. Then always give them a good-night kiss. It will be very difficult to break the Word of Wisdom and come home and kiss Mom without getting caught.

A few years ago I had an opportunity to speak at the BYU–Idaho Education Week. I loved the experience shared by Elder Neil L. Andersen at the devotional. He said,

> I remember a few years ago when our youngest son, Derek, lived with us in our home. He would get ready to leave in the evening for a night with his friends and his mother would say, "Derek, We'll be waiting for you when you get home so we can have a prayer with you." He would respond, "Let's pray now. You can go to bed. I'll be home." She would insist, "No, Derek, we want to pray with you when you return." I would spend the evening slapping cold water on my face to stay awake knowing that Derek would step through the door just before the set curfew hour. Then, we were on our knees and you could hear her pray, "We thank thee, Father in Heaven, for watching over Derek, for helping him to keep his covenants, and obey the commandments. We thank thee for the good son he is and for his commitment to do right.[15]

Benefits

Catch Problems Immediately

My friend Bill is an institute director whose family joined the Church when he was fourteen years old. They were a very religious family even before joining the Church. One of the first things Bill did after his baptism was go to a party with his younger brother at the home of an LDS family. While there, someone spiked the punch, and the boys unknowingly drank it. When they came home, their mother was up waiting up for them as she always did. She talked with the boys about the night, then gave Bill her traditional nightly kiss. As soon as she did she said, "You've been drinking, haven't you?" He denied doing it, saying that he had only drunk punch at the party. She then called her husband in. Both smelled the breath of each son. Bill was caught the very first time he tasted alcohol. The boys finally convinced their parents they did not intentionally drink. Bill then said that he has never tasted alcohol again since that experience.

The best chance to cure cancer is to catch it in its very early stages. The best chance of helping youth avoid serious sin is to catch problems in a less serious stage, before the chains are wrapped tight. If a family member was upset when he came home, could you tell without him saying anything? Of course you could. As soon as he walked through the door you would know something was wrong. When you are around someone for a long period of time, you get to know that person. You can read body language and know when that person is upset. Very seldom do LDS youth, who have been trained, fall quickly into serious sin. They usually have to be broken down over time. By being at the crossroads and looking at their countenances every day and night, you can almost always know immediately if anything is wrong.

However, you can't lie in bed and have them yell they are home. You must be able to look them in the eye and talk to them. The next morning is too late to get the connection. How could they smoke, drink, or be immoral, and then look you in the eye, and talk and act as if everything is fine? The only way they could do that is if they become hardened. The only way to become hardened is to repeat the sin. That is why it is so important to try and stop inappropriate behavior as soon as it starts.

More Likely to Meet Curfew Times

When children know you are waiting up for them, they are far more likely to meet their curfew and to call if they will be late. Every child needs a curfew, but only about 49 percent of high school students have a specific time to be home. One cure is for parents to wait up for their children. Few parents would be willing to wait up for kids who were consistently coming home during the early morning hours. Something would obviously change. What time should curfew be? That's easy! It should be the time it takes to get home from wherever their activity was held. Why have midnight curfews if an activity is over at 9:30 p.m.? There is great danger in having too much unplanned time. No matter where they are, they should have a default curfew time. President Ezra Taft Benson said, "Some of our worst sins are committed after midnight."[16] If children are not able to make their curfews, they should be taught to call and explain the situation.

Great Bonding Time

Even before your children start to date, there are plenty of times to wait for them. Make sure you are awake and excited to talk to your children any time they arrive home from stake dances, activities with friends, and so on. Some of the best conversations my children and I have ever had were after their activities and dates. I have never gone to bed when one of them was out. I made it a policy as long as they continued to talk, I would not ask them to go to bed. There were occasions when we would stay up into the wee hours of the morning talking, even though I would have early morning meetings. Some days, I was so tired I could hardly function, but I would not have traded those nighttime talks for any amount of sleep.

Return and report is the Lord's way. If every parent would vow to be at the crossroads of their children's lives, we would eliminate many of the mistakes of our young people. You know them and their body language. Our youth are not broken down overnight. Gradual steps lead to serious sin. Looking them in the eye and talking to them daily when they come home will help keep them clean. I believe parents will lose less sleep in the long run by waiting up for their children than they will by going to bed. They need our continued love and attention. Waiting up is one way to help them feel secure and keep them within safe boundaries as society's ills rage around them.

Notes

1   Ezra Taft Benson, "To the Mothers in Zion," parents' fireside, Salt Lake City, UT, 22 February 1987.

2   *ABC Nightline*, 17 February 1995.

3   Spencer W. Kimball, *The Miracle of Forgiveness* (Salt Lake City, UT: Deseret Book, 1969), 213.

4   Jenny Deam, "The New Latchkey Kids," parents.com, December 2011.

5   Ezra Taft Benson, *Come, Listen to a Prophet's Voice* (Salt Lake City, UT: Deseret Book, 1990), 32.

6   Frances Kemper Alston, "Latch Key Children," New York University, Child Study Center, May 1, 2007.

7   American School Board, June 2004: Vol. 191, No. 6.

8   Gordon B. Hinckley, in Conference Report, October 1996, 93.

9   Larry R. Lawrence, "Courageous Parenting," *Ensign*, 99.

10 Heber J. Grant, *Gospel Standards* (Salt Lake City, UT: Deseret Book, 1941), 55.

11 *Family Planning Perspectives*, May/June 1988, 75.

12 Randal A. Wright, "Family, Religious, Peer and Media Influence on Adolescence Willingness to Have Premarital Sex" (PhD dissertation), Brigham Young University, 1995, 117.

13 Ibid.

14 Caroline Eyring Miner, *Camilla* (Salt Lake City, UT: Deseret Book, 1980), 109.

15 Neil L. Andersen, "Patterns of Righteousness," BYU–I Education Week devotional, August 1, 2008.

16 Ezra Taft Benson, *God, Family and Country* (Salt Lake City, UT: Deseret Book, 1974), 240.

FAMILY
TRADITIONS

MISTAKE: Failure to have family traditions that teach, indoctrinate, and unify.

"The tradition that we had in my home growing up was that we had no family traditions. My parents even made us feel like holidays and birthdays were a chore for them rather than occasions to celebrate together as a family and increase unity. I think that is one reason that we have very little interaction with each other now that everyone is grown and married."

What is the first thing that comes to your mind when you hear USC, Florida State, Notre Dame, Michigan, Ohio State, Texas, Oklahoma, Alabama, Penn State, Miami? Most people would likely say football. Almost without fail, the teams from these colleges will be ranked in the top twenty-five of the national polls every year. They have what you call strong football traditions. All of these schools devote tremendous amounts of resources to keep their programs on top. Each school has many traditions based around their football team. For example, the Red River Shootout between Texas and Oklahoma has been played for one hundred years. It is always played at the Cotton Bowl, which is a neutral site located on the grounds of the Texas State Fair in Dallas. Because of strong traditions, these schools are able to consistently recruit the top football players in the nation. Other schools that traditionally have losing programs are not able to recruit the top talent. The top football recruit in the nation would never consider going to a traditional loser. He wants to be on a

41

team with strong winning traditions. Children want to be in families that have strong traditions as well.

In the Church, we have many traditions established over the years. Most faithful members would never think about going against these traditions. And yet, we have no idea where some of these traditions even came from. For example, where in the scriptures are we instructed to

- Call each other *brother* and *sister* at church?
- Call some leaders by titles and their last names, such as President _____, Bishop _____?
- Call all missionaries Elder _____ or Sister _____ and their last name?
- Call members of the Quorum of the Twelve Elder _____, even though they are apostles?
- Always include an initial when calling the General Authorities by name?
- Stand and sing "We Thank Thee O God for a Prophet" when he walks into a room?
- Have all male missionaries wear white shirts and nametags?
- Abbreviate everything church related: LDS, FHE, CTR, CES, MTC, BYU, YSA?
- Shake hands with other members at church meetings?

Most of us probably cringe a little when hearing a new convert say something like, "Boyd Packer said. . . ." We would never say George Smith, David McKay, Spencer Kimball, Ezra Benson, Howard Hunter, or Gordon Hinckley. When someone goes against this little tradition, although it is not scripture-based, it seems like it is almost a sin. That is simply not something we faithful members do. Why? Because it is wrong. Why? I don't know—it's just a tradition.

If you were to think of another religious group with many strong traditions, what group comes to your mind? Many would say the Jewish faith is steeped in tradition. Is this the reason this religion has held onto their members through the centuries, even while enduring extreme persecution and isolation from their land of promise? Faithful Jews have observed traditions like the Feast of the Passover since their days of slavery in Egypt. I have often wondered how Jews, who were scattered all over Eastern Europe and the old Soviet Union, remembered they were Jews. I believe the answer to that question can be summed up in one word—tradition. It tells them who they are and what they believe. Faithful Jews, who really practice the traditions of their forefathers, would never consider leaving their faith.

Whether or not our own children remain faithful to the Church of Jesus Christ of Latter-day Saints will in large part depend on the traditions they are exposed to in the family. The word *tradition* has several meanings: 1. the handing down of statements, beliefs, legends, and customs from generation to generation by word of mouth or by practice; 2. a long-established or inherited way of thinking or acting; 3. acts repeated so often they become almost automatic. Speaking of the power of traditions, President Brigham Young said, "The traditions of my earliest recollection are so forcible upon me that it seems impossible for me to get rid of them. And so it is with others; hence the necessity of correct training in childhood."[1]

Traditions Are Numberless

The number of traditions that exist are infinite. Cities, states, countries, schools, religions, and families have traditions passed on through the generations. *Not* having any traditions can become a tradition. There are fun traditions and serious traditions. There are righteous traditions and wicked traditions. One thing is certain. Traditions have a powerful influence on individuals, families, and society in general.

In the Book of Mormon, Laman started wicked traditions, which led to the complete annihilation of the Nephite nation. Their traditions are summarized with these words: "And thus they have taught their children that they should hate them, and that they should murder them, and that they should rob and plunder them, and do all they could to destroy them; therefore they have an eternal hatred towards the children of Nephi" (Mosiah 10:17). One thousand years later, Laman's descendants, who still called themselves Lamanites, slaughtered and subjected the Nephites to rulers whom they believed had the right to lead. How many people do you think have died through the generations because of wicked traditions? How many people have refused to listen to the message of the restored gospel because of the traditions of their fathers?

President George Q. Cannon spoke of the power of false traditions with these words:

> The greatest obstacle that has ever opposed the spread of truth and the diffusion of correct principles is the traditions of the people. So potent is their influence and so much importance is there attached to them that truth is but seldom received, even when supported by the best of reasons and evidence, if it comes in contact with them. They are set up as a standard or criterion by which every new principle or idea must be measured and judged; and whether they be true or false, correct or incorrect, by its agreement or disagreement with them must it be accepted or rejected.[2]

Are there any traditions you have in your family that would be considered wicked? If so, history and prophets' words suggest there is a strong possibility that your posterity will continue them.

Nephi, on the other hand, taught us that righteous traditions can have just as powerful an influence on people as wicked traditions. Nephi loved his brethren in spite of their hatred toward him and his family. He constantly prayed for them and taught them the word of the Lord to bring them back to the fold. One thousand years later, his direct descendants, still calling themselves Nephites, were trying to bring them back. In the last chapter of the Book of Mormon, we read, "Now I, Moroni, write somewhat as seemeth me good; and I write unto my brethren, the Lamanites" (Moroni 10:1).

There is another group in the Book of Mormon that is not mentioned much. They can, however, teach as many valuable lessons as the wicked traditions of the Lamanites and the righteous traditions of the Nephites. This group is sometimes referred to as the Mulekites. You may ask what kinds of traditions this group had. They apparently had a tradition of having no traditions. This group came to the Americas around the same time as the descendants of Lehi and subsequently built a large city called Zarahemla. When Mosiah and his small group of strangers called Nephites came to Zarahemla, the Mulekites did something very strange. They made Mosiah their king. Luckily for the Mulekites, Mosiah was a righteous king. This experience teaches that having no traditions allows people to be influenced by the first strong leader that comes along, whether wicked or righteous. Perhaps this is one of the reasons we are losing so many of our children to the world.

In our time, as then, having no traditions can also put family members in extreme danger.

The Book of Mormon teaches that righteous traditions can help save families, and wicked ones can destroy them. How many people have been saved through the generations because of strong righteous traditions? Are there any traditions that you have in your family that are considered righteous? If so, there is a strong possibility your posterity will continue them. There are so many good family traditions, I hesitate to even mention any, but here are two that perhaps you can add to those you already have.

Have a Family Mission Statement

Many years ago, I was sitting in a BYU class, and the professor shared a family mission statement that had become a tradition in his home. He said this statement had guided almost every decision they made and had become a family tradition: "Be where you are supposed to be, when you are supposed to be there, doing what you are supposed to be doing." As soon as I heard this statement, I wrote it down and shared it with my wife when I got home. We both agreed that we also wanted this to be a tradition in our family. Let's look a little closer at the three parts of this statement.

Be Where You Are Supposed to Be

I hate to brag about this, but my children won a lot of ribbons for all of the contests and events they entered while growing up. All five children have memory books where these ribbons are displayed. Most of these ribbons are the exact same color, with the same color lettering across them. The ribbon color is green, and the lettering says in bold gold letters—"Participant." There are few blue ribbons in our family, and that is fine with me. I'm extremely proud of those green ribbons because I believe that all the Lord expects of us is to show up and do our best, even if we are not number one. I've learned through the years that if you just show up and do the best you can, good things happen.

My boys are both Eagle Scouts, but I would be the first to admit that they were not very good Scouts. Then how did they obtain that high rank? There is only one explanation: They were always where they were supposed to be. It was our family tradition. On Wednesday nights, they always went to their Scout meetings. If there was a campout, merit badge activity, or anything else, they were in attendance. I have noticed if youth go to seminary every day for four years, they will graduate. If they go to high school for four years, they will graduate. I have also seen that if students go to college every day, taking a full load for four years and study, they will be college graduates. It is the same with life in general. Most success in life is showing up and sticking to the task at hand. Elder Joseph B. Wirthlin said, "I believe that perseverance is vital to success in any endeavor, whether spiritual or temporal, large or small, public or personal. . . . All significant achievement results largely from perseverance."[3]

King David, unfortunately, did not establish a tradition of being where he was supposed to be. Otherwise, he may have been spared the terrible sin he committed with Bathsheba. One of the reasons he fell is clearly pointed out in this verse: "And it came to pass, after the year was expired, at the time when kings go forth to battle . . . David tarried still at Jerusalem" (2 Samuel 11: 1). David was the king of Israel. Where was he supposed to be? He should have been in battle with his men. Instead, he stayed behind, which led to his downfall to immorality. How many of our children could be saved from the world if they were raised with a tradition of always being where they were supposed to be?

When You Are Supposed to Be There

Not only should we be where we are supposed to be, it should be when we are supposed to be there. We often hear people joke about Mormon standard time. But we, of all people, should be punctual. After all, a standard is something established as a rule or basis of comparison. Who do we look to as a basis of comparison on earth? The Lord has provided us with living prophets and General Authorities to be our standard bearers. Are our spiritual leaders punctual people? Let's think back for a moment about our general conferences. How many times have you seen a General Authority walk onto the stage in the conference center late to general conference? Can you imagine our prophet or a member of the First Presidency or Quorum of the Twelve explaining he didn't make it to conference on time because he forgot to set the alarm or couldn't find his shoes? Can you even imagine members of the Tabernacle Choir walking onto the stage late? What would be the results if a television cameraman, the organist, or the custodians who open the tabernacle doors were not punctual people? Our real standard, as demonstrated repeatedly by our leaders, is to be punctual. When we are routinely late, it is not Mormon standard at all, but exactly the opposite.

Perhaps being non-punctual is a dangerous tradition in some families. When we get in the habit of not doing things at the proper time, we establish a habit that becomes a family tradition. Timing in many other areas of life may be affected. By not doing things at the proper time, we increase the chances that our children will also not do things when they should be done.

Mormon standard time, in reality, should mean to be *on time*, not late. We define what's important to us by the things we are consistently late to and the things we arrive on time for. If we are always on time to the movies and always late to sacrament meetings, we send a strong message to our children of what is truly important in our lives. Great blessings are promised to those who are at the right place at the right time. President Brigham Young said, "Let promptness and punctuality be the standard with you and the God of peace will pour out blessings upon you that there shall not be room enough to receive them."[4]

Doing What You Are Supposed to Be Doing

We have never refused an assignment from Church leaders. The benefits of this practice became clearer with an experience I had with one of my daughters. One Sunday, a member of the Primary presidency told my wife, Wendy, that our five-year-old Nichelle was assigned to give a talk the following week. Wendy told Nichelle to remind her throughout the week, so they could prepare the talk together. However, they both forgot about it. My wife was our stake Young Women president and visited another ward the Sunday our daughter was to speak. She totally forgot about Nichelle's talk and did not inform me either. When Nichelle went to Primary, a member of the presidency asked if she had her talk. Remembering her mother's word the previous Sunday, she said yes. She was asked to come up to the front and sit with those participating in the program. When it was her turn, she went to the podium and stood there smiling. The Primary counselor became uneasy with her silence, and said, "Nichelle, do you have a talk in your pocket?" She replied, "No." The counselor inquired, "Did your mom help you prepare a talk this week?" Nichelle said, "No." The counselor pressed, "Did your dad help you get a talk?" She answered, "No." She was still smiling when the counselor said, "Boys and girls, Nichelle will give her talk another time." I was very embarrassed, yet proud of this obedient five-year-old who carried out *her* assignment. She did her part in what she was supposed to do. I guess she did give her talk that day. Her talk was on smiling through adversity.

There is also great risk in not doing our duty, whatever that duty may be. President Brigham Young said, "Omission of duty leads to apostasy."[5] On the other hand, there is great protection that comes from doing our duty.

Make Special Events Special

As mentioned earlier, those of the Jewish faith have done a remarkable job of passing on traditions to their family members throughout the centuries. How do they do it? One way is by making important events special. For example, in Jewish law, a boy is deemed a "bar mitzvah" when he turns thirteen. A Jewish girl becomes a "bat mitzvah" when she turns twelve. At this time, they become full-fledged Jewish adults. Bar and bat mitzvahs are celebrated with a festive meal, with family and friends in attendance to celebrate their entrance into adulthood. The meal is often accompanied by encouraging speeches from friends and relatives to the bar or bat mitzvah. The speeches focus on their new role as a full-fledged Jewish adult, having joy while striving to add spirituality to their lives. Friends and relatives will travel from all over the world to attend these special events. Those who attend often give gifts and money, which makes the young person feel very special.

Let's contrast that with what happens when a young man in our church turns twelve and receives the holy priesthood. This obviously should be one of the most special and memorable days of his life. In all too many cases, however, the day a boy is ordained to the priesthood is just an ordinary day. Often a boy is ordained in his quorum, and family members are not even invited in. This event should be a time of special gifts, festive dinners with friends and relatives, father's interviews and blessings, pictures, unique trips, and so on. A similar scenario should be established for our young women who enter the Young Women program.

In the Church, we have numerous events that should lend themselves to special family traditions. The obvious events are baby blessings, baptisms, ordinations to the priesthood, turning sixteen, Eagle Scout awards, Young Womanhood Recognition, patriarchal blessings, seminary graduation, and mission calls. The Church will not establish family traditions for you. Remember, at some point in time, a Jewish family started the bar and bat mitzvah celebrations that keep their children Jewish for centuries. What traditions have you established for special events in your family?

Remember the three meanings of the word *tradition*: 1. the handing down of statements, beliefs, legends, customs, etc. from generation to the next by word of mouth or by practice; 2. an inherited way of thinking or acting; 3. acts repeated so often they become almost automatic. In terms of teaching children the gospel, all of these definitions have powerful implications. The wonderful, or frightening, thing about traditions is they can be started by anyone, and with consistency, passed on through the generations. If we will establish righteous traditions, they will be a source of great protection for family members not only now, but in the future.

Notes

1   Brigham Young, "The Power of Tradition on the Human Mind," *Journal of Discourses*, 13:243, September 25, 1870.

2   George Q. Cannon, *Gospel Truth* (Salt Lake City, UT: Deseret Book, 1957), 294.

3   Joseph B. Wirthlin, "Never Give Up," *Ensign*, November 1987, 9.

4   Brigham Young, *The Journal of Brigham: Brigham Young's Own Story in His Own Words* (Springville, UT: Cedar Fort, 1980), 126.

5   Brigham Young, "Duties of the Saints—Obedience to Counsel," *Journal of Discourses*, 11:108, May 15, 1865.

CHILDREN'S
FRIENDS

MISTAKE: Allowing children to associate too closely with friends who do not share their same standards.

"My parents let me hang out with people who did not have the same standards as our family. I went out with some shady characters and got into more trouble than I should have. Instead of raising their standards to mine, I'm afraid I lowered mine to theirs. My parents should have been more concerned with my friends and the things that I was involved in. Now that I think of it, they really never even talked to my friends."

Years ago, we lived in a rural area that had no leash laws for pets. Our children had a very mild-tempered cocker spaniel named Mick, who often roamed the neighborhood. One day, as I was driving home from early-morning seminary, I saw our dog trotting down the road with four other dogs. The lead dog was a Rottweiler, with three Doberman pinschers and Mick following closely behind. These four dogs had bad reputations, and I wondered why our innocent dog was hanging out with them. I recall that it looked as if Mick thought he was really "cool" running with the bad dogs. Later, as I returned home from work, I saw the leader of the pack lying on the side of the road, dead. As I drove into our driveway, I saw Mick limping badly from an injured leg. The dogs had gotten a little too close to the highway, where one was killed and at least one injured when hit by a car. That night, I thought about how our children must be extremely careful with whom they spend their time. H. Burke Peterson said, "We pick up our worst habits from our best friends."[1] It is a dangerous world that we live in, and poorly chosen friends can often lead our unsuspecting children down dangerous paths.

President Gordon B. Hinckley gave valuable counsel to the youth of the Church:

> Choose your friends carefully. It is they who will lead you in one direction or the other. Everybody wants friends. Everybody needs friends. No one wishes to be without them. But never lose sight of the fact that it is your friends who will lead you along the paths that you will follow. *While you should be friendly with all people, select with great care those whom you wish to have close to you.* They will be your safeguards in situations where you may vacillate between choices, and you in turn may save them.[2]

Shortly after the incident with the dogs, my friend Dale, a biology teacher with a fondness for snakes, told me about a past experience. With several snakes at school, and a king snake in a cage near his home, he still wanted to catch a blue racer for his collection. But blue racer snakes are very difficult to catch because of their natural quickness. King snakes are also unique because of their tendency to prey on other snakes. Although harmless to man, king snakes coil around their prey and squeeze them to death.

One day, Dale and his son were driving home when they saw a blue racer cross the road. Excitedly, Dale stopped his truck and began a chase. After much effort, the two finally cornered the snake and captured it. Realizing he didn't have an empty cage for his new prize, Dale decided to house the blue racer in the cage with his king snake as he quickly built a new one. Fully aware of the king snake's bad reputation, Dale planned to leave his blue racer in the cage for only a short period of time. As he hurriedly built the new cage, his daughter ran over and exclaimed, "Dad, the king snake is wrapped around your blue racer!" Dale ran as quickly as he could, but it was too late. The king snake had killed his prized blue racer.

Our experience with our dog, Mick, and my friend's blue racer snake reminded me that we, as parents, need to be careful not to let our children associate closely with those who could lead them astray. Even though most are strong, they are often no match for some of the "bad dogs" and "king snakes" of our permissive society. Too many parents think simply because they are teaching their children in the home, their children's friends will have little influence on them. That is not the case. Friends have been shown, in repeated research, to have a huge influence for good or bad on our children.

A former stake president said, "If you want to get a good look at yourselves, take a look at the friends you have. They almost always reflect your values." By the same token, if you want to know how your children are doing, look to their friends. Good friends almost always do the same kinds of things. This is not coincidental. Friends are often chosen on the basis of similarities with another. By the same token, one who wants to join a group of friends will often modify their behavior to conform to the values of the group with which they associate. For example, think of the type of music your children listen to. Is it coincidental that their friends like the same type of music? The old saying "Birds of a feather flock together" is usually true.

Consider carefully the significance of a statement by President Thomas S. Monson. He said, "In a survey which was made in selected wards and stakes of the Church, we learned a most significant fact. Those persons whose friends married in the temple usually married in the temple, while those persons whose friends did not marry in the temple usually did not marry in the temple. The influence of one's friends appeared to be a more dominant factor than parental urging, classroom instruction, or proximity to a temple."[3] Did you catch what he said? Friends have more of an impact than parents, seminary, YM/YW, or where you live. Research consistently indicates those who associate with friends who smoke are likely to smoke themselves. How many times have you seen a group of teenagers smoking at the same time? The friends of those using drugs will usually turn to drug usage themselves after time. The same holds true for drinking and morality. Those who associate with sexually active friends are likely to become sexually active in time. When children closely associate with those of differing standards, the results can be devastating. We should be extremely vigilant in monitoring our children's friends. We learn a great lesson from the Book of Mormon, "Yea, and we also see the great wickedness one very wicked man can cause to take place among the children of men" (Alma 46:9).

When I asked a large group of youth teachers to make a list of some of the indicators that a youth might be struggling, almost everyone mentioned the quality of his or her friends as a huge factor. Keep in mind that if our children are spending time with friends who are struggling with the standards, there is a good chance our kids are struggling also, or they soon will be, unless something changes. Of course, this can be a delicate situation. Trying not to come across to others as self-righteous or superior can be tricky. What can we do to help ensure that our children have friends that lift them up instead of bringing them down?

Pray for Good Friends

While it is true that friends can have a detrimental effect on our children, it is also true that good friends can have a positive influence. Many years ago, Elder Francis M. Lyman pointed out, "Children . . . will never go astray while they are in good company."[4] What a wonderful promise this is. Since it is so difficult to go against the norm of a group, this can work in a positive way also. If our children are always in good company, then they will be safe. As parents, we must pray for our children to have good friends and then work to make it happen. I have seen the power of this principle on numerous occasions working with youth and young single adults. Over the years, many young men and women who were struggling spiritually have walked into the institute building where I teach. I believe many of these individuals walked through the doors because of the prayers of worried parents. Whenever this happens, a group of active LDS students have always reached out to them. I have seen many miracles occur when parents have prayed for their children and then made the effort to inform leaders of their children's needs.

I believe there is great power in prayers offered in behalf of our children. When we got the call to move to Utah, it couldn't have come at a worse time for our oldest son, Nathan. He was going into his senior year of high school and was especially looking forward to playing basketball with a group who had been together since the seventh grade. He had also grown up around his cousins who were not only good friends but great examples as well. We were very concerned about who his friends might be. We prayed every night that he could find a good friend in Utah.

Just a few weeks after moving to Utah, I got a call from Rhonda, a family friend, and one of my former seminary students from Texas. She had married a returned missionary who was attending BYU. Her mother-in-law was the sister of our former stake president, and her father-in-law was a BYU professor. They happened to live in the same area where we had just moved. When Rhonda called, she said, "I had a dream about your son, Nathan. I dreamed that Nathan and my brother-in-law, Jason, needed to be friends." She then asked if we would come over for family home evening the next Monday night at her in-laws' home. Of course we went, and that night Nathan met Jason, a senior at the same high school our son was attending. Jason was an outstanding young man, and they became good friends that night. This friend helped Nathan have a good experience his senior year and helped him prepare for his mission. Some may say that this was just a coincidence, but I have a testimony that the Lord watches over our children and gives them opportunities to cross paths with others who will help.

Invite Families Over

It is not enough to just pray for good friends for our children; we must take an active role in seeing that it happens. One thing we can do to help our children have good friends is to have lots of friends ourselves. Sometimes we get so busy when we have children that we fail to cultivate relationships with our own peers. Make sure to invite exceptional families over with children similar in age to your own children. Play games, go camping, and do things that will help bond your families. I have watched many families over the years do exactly this. In many cases, close friendships are formed between the children of good friends. President Spencer W. Kimball said, "Always keep good company. Never waste an hour with anyone who doesn't lift you up and encourage you."[5] When we follow this counsel ourselves, we expose our children to friends who will lift and encourage them.

Open Your Home

Another way to help your children have good friends is to make your home the center place for youth. Many parents will gladly let you take on this role, since having your home the "place to be" comes with a price. You will most likely have to clean up after them, provide food for them, and have your routine interrupted. But the benefits of this practice can be tremendous. When your children's friends congregate at your home, you get to observe them closely to see what kind of friends they really are. Maybe just as important is the opportunity you have to influence your children's friends in a positive way. Many youth today do not have the good fortune of coming from homes where gospel principles are taught. When parents take the time to interact with their children's friends, many positive benefits can occur. President Gordon B. Hinckley gave the following inspired counsel to mothers:

> I mentioned to the Relief Society women several specific things that they ought to teach their sons and daughters. I repeat them briefly, perhaps in different language.
>
> The first is to encourage them to develop good friendships. Every boy or girl longs for friends. No one wishes to walk alone. The warmth, the comfort, the camaraderie of a friend mean everything to a boy or girl. That friend can be either an influence for good or an influence for evil. The street gangs which are so vicious are an example of friendships gone afoul. Conversely, the association of young people in church and their mingling in school with those of their own kind will lead them to do well and to excel in their endeavors. Open your homes to the friends of your children. If you find they have big appetites, close your eyes and let them eat. Make your children's friends your friends.[6]

Of course, we know that President Hinckley married a girl who grew up in that kind of open and warm home. Marjorie came from a home that was the center of neighborhood activities. Sheri L. Dew said, "Georgetta and Roy [Pay] were warm, generous people who opened their home in a comfortable way that drew friends and family to them. On Sunday evenings Marjorie and her friends came home after sacrament meeting for waffles—a weekly ritual so sacred that when the waffle iron quit working, Marjorie's friends pooled their money to buy the Pays another one."[7]

Become Friends with Children's Friends

One day I came home early from work and sat down in the living room to work on a project. My wife was upstairs, and our two youngest daughters, Natalie and Nichelle, were gone. I was surprised when I heard the front door open and wondered who it could be. All of a sudden, I heard a voice say, "Oh hi, Brother Wright." I responded, "Hi, Melinda." She is one of Natalie's best friends. She just went to the refrigerator, opened it, looked around, and then shut it. Then she opened up the freezer, looked in, and then shut it. Next, it was the pantry where she looked around for a minute and then yelled up to my wife, "Sister Wright, where are the Swiss cake rolls?" I heard my wife say, "I forgot to buy them, but I'll get some soon." Melinda then said, "Is Natalie home?" I told her that she was still at work. Melinda went upstairs and talked to my wife for over an hour. When that happened, I had a very warm feeling pass over me and a new love and appreciation for my wife. I knew that she was Melinda's friend and that somehow she was helping our own daughter in the process.

Many parents become so busy that it is difficult for them to keep up with the friends of their children. Do you know who your children's friends are? Do you know their parents and the type of family they have? Elder Joe J. Christensen gave this valuable counsel, "You may need to get together with the parents of your children's friends and mutually agree on acceptable standards of entertainment, hours, and activities. When discussions about standards are held, either at home or with the neighbors, involve the children, whenever possible. If they have a part in the decisions made, they will more likely 'own' them and be more inclined to live up to them."[8]

Do you have those friends in your home frequently so you can spend time together and get to know them? When parents are friends with their children's friends, those friends will be less likely to try to get your children to do anything against your family rules. Over the years I have heard many youth talk about the parents of their friends. I have often heard the words, "Your parents are so cool." If your children hear that from their friends, they will then be more likely to listen to your counsel.

Social Skills

As parents, we should also help our children develop the skills it takes to form healthy friendships with others. One way to do this is to model good social skills ourselves. Invite friends over who have children similar in age for a barbecue, party, holiday, or birthday celebration. Our children watch and imitate us much more than we realize. When children see parents socialize warmly with friends, the tendency is for them to do the same with their peers. If we isolate ourselves socially, then chances are that our children will follow our example.

Those without the social skills needed to develop healthy friendships are often drawn to anyone who will accept them. Many in this situation will compromise their own standards rather than be left out. It is very important for our children to learn how to be social so they can be influential themselves. There are many things that can help your children be more social. I will mention two that are closely related.

Friendly Greetings

It goes without saying that if we want to have friends then we must be friendly. A great example of this principle was President Spencer W. Kimball. He was a master at developing lifelong friends. What was the key to his success? He had an amazing ability to make people feel loved. By all accounts, he was extremely friendly. He said, "In Salt Lake as I go down the street, I say hello to everybody, a stranger or otherwise. I know that they do not know me, but I like to say hello and I think they appreciate it. I notice their faces light up with a smile."[9]

When I first moved to Texas, I was assigned to be a home teacher with Nate, one of the young men in the ward. He was a ninth grade student and a talented football player. One night as we were driving along to our next appointment, he told me how the kids at his high school gave the members of the Church a hard time. He said that his friend, Gary, would argue with those who said derogatory things about the Church, but he had learned this never helped. He told me that he just tried to be a good example for those who were not members of our faith. I asked him if everyone at the school gave the members a hard time. At first he said yes, but then he pondered the question a little longer and said, "Well, almost everyone. Those in the choir or the drama department are very nice to us." I asked why he felt this was the case and he replied, "Because of Ryan." Ryan, a senior in high school, was in choir and drama. Nate then said, "If people know Ryan, they don't give us a hard time since everyone loves Ryan." He said, "Ryan is friends with everyone. He's a friend to the jocks, the skaters, the druggies, the hicks, the goths, and all the cliques. He smiles and is friendly to everyone no matter what group they are in. Everyone loves Ryan." Then looking straight ahead, obviously talking to himself instead of to me, he said, "If I ever said anything bad about Ryan, I would feel really bad. Man, if anyone ever said anything bad about Ryan they should feel really bad. Man, if anyone ever said anything bad about Ryan that would be like stealing a car from a church!" As we continued down the road, I pondered his message. Football players are not usually that impressed with those in choir and drama. But Nate was very impressed by an LDS priest in his ward who was friendly to everyone. Are we friendly to everyone? Are we teaching our children to smile and greet people with enthusiasm? Those who master this art usually have many friends.

Call People by Name

Once I spoke with a successful stockbroker during a youth conference. We talked about making good friends, and he shared an experience from his own life. He said that as a junior, he moved to a new high school where he didn't know a single person. This was a hard move, and he was uncomfortable going to school without friends. Talking over the problem with his parents, they came up with a plan. He bought a yearbook from the previous year and began to study the names of everyone in his school. When he walked down the hall at school, he said hi and then called people by name. Most of his classmates seemed surprised that he knew their names, but not one person asked how he learned their names or what his name was. Before long, however, he would say hi and call the person by name and they would greet him, calling him by name. He never asked them how they knew his name either. He was using a technique taught by Dale Carnegie, who said, "Remember that a person's name is to that person the sweetest and most important sound in any language." Why did his classmates know his name without asking him? I believe they were too embarrassed to ask him his because he already knew theirs. So they would ask people behind the scenes who he was. Soon almost everyone in the school knew Jim. He was elected the student body president the following year. This simple little technique works like magic. Someone once said, "The average man is more interested in his own name than he is in all the other names on earth put together."

Friends of our children can be a great support in helping you reach your family goals. Dyer and Kunz found in their study of effective families that "eighty-five percent of the families in the survey indicated that their children's friends have been a 'very helpful' influence."[10] The same can be true of our children's friends by monitoring them in our homes, and by teaching our children how to be a true friend.

Ezra Taft Benson said, "Have good associates or don't associate at all. Be careful in the selection of your friends. If in the presence of certain persons you are lifted to nobler heights, you are in good company. But if your friends or associates encourage base thoughts, then you had best leave them."[11]

Finally, Elder Larry R. Lawrence expressed his concern about having friends spend the night at each other's homes. He said, "May I express my personal warning about a practice that is common in many cultures. I am referring to sleepovers, or spending the night at the home of a friend. As a bishop I discovered that too many youth violated the Word of Wisdom or the law of chastity for the first time as part of a sleepover. Too often their first exposure to pornography and even their first encounter with the police occurred when they were spending the night away from home."[12]

Notes

1 H. Burke Peterson, in Area Conference Report, August 1973, 62.

2 Gordon B. Hinckley, "A Prophet's Counsel and Prayer for Youth," *Ensign*, January 2001, 2.

3 Thomas S. Monson, CES Fireside for Young Adults, November 6, 2005, Brigham Young University.

4 Francis M. Lyman, in Conference Report, October 7, 1915.

5 Edward L. Kimball, ed., *The Teachings of Spencer W. Kimball* (Salt Lake City, UT: Deseret Book, 1982), 262.

6 Gordon B. Hinckley, "Great Shall Be the Peace of Thy Children," *Ensign*, November 2000, 50.

7   Sheri L. Dew, *Go Forward with Faith: The Biography of Gordon B. Hinckley* (Salt Lake City, UT: Deseret Book, 1996), 110–11.

8   Joe J. Christensen, *One Step at a Time: Building a Better Marriage, Family, and You* (Salt Lake City, UT: Deseret Book, 1996), 74.

9   Edward L. Kimball, ed., *The Teachings of Spencer W. Kimball* (Salt Lake City, UT: Deseret Book, 1982), 261.

10 William G. Dyer and Phillip R. Kunz, *Effective Mormon Families* (Salt Lake City, UT: Deseret Book, 1986), 128.

11 Ezra Taft Benson, *God, Family and Country* (Salt Lake City, UT: Deseret Book, 1974), 241.

12 Larry R. Lawrence, "Courageous Parenting," *Ensign*, November 2010, 99–100.

PEER
PRESSURE

MISTAKE: Failure to teach children how to deal with the tremendous pressures they will face.

"My parents tried to tell me growing up that if I would live the gospel standards, all the kids at school would admire me for it. Nothing could have been further from the truth. I was not prepared to deal with the pressure and mocking that I faced and unfortunately gave in to it."

It was a beautiful summer day, and my friends and I were looking forward to a fun afternoon of water skiing. We had a powerful boat to pull us down the river, but our skis left a little to be desired. One was a slalom ski, the other a regular ski for the right foot, with its match missing. We had a hard time getting up as the boat tugged on our tow rope since one ski was approximately a foot longer than the other. We were having a really good time, and I was proud of myself for mastering this inconvenience, especially since I had been skiing only a few times in my life. As the boat pulled me down the river, we passed a ski jump ramp owned by the local ski club. Friends in the boat started coaxing me to attempt the jump. As Jim, the driver, circled past the ramp several times, I thought, "Yeah, right. I barely know how to ski. I'm sure not going over any ski ramp!" But they continued encouraging me to jump, adding a few words that implied that maybe I was afraid. They had that part right. The thought of making that jump scared me to death! However, before long another thought crossed my mind—it'd be really cool to be the only one brave enough to go over the jump. When I yelled back to take me toward the jump, a cheer went up from my friends. I could sense their surprise that I would really go through with it.

As I neared the ramp, I felt almost confident about what I was about to do. I knew I would be a hero of sorts to the wimps in the boat because of the feat I was about to accomplish. I was ready as the ramp approached. But the second I hit the ramp, I realized I was in trouble. Jump skis don't have rudders on the bottom, but the two mismatched ones I was wearing did. And yet, with all the scraping and shaking that occurred as the skis touched the jump, I managed to stay upright. I actually cleared the end of the ramp standing up, and I felt like I had just won a world championship. I heard the cheers from the boat as I quickly made my way down toward the water. I was so excited about clearing the end of the ramp, though, that I forgot to concentrate on my landing. Later, I learned that when you land after jumping, it is essential to keep your skis pointed slightly upward. Mine, according to those in the boat, were pointed directly down. I remember entering the water at high speed, going just a few feet farther once I landed. Apparently, the longer ski hit the water first. Since both skis were pointed toward the water, my forward motion stopped almost immediately. It was like doing a complete belly flop off a fifty-foot high dive. I hit the water so hard that I seriously thought I would lose my eyesight. I was red from head to foot. Of course, my friends thought it was hilarious, once they determined I wasn't dead. I was very lucky to not be seriously hurt. Others who have followed the pressure of the crowd have not been so lucky. I had failed to learn the lesson that President Spencer W. Kimball taught when he said, "When you do not worry or concern yourself too much with what other people do and believe and say, there will come to you a new freedom."[1]

The desire to be accepted often means conforming to peer standards. These peer standards can be positive in some areas, harmless in others, or devastating in yet others. The group has the power to accept or reject based on their terms. Businesses love it, because they come up with the clothing and music for each group. Every high school has cliques, and every clique has something to say about the other that is not flattering. No matter what group our kids are in, someone is going to not like them. Enormous pressure to conform to the norm of the group and not be a loner is placed on children. Individuals are often singled out for ridicule because they do not fit into the group's norm. The crowd can be very cruel. Many young people find it easier to give in rather than stand up for what they believe in. Elder W. Eugene Hansen said, "There is a compelling desire to belong—to be one of the group. If he can get just one person to influence others to choose the wrong way for whatever reason, Satan wins. Often the easiest and simplest nudging is that 'everyone is doing it' or 'it's the cool thing' or 'how do you know it's bad if you haven't tried it?'"[2]

There are many reasons youth have trouble dealing with pressure from peers. One reason youth give into peer pressure is their friends provide them what they are not getting at home. With family members going in so many different directions, many of our youth spend more time with their peers than with their families. Youth who enjoy being with their families have less need to conform to peer demands and are known to be less permissive in their sexual attitudes. Our youth will ultimately make the final decision to be virtuous or not. If their home life is happy, teenagers often desire this same happiness for themselves and are more likely to listen to parents' counsel and follow parental examples. When confronted with crucial decisions, parental rather than peer opinions are accepted. President Spencer W. Kimball once observed, "Home life, home teaching, parental guidance is the panacea for all the ailments, a cure for all diseases, a remedy for all problems."[3]

In times past, home has been a safe haven from the world. But now the home and family are under attack. The casualties in this great battle have been millions. Many teens are growing up in homes where contention and turmoil are the norm. Numerous couples are not in harmony. Too many are out chasing after the things of the world. We would all do well to remember the words of President David O. McKay's oft-quoted statement: "No other success can compensate for failure in the home. The poorest shack in which love prevails over a united family is of greater value to God and future humanity than any other riches. In such a home, God can work miracles and will work miracles."[4]

Not Just Youth

Would you or I wear a pair of faded blue jeans, a T-shirt, and tennis shoes to sacrament meeting? Why not? Our youth often feel the same way about being different from the crowd. Sometimes adults have little compassion for youth who give in to the pressure of the crowd. Many of us have no idea what our children are going through with their peers. It's easy for parents to say, "Stand up," when they are not the ones being laughed at. As adults, we seldom feel the pains of rejection and often have short memories about our own teen years.

However, we should remember that adults face tremendous amounts of pressure also and often give in as much as youth. Are we influenced by what other parents do? How many times have you heard things like: "The Smiths let their kids go to the prom before age sixteen and they turned out fine," or "The Joneses let their children steady date, so I don't see the big deal," or "The Williamses bought all of their kids a car when they got their driver's licenses, so why can't I have one?" The truth is that few of us, whether old or young, want to go against the norm and be different from those around us.

I found out that the pressure to give in to the crowd never goes away, no matter what the age. I wrote the following about an experience I had many years ago when serving on the high council:

About twenty young single adults and I enjoyed an activity in Dallas, Texas, at a water amusement park that had swimming pools, water slides, wave pools, and various other water attractions.

We were all having lots of fun when someone suggested we go down the dreaded "black hole," an enclosed tube about six stories high in which you twist and turn in every conceivable way in total darkness until you finally shoot out the end at high speed into a small pool of water. I assured the person who made the suggestion that I was doing just fine without going down this tube. But when someone else accused me of being "chicken," I had no choice but to ride the "black hole." It turned out to be as bad as I had envisioned it. I was completely disoriented while going down, and my head was spinning badly by the time I hit the shallow pool of water at the bottom. But at least I couldn't be called a chicken, and I felt good about that.

A few minutes later, we were joined by another group of young single adults. Among this group was an energetic, young returned missionary named Benny. After some small talk, Benny came up with a frightening suggestion—at least it was scary to me! He said, "You know what would be totally awesome? To go down the black hole backward!" I exclaimed, "That ride is terrible going down frontward! Why would any normal person want to go down backwards?" Some of the group agreed, but another member of the group, Danny, said, "Let's go for it. It *will* be awesome!"

With that remark, like a bunch of sheep, we followed Benny and Danny up the stairs to the top of the black hole. As we waited for our turns, Benny turned to me and asked if I was going down backward. I replied, "Why don't all of you guys go first and show me how it's done." All of the group in front of me went down the tube backward, and with them went the pressure to give in for fear of being laughed at. My guess was that they would be so dizzy at the end of the ride they would never notice that I was going to come down frontward.

Then, to my surprise, Angie, the young woman behind me, asked if I was going backward. Chuckling, I said, "No. I am going frontward. The guys will never know the difference." Then she added, "I can't believe it. Randal's a chicken! Even I am going down backward!" Well, that's all it took. I wasn't going to have anyone laughing at me and calling me a chicken for being afraid. So I went down backward, and as I expected, I hated every minute of it. By the time I reached the bottom, I couldn't tell whether I was going frontward, backward, or sideways. I was so disoriented.

The consequences of our actions came immediately. I staggered over to some chairs after the ride and sat down. Benny was sitting down on the grass looking about the same color as his green surroundings, while Danny leaned against a fence post and moaned with discomfort. Several of us felt ill for the rest of the day. And to my amusement, Benny and Danny were the sickest of all.

I've done a lot of thinking since that event and have decided that the process we were involved in that day is closely related to the techniques the adversary uses to ensnare us in sin.

Luckily for our group, going down the black hole backward was not a sin. But the process used to get us to do it is similar to the one that Satan uses. It goes something like this: Someone does something wrong. He tells his friends it was "totally awesome." If the friends don't do it also, others will laugh and call them "chicken," a "goody goody," or a similar name. Finally, they give in. Once these friends try the forbidden, they use the same methods to talk others into doing the same thing. And like the young adults' experience with the black hole, most victims do not think of the consequences of their actions until it is too late. Sometimes it takes years to see the effects of smoking, drinking, immorality, and other sins in a person's life.[5]

Mocking is one of the most powerful weapons in Satan's vast arsenal to get us to give into pressure. We must learn to pay no heed to peer pressure if we are to make it safely back home. Explaining his father's vision, Nephi said, "And great was the multitude that did enter into that strange building. And after they did enter into that building they did point the finger of scorn at me and those that were partaking of the fruit also; but we heeded them not" (1 Nephi 8:33).

Pressure with Appearance

I gave a talk to the teenagers in a local stake about the pressure many feel to dress similarly to those they hang out with. The next day, one of my institute students said his seventeen-year-old brother, John, was at the fireside and wanted him to give me a message. He said that I was wrong about pressure from friends. He said his friends never pressured him to do anything. He said he could wear any kind of clothes and they wouldn't say anything. I knew John and also knew that he wore clothes from Goodwill like old Dairy Queen shirts, mechanics shirts with the former owners names still on them, and the like. Coincidently, his friends dressed the same way. John also had hair down the middle of his back that was seldom combed—just like his friends.

I knew exactly why his friends didn't pressure him. It was because he had already given into their pressure and was doing almost everything they did. So, of course, they would not pressure him. I told John that I loved to do research and would give him fifty dollars if he would wear the clothes I would provide for him during three consecutive days to school. I told him I wanted to see if his friends would say anything if he went against their norm. Day one I told him would be "prep" day. I would supply him with a polo shirt and pants and penny loafer shoes. Day two would be "hick" day and I would supply him with a cowboy shirt, Wrangler jeans, cowboy boots, belt, and hat. Day three would be "scout appreciation" day. His clothes would be a complete boy scout uniform with shirt, shorts, long scout socks, and a sash with merit badges. If anyone asked him why he was wearing the scout uniform, he would say that he was "trying to build scout spirit" at his high school. With each new outfit, the deal was that he couldn't say one thing to his friends about why he was doing it. He just had to say "Because I like them" if his friends asked why he was doing it.

I pointed out that if he refused to wear the clothes I provided, it would prove that he was giving into pressure from his friends to dress only a certain way. At first John talked big as if he would take the challenge, but in the end, just as I predicted, he wouldn't do it. I raised the payoff to a hundred dollars to wear the clothes I picked out, but he still refused. It is interesting that the boy who wore clothes from secondhand stores refused to wear the brand new clothes I would provide him. Why? Each of his friends wore the same grungy clothes that he did because this was the group's unique trademark style. Of course almost every high school in the nation has a similar group. They refuse to wear anything but what is approved by the group and would never be caught wearing preppie or cowboy clothes. Many youth feel as if they are not being pressured when in reality they have *already* totally given into the pressure of the group so there is nothing to pressure them about.

Immorality

One of the more curious terms of derision used by kids today is the word *virgin*. In many peer groups it is an insult to be identified as never having had sex. Some who insist on maintaining their virtue are even rumored to be homosexual. Virgins—both boys and girls—are made to feel they don't fit in and that something is wrong with them.

David Gelman said, "One reporter summed up the situation well when he said, 'Once chastity was something to be guarded—or lied about when lost. Now an uncommonly virtuous teenager lies to protect the dirty little secret that she is still a virgin. There is more pressure than ever for a girl to 'get it over with.'"[6]

This direct pressure can be intense once the crowd learns that a youth is still a virgin. Ridicule and mocking often follow the news. Recently, one of the star LDS athletes at our local school was called a wimp by a group of cheerleaders because he chose to remain virtuous. Fortunately, his high self-image, the support of his family, the possession of many talents, and his strong religious beliefs allowed him to ignore the ridicule and actually laugh about the incident. Others are not able to endure this kind of pressure.

Word of Wisdom

There is tremendous pressure on youth in our day to try alcohol. Youth see alcohol ads everywhere they turn. It is in the magazines they read and on television programs they watch. An analysis of prime time television found that fifteen characters out of sixteen accepted an alcoholic drink when they were offered. Multiple studies have shown that exposure to alcohol advertising serves as a form of peer pressure and increases the chances that young people will begin drinking, or drink more if they are already consuming alcohol. The bombardment to pressure youth to drink continues unabated. For example:

- The alcohol industry spent more than $8 billion on 2.7 million product advertisements between 2001 and 2009.[7]
- The average annual number of alcohol ads seen by youth watching television increased from 217 in 2001 to 366 in 2009. This is approximately one alcohol ad per day.[8]
- From 2001 to 2009, youth were twenty-two times more likely to see an alcohol product ad than an alcohol company–sponsored "responsibility" ad.[9]
- Every day in the United States, 4,750 young people under the age of sixteen have their first full drink of alcohol.[10]
- Youth who start drinking before age fifteen are four times more likely to become dependent on alcohol than those who wait until age twenty-one.[11]
- Ninety-five percent of all violent crime on college campuses involves the use of alcohol by the assailant, victim, or both.[12]
- Ninety percent of acquaintance rape and sexual assaults on college campuses involve the use of alcohol by the assailant, victim, or both.[13]
- Each year, approximately 5,000 young people under the age of twenty-one die as a result of underage drinking; this includes about 1,900 deaths from motor vehicle crashes, 1,600 as a result of homicides, 300 from suicide, as well as hundreds from other injuries, such as falls, burns, and drownings.[14]

- Youth are eleven times more likely to be in a physical fight after drinking.[15]

Other consequences include:
- School problems, such as higher absence and poor or failing grades.
- Legal problems, such as arrest for driving or physically hurting someone while drunk.
- Unwanted, unplanned, and unprotected sexual activity.
- Disruption of normal growth and sexual development.
- Memory problems.
- Abuse of other drugs.
- Changes in brain development that may have lifelong effects.
- Death from alcohol poisoning.[16]

We live in a world that realizes the consequences of alcohol on a daily basis. It is highly associated with death on the highway, loss of virtue, crime, abuse, loss of health, and addiction. And yet, non-drinkers are the ones called weird. Evil and conspiring men of our day have been extremely successful convincing youth to drink.

Had a Drink in the Last 30 Days;
Had a Drink in the Last Year

Eighth graders 13.8%; 29.3%
Tenth graders 28.9%; 52.1%
Twelfth graders 41.2%; 65.2%[17]

What can families do to help members stand up to the onslaught of pressure that surely will come in our day?

Make Up Their Minds Beforehand

A few years ago, I took my wife, Wendy, our daughter Nichelle, and her friend Tiffany to an amusement park in Pennsylvania. I knew they had one of the top wooden roller coasters in the nation and wanted everyone to ride it, just so we could say we had done it. We talked about riding it on the way to the park. Wendy and Tiffany announced in no uncertain terms before we even arrived that they were not going to ride it. I tried to pressure them a little, but I could tell by the way they said "no" that they meant it and that I was wasting my time with them. Nichelle, however, didn't say anything before we arrived. That meant to me that she hadn't really made up her mind. When we were all beneath the huge roller coaster, I began to pressure all three girls to ride it by saying it was a chance in a lifetime and for them to not be babies. Wendy and Tiffany were still very firm and proceeded to sit down. Nichelle, on the other hand, started laughing and said, "No, Dad, I'm not riding it." Of course, her laughter told me she was vulnerable and that if I kept up the pressure, she would eventually give in. So, I turned away from my wife and Tiffany and kept up the pressure with Nichelle. Since she had not made up her mind beforehand, she finally gave in to the pressure. You must make up your mind before temptation comes and then be firm when it does come.

Perhaps everyone in the family can make up a list of the things they *will* do and the things they *will not* do. Then when the pressure comes, the decision will already have been made, and it will be much easier to resist.

Not Always Admired

Some youth feel misled by parents and leaders when told if they stand up for what they believe in, the other youth will admire them for it. The truth is that youth with high standards are not universally admired in popular social groups at their schools. Many are even detested and laughed at because of their standards. If there is secret admiration, it certainly does not manifest itself in all circles. President George Albert Smith said, "We will not be popular with those who are unrighteous."[18] That they will always be admired is simply not guaranteed. Paul describes the last days by saying, "Men shall be lovers of their own selves, covetous, boasters, proud, blasphemers, disobedient to parents, unthankful, unholy, without natural affection, trucebreakers, false accusers, incontinent, fierce, *despisers of those that are good*" (2 Timothy 3:2–3; emphasis added).

Many youth become disillusioned when they find out they are not always admired for living gospel standards. Some will respect you, and some will not. Even Latter-day Saints who are not doing what they should will sometimes mock those who are keeping the standards of the Church. "Yea, and all that will live godly in Christ Jesus shall suffer persecution" (2 Timothy 3:12).

Recently, I heard a young man speaking at a stake general priesthood meeting right before he left on his mission. He had lived in a home where he was taught to stand up to pressure. This prevented him from worrying as much about what others said. At one point in his talk, he said: "To the kids at school I wasn't cool, and I was proud of it."

Ask How Can I Do It?

The best time to look for an emergency exit is before an emergency occurs. The scriptures say, "Flee youthful lust" (2 Timothy 2:22). Joseph of old was faced with a moral dilemma when Potiphar's wife tried to persuade him to violate his standard of morality. How he responded to this is a great example to all of us when faced with pressure to sin. He simply asked himself a question and then ran from the situation. The question was "How then can I do this great wickedness, and sin against God?" (Genesis 39:9). All of us should ask the same question when faced with pressure to go against the teachings of the Lord. The scripture says, "And she caught him by his garment, saying, Lie with me: and he fled, and got him out" (Genesis 39:12). Sometimes the best solution to a tempting situation is to just run. Joseph did not run because he was a coward. He ran because he realized this principle: "Can a man take fire in his bosom, and his clothes not be burned?" (Proverbs 6:27).

There are times, however, when you simply cannot run away from the pressure like Joseph did. You just have to take a stand. William Travis and his men chose to do just that at the Alamo. He and all those who chose to follow him decided they would not flee, but stand up to the enemy. There are times when there is nowhere to go and we must stand up to the pressure.

Self-Esteem and a Sense of Humor

As I have worked with the youth of the Church, I have taken notes on those who seemed to be the least affected by negative peer pressure. I have noticed that there are some who are better equipped to handle it than others. Those who have high self-esteem are definitely better able to deal with it than those with low images of themselves. Those talented in sports, music, drama, and so on seem to cope better than others with few visible skills or hobbies.

I have also noticed that those who really live the gospel have a good sense of humor, are fun to be around, and are less affected by worldly pressure. Clark was one of those whose personality made everyone love to be around him. He was extremely funny, yet he lived the standards. At the Philmont Scout Ranch, he got on a table and sang "Jesus Wants Me for a Sunbeam" with all the actions in front of about six hundred scouts from around the world. What do you think the other boys thought of him? They thought he was so cool that no one even tried to pressure him to do anything against his standards, because they loved to be around him. President Gordon B. Hinckley said, "We need to have a little humor in our lives. If the time ever comes when we can't smile at ourselves, it will be a sad time."[19]

Good Friends

Since a lot of the pressure we feel comes from friends, it is imperative that we help our children choose good ones. Elder M. Russell Ballard gave this advice to youth: "Choose friends who share your standards, both members and nonmembers. Such friends will make peer pressure uplifting and positive."[20] One of the best means of protection is to openly discuss values with our friends. By letting them know where we stand on moral issues, they will quickly spread the word to others. We will begin to attract the type of people we want to be around. Word spreads just as quickly about those with high standards as it does about those with low standards. This gives a clear message to those with standards below our own: "I'm not available." Some youth may find themselves dating more, while others may find themselves dating less. In the long run, however, this strategy will pay off, and they will become priceless to a worthy mate. "Who can find a virtuous woman? For her price is far above rubies" (Proverbs 31:10.) Family members need not come across as "holier than thou." We can disagree without being disagreeable or judgmental of others. Who knows how many modern-day Sams (those who follow rather than lead) will come forward when a Nephi is taught to take a stand?

Notes

1   Edward L. Kimball, ed., *Teachings of Spencer W. Kimball* (Salt Lake City, UT: Deseret Book, 1982), 236.

2   W. Eugene Hansen, in Conference Report, April 1996, 54.

3   Spencer W. Kimball, in Conference Report, April 1965, 65.

4   David O. McKay, in Conference Report, April 1964, 5.

5   Randal A. Wright, *Families in Danger: Protecting Your Family in An X-Rated World* (Salt Lake City, UT: Deseret Book, 1988), 23–25.

6   "The Games Teenagers Play," *Newsweek*, September 1, 1980, 51.

7   "Youth Exposure to Alcohol Advertising on Television, 2001–2009," the Center on Alcohol Marketing and Youth, July 23, 2012.

8   Ibid.

9   Ibid.

10 "Prevalence of Underage Drinking," The Center on Alcohol Marketing and Youth, fact sheet, July 2011.

11 B.F. Grant, *Alcohol Health and Research World*, Volume 22, 1998.

12 "Alcohol, Drugs and Crime," National Council on Alcoholism and Drug Dependence, Inc., fact sheet

13 Ibid.

14 "Underage Drinking," National Institute on Alcohol Abuse and Alcoholism, No. 67, January 2006.

15 R. Hingson, T. Heeren, R. Zakocs, "Age of Drinking Onset and Involvement in Physical Fights," *Pediatrics*, 2001, 108 (4):872–77.

16 "Alcohol and Public Health," Centers For Disease Control and Prevention, fact sheet, October 29, 2012.

17 L.D. Johnston, P.M. O'Malley, J.G. Bachman, and J.E. Schulenberg, "Monitoring the Future National Results on Adolescent Drug Use," Ann Arbor, MI: Institute for Social Research, 2010.

18 George Albert Smith, in Conference Report, October 1921, 161.

19 Interview with *Church News*, 1 September 1995.

20 M. Russell Ballard, in Conference Report, October 1990, 48.

TELEVISION

MISTAKE: Failure to limit children's exposure to inappropriate television programming and allowing children to have televisions in their bedrooms.

"Television was out of control in our home when I was growing up. We had TVs in every room including our bedrooms. Most were turned on in the morning and stayed on all day. My parents never placed any controls on what we watched or how much we watched. I think that is one of the reasons we don't really know how to talk to each other even to this day."

As a member of a bishopric many years ago, I was often asked to give spiritual thoughts to the Primary children during sharing time. One Sunday, speaking to the younger group of about thirty kids, I asked them to raise their hands if they knew the answer to a question. The question was, "How many of you can name the four Teenage Mutant Ninja Turtles?" Every hand in the entire Primary went up, except for two small girls. The first four children I called on revealed the names of the four turtles. I then asked four-year-old Lydia how she knew their names. She proudly announced with a huge grin, "Because I watch them every day!" Then I said, "Okay, kids, I have another question for you." They were visibly excited. My question was, "Name one of the four sons of Mosiah in the Book of Mormon." At first, they glanced at me with a look of "What channel do they come on?" Then they looked at each other with blank stares. Not one child could name them. After a long silence, one little girl slowly raised her hand. I said, "Okay, Erin, name one of the sons of Mosiah." She said in an uncertain tone, "Michelangelo?" I said, "That's a good guess, Erin, but that's not quite right. Can anyone else think of one?" Finally, after many confused looks, they all gave up. I then turned back to Lydia and asked her why she didn't know the names of the four sons of Mosiah. She was quick to answer, "Because I don't watch them every day." Some of us are apparently not doing a very good job teaching our children the scriptures. It appears if we do not teach our children, the television will. Television has won the hearts and the time of Americans like nothing else in our history. Members of the Church are not exempt from television's influence.

After a presentation at Education Week, a sister came up to me in front of several other people and said that she had eight TVs in her house. She didn't seem the least bit embarrassed by it and said she turned them all on at 7 a.m. and turned them off at 11 p.m. every day but Sunday. When I asked her why she had them on for so long, she said with a chuckle, "I can't stand the quiet." She then told me that she really didn't watch them that much but that she only had them on for the noise. As she walked away, I thought of two things: First, everyone in that house was subjected to 96 hours per week of noise, and second, one of the characteristics of the Spirit is that He whispers.

How TV Influences Viewers

Lucifer is the master of deceit, and he has many tools in his bag. Few tools have had the same impact that television has had on our society. And yet, few seem concerned about this powerful medium. Elder Joseph B. Wirthlin said, "Television is out of control in some homes; the set is rarely turned off, regardless of the programming. Some programs are filthy and evil and are poisoning the minds of God's children today . . . Satan has made the television and film media among his most effective tools to destroy minds and souls."[1]

Time Waster

The mass media has invaded our homes and families, with a detrimental effect on all who abuse it. The time spent by the average American teenager with media is staggering. Research has shown that most people tend to badly underestimate the amount of TV being watched in their homes and rationalize the programs they view. "The average American teen spends one-third of each day with various forms of mass media, mostly without parental oversight."[2]

Usually placed at the center of our most-used rooms with furniture facing toward it is a television set. In far too many homes, this medium is blaring for hours and hours per day. "By the time the average person reaches age 70, he or she will have spent the equivalent of 7 to 10 years of their lives watching television."[3]

The scriptures warn us about time wasters. "But wo unto him that has the law given, yea, that has all the commandments of God, like unto us, and that transgresseth them, and that wasteth the days of his probation, for awful is his state!" (2 Nephi 9:27.)

Research notes that typical teenagers will spend almost twice as much time in front of the television as they will in the school class-room by the time they graduate from high school. It is also believed that by the time a child is eight years old, they will have spent as much time watching television as they will conversing with their fathers during their entire lifetime.

According to the latest Nielsen report, "The average American over the age of 2 spends more than 34 hours a week watching live television, plus another three to six hours watching taped programs."[4] If those figures are correct, even without counting any taped programs, a typi-cal American will watch 1,768 hours of TV per year, the equivalent of 221 eight-hour days. What would happen if all 316,600,000 people who live in America cut their viewing time in half and then spent that time in personal, family, and community improvement? Think of the billions of combined hours that could be used to read good literature, visit friends and relatives, obtain college degrees, do volunteer work, be involved in civic or church affairs, develop talents, plant gardens, or thousands of other worthwhile endeavors that build individuals, fami-lies, and society. What would our world be like if everyone took the challenge to watch less TV and use the time in a worthwhile cause?

President Gordon B. Hinckley stated, "I am suggesting that we spend a little less time in idleness, in the fruitless pursuit of watching some inane and empty television programs. Time so utilized can be put to better advantage, and the consequences will be wonderful. Of that I do not hesitate to assure you."[5]

Addiction

Not only is television a tremendous time waster, but it also has the possibility of being psychologically addictive. Some perhaps question this assertion, but there is a very simple way to tell if you or any member of your family has an addiction. Shut off all media for seven days and see how everyone reacts to the experiment. Over the years, I have challenged thousands to give up television for a seven-day time period. I usually begin the challenge by asking parents if they would leave their kids for seven days to go to Europe with their spouse? Most would not have a problem. Then I ask the youth if they would mind leaving their parents for a week to go to Hawaii with a good friend. Most readily agree. Then I point out that if they wouldn't mind leaving their close family for seven days, then surely they wouldn't mind leaving their television for seven days. For those who accept the challenge, I have asked them to keep a journal for the week and send me a copy after they finish. The following two excerpts are from an adult and a child who accepted the challenge and then wrote up their experiences.

From a mother:

Day one: I made the commitment! After the kids left for school it was like death! No noise, except the neighbor's chickens clucking. I don't feel I need the TV shows, just the noise. During this withdrawal period, I went to the store and killed two hours. An amazing thing happened after the kids were home. Our teenage daughter cleaned her room! Our twelve-year-old discovered that the *Reader's Digest* was interesting—read it until bedtime and took it to the bus stop on day two.

Day two: Temptation set in about 1:30. Turned educational TV on just for the noise. After 5 min., decided that it was the wrong noise. Not as exciting as game shows or soap operas! Did a load of laundry, just to hear the noise. Studied seminary lesson. Another trip to the store.

Day three: Slept in. Company for two hours. Finished 500 piece jigsaw puzzle. Cleaned whole house. Fed missionaries. Kids went to bed early.

Day four: Piece of cake. Gone all day with no radio in the car.

Day five: I fell completely off the wagon today, but didn't tell the family.

Day six: I did aerobics for four days this week with a VCR tape. *ME*, exercising?

Day seven: We held a family council and have dramatically cut down on TV hours. *We are spending more quality time with our children* and with uplifting literature.

From a five-year-old girl (actual words written down by her mother):

Day one: I went the whole day without TV and radio and cartoons. I spent my day playing inside, coloring, and playing with my brother.

Day two: I'm sorry I slipped today. I watched a little "Nintendo" at Leo's (the neighbor). I feel sad.

Day three: I didn't watch any TV. I won't let Linda (another neighbor) turn on the TV.

Day four: I didn't watch any TV. I feel happy. I played at the park. I met some new friends—Kelly, Lacey, and Mariah. I colored in my coloring book.

Day five: We went to another park today. We saw animals and a brand-new bunny.

Day six: I didn't watch any TV because I wanted to be good and do what my mom said. I did not watch Saturday morning cartoons because we went out to breakfast at the park. Tonight we went to see a play. It was different than TV. I like plays better. We went to the library to get me some reading books. I read about a cat that was fat.

Day seven: We went to Church, read books, and had fun. I've learned to be happy without TV. It gave me some time to do some other things. Heavenly Father doesn't want us to watch too much TV.

The first time I ever issued the TV challenge, a mother approached me after my talk and told me what her six-year-old son said. Upon hearing the invitation, the young boy leaned over to his mom and asked, "Are we going to do that?" to which the mother replied, "Yes." He then said, "I hate him!" I don't want anyone to hate me, but wouldn't it be fun to see if anyone in your home is a little too involved with the media?

Sexual Influence

Unfortunately, television communicates the same information to everyone simultaneously, regardless of age, level of education, or

POWER PARENTING

experience. In the quest for new material to involve audiences, TV programs expose viewers to sexually oriented subjects, which have been traditionally considered forbidden.

Television has become a powerful sex educator. Youth appear to be influenced by the immoral behavior their favorite TV characters depict. Many copy these models, reasoning if the stars do it, it must be okay. What these TV models do with the immense power given them is now evident.

Several years ago, President Spencer W. Kimball warned of a connection between watching inappropriate television and sexual immorality. He said, "The path to the grievous sins of fornication, adultery, and homosexuality can begin, too, with the viewing of some of the sex and violence-oriented programs now being shown on television, including network television."[6]

We are being bombarded in our own homes with content that is repulsive to lovers of truth. Not only are temptations blasting into our living rooms, but in recent years television has invaded even the once private domain of our bedrooms. Research has found that, "Nearly 70 percent of young children have TVs in their bedrooms today; nearly half (49 percent) have video game systems in their bedrooms; 46 percent have VCRs; 37 percent have DVD players; 35 percent have cable or satellite TV service; 24 percent have PCs and 18 percent are hooked up to the Internet in their bedrooms."[7] With widespread availability of the smartphone, individuals now have instant television or video game access with them at all times.

It seems very strange that we place deadbolt locks on our doors to prevent evil people from entering into our sacred homes, and then we turn around and invite the same type of people in through television programming. Television is saturated with inappropriate sexual content. This material is getting more frequent and more graphic with time. The Kaiser Foundation found that

Seventy percent of all shows have sexual content, up from 56 percent in the first study in 1998 and 64 percent in 2002. Two-thirds (68 percent) of all shows include talk about sex, and 35 percent of all shows include sexual behaviors. The proportion of shows with sexual content in prime time on the major broadcast networks has also increased. Nearly eight in ten such shows (77 percent) include sexual content, compared to

82

67 percent in 1998 and 71 percent in 2002. In those shows that do include sexual content, the number of sexual scenes per hour is also up, to an average of 5.0 scenes an hour in the full composite week sample. In fact, because of increases in both the percent of shows that have some sexual content and the number of sexual scenes in those shows, the total number of sexual scenes in the program sample has nearly doubled since this study was first conducted in 1998 (up 96 percent from 1,930 to 3,783). . . . Among the top 20 most-watched shows by teens, 70 percent include some kind of sexual content, and nearly half (45 percent) include sexual behavior.[8]

Research has repeatedly shown that teenagers who watch television programs with strong sexual themes increase their chances of engaging in premarital sexual behavior. A study by the Kaiser Family Foundation on the media habits of young people found that "Today, 8–18 eighteen-year-olds devote an average of 7 hours and 38 minutes (7:38) to using entertainment media across a typical day (more than 53 hours a week). And because they spend so much of that time 'media multitasking' (using more than one medium at a time), they actually manage to pack a total of 10 hours and 45 minutes (10:45) worth of media content into those 7½ hours."[9] "The most recent content analysis of television found that more than 75 percent of prime-time shows on the major networks contain sexual content, but only 14 percent of incidents include any mention of the risks or responsibilities of sexual activity or the need for contraception."[10]

As pointed out in the home environment chapter, the more media a teenager is exposed to in their bedrooms, the more willing they are to engage in premarital sexual behavior. Everything should be done to try to protect youth from these immoral influences. As Michael Rudinski said, "The thing about young people is when they see things in the mass media and they think it's going on, they start doing it."[11]

I have often heard people say that they were flipping through the television stations and were shocked by what they saw. Is that really true? Why would we be shocked? Don't we really know that if we turn on the TV that we are going to see something inappropriate?

Communication

Perhaps one of the most overlooked consequences of television is the devastating effect it has had on family rituals, traditions, and communication. Too much television can not only produce negative consequences, but it can also prevent positive behavior. As a child, I remember families coming over to visit. Everyone sat on the porch and just talked. Those days have long since past. What happened? In a day when we have more time-saving devices than at any time in history we don't have time to communicate. Why? Maybe Ellen B. De Franco found the answer when she said, "Before television, children played together more often, played outdoors more, spent more time being creative and inventive, and read more. Parents and children spent more time together, talked together more, shared more joint projects and chores, and ate more meals together.[12]

Family researcher Urie Bronfenbrenner had this to say about the power of television: "Like the sorcerer of old, the television set casts its magic spell, freezing speech and action, turning the living into silent statues so long as the enchantment lasts. The primary danger of the television screen lies not so much in the behavior it produces, although there is danger there, as in the behavior it prevents: the talks, the games, the family festivities . . . through which much of the child's learning takes place and through which his character is formed. Turning on the television set can turn off the process that transforms children into people."[13]

Violence

A popular statement to justify watching programming with violence or playing violent video games is that "it didn't have any sexual scenes in it, so it was okay." Sometimes we forget that sexual immorality is the sin that is next to an even more serious one. Violence is rampant through much of the programming in today's television. Elder M. Russell Ballard stated,

> Televised violence has become so pervasive that the average high school student by graduation has seen eighteen thousand murders and many other acts of violence and sin. This being the case today, more parental review and monitoring is needed to protect our families from the current flood of TV violence and the effect it has on us.[14]

Current studies show that as much as two thirds of all television contains violence and that shows for children contain more than other television programs. Our children are being bombarded with a steady diet of violent images, and it is not slowing down. For example, during the week of September 2005, "There were 63 dead bodies visible during prime time on the six broadcast networks. That's up sharply from the 27 bodies counted during the same week in 2004."[15] Media violence is usually glamorized, and the perpetrators often go without punishment. All of these images are taking a heavy toll on our society and in our families. Some research has suggested as much as 20 percent of real-life violence may be correlated to media violence.

Perhaps one of the most frightening consequences of viewing media violence is that it desensitizes those who are involved. Fedric Wertham pointed out this phenomenon many years ago when he said,

> The desensitization manifests itself on different levels. Children have an inborn capacity for sympathy. But that sympathy has to be cultivated. This is one of the most delicate points in the education process. And it is this point that the mass media trample on. Even before the natural feelings of compassion have a chance to develop, the fascination of overpowering and hurting others is displayed in endless profusion. Before the soil is prepared for sympathy, the seeds of sadism are planted. The clinical result is that feelings for others are interfered with. These youngsters show a coarsening of responses and an unfeeling attitude.[16]

Video Games

In our day the adversary has found a new way to use television and smartphones to deliver his immoral and violent messages to our youth. Video games are extremely popular, and violence is common in many of the most popular games. Brad J. Bushman, Ph.D., a Professor of Communication and Psychology at the Ohio State University had this to say:

> We recently conducted a comprehensive review of 136 articles reporting 381 effects involving over 130,000 participants around the world. These studies show that violent video games increase aggressive thoughts, angry feelings, physiological arousal (e.g., heart rate, blood pressure), and aggressive behavior. Violent games also decrease helping behavior and feelings of empathy for others. The effects occurred for males and females of all ages, regardless of what country they lived in. This review also sheds light on why violent video games increase aggression. Someone who has aggressive thoughts, feels angry inside, lacks empathy for others, and is highly aroused should be more likely to behave aggressively.[17]

Another frightening aspect of this phenomenon is that "90 percent of teenagers say that their parents never check the video game ratings before allowing them to rent or buy computer or video games."[18]

M. Russell Ballard warned of the addictive nature of much of the media available in our day when he said,

> Remember, brothers and sisters, any kind of addiction is to surrender to something, thus relinquishing agency and becoming dependent. Thus, video-gaming and texting on cell phones need to be added to the list. Some gamers claim to spend up to 18 hours a day going through level after level of video games, neglecting all other aspects of their lives. Texting on cell phones can become an addiction, causing the important interpersonal human communication to become lost.[19]

View TV as a School

One thing that has helped me over the years is to view television as a school. The next time you turn the television on, think about those who appear on the screen as your family's teachers. As an educational institution, the TV School is by far the most successful school system in the history of the world.

- *Community Involvement*: Nearly 99 percent of the nation's population is enrolled in TV school, unequalled in history. No nation has ever had so many students voluntarily enrolled in the education system.
- *Dropout Rates*: Rarely do we find those who drop out of the TV school. No mandatory attendance laws exist. This school does not have an attendance officer.
- *Class Times*: Classes are offered 24 hours per day, 365 days a year. The school never closes—unparalleled in history.
- *Tuition*: Hundreds of classes are taken each week free of charge, with others offered for a small monthly fee.
- *Babysitter*: For those with small children, the school provides free babysitting service.
- *Basis of School Support*: Businesses pay school officials huge sums of money, which allows them to come into the home classrooms and try to sell products to the students. Teachers (actors) are paid by these businesses. These teacher/actors are the highest paid teachers in the history of the world.

- *Time in Class*: The average American spends approximately 28 hours per week in TV classes.
- *Class Offerings*: No school system has ever offered such a variety of classes. Students can choose from classes in music, games, drama, dancing, local news, world news, nature, religion, murder, rape, drug use, immorality, profanity, and so on.
- *Teachers' Characteristics*: While there are many teachers with high moral standards, there are also many who would never be allowed to teach in public schools because of their immoral lifestyles.
- *Consequence*: When we turn on the knob, we enter a class. Constantly ask the question when you are in class: What are you being taught?

Analyze Content

You might want to try viewing movies and television with a pencil and paper in hand to analyze the content. You will be amazed at the messages, both good and bad. In analyzing the content, use gospel principles to determine what is negative or positive. Here are some aspects to consider:

Theme: What is the purpose or the message of the movie or program? Why did the producers spend so much money to bring you this message? How would you characterize the overall message—good, bad, spiritual, immoral, silly, patriotic, or something else?

Language: What kind of language is used? Are people respectful in communicating with one another or do they ridicule or mock? Are off-color, vulgar jokes or dialogue included? How many profane words are used? Is the Lord's name used in vain? How many times?

Violence: How many acts of violence are shown? Why were they included? Are they essential to the plot?

Immorality: Were sexually related scenes shown or implied? Were there any portrayal of couples living together unmarried? Were the heroes portrayed as sexually promiscuous or virtuous? Were there any consequences shown for immorality?

Other Inappropriate Behavior: How much drug, tobacco, and alcohol abuse is shown? How is marriage and family life portrayed? What crimes were committed, and what were the consequences?

Once you have established your guidelines and watched a movie or program critically, using a pencil and paper to keep counts and make notes, inappropriate scenes will almost jump out at you from the screen. If you have never listened closely to the language being used in the media, you may be in for a big surprise when trying this idea. You will see and hear things that you have never noticed before and in the process will build up a wall of protection, becoming more aware and ultimately eliminating from your view those films that do not meet your standards.

Making Changes

When I was a young man, my father told me an old story of a mother who gave her young son some advice. She said, "Son, I'm going to town, and while I'm gone, whatever you do, don't pull the chair over to the kitchen counter, climb up, pull down the bean jar off the top shelf, open it up, and stick a bean up your nose." Today, the story is a little different. It goes more like this: "Son, I'm going to get a massage and a pedicure, and while I'm gone, whatever you do, don't go into your bedroom and turn on the premium cable TV channel to the graphic channels or get on the high speed Internet on your computer, tablet, or smart phone and look at those raunchy music videos or pornography sites!"

We live in a very dangerous world. There are temptations coming at us from all directions. Reo M. Christenson of Miami University gave this now prophetic warning before the wall of communism came tumbling down, as he said, "When the next Gibbon writes about the Decline and Fall of America, he won't be talking about communism; the entertainment industry will be the villain. It is winning America's heart while ravaging its soul."[20] We have lived to see this prediction come to pass. We must stand up and limit the access our children have to the filth now available.

Finally, Elder M. Russell Ballard gave this counsel, "We need to limit the amount of time our children watch TV or play video games or use the Internet each day. Virtual reality must not become their reality."[21]

Notes

1   Joseph B. Wirthlin, "The Priesthood of God," *Ensign*, November 1988, 36.

2   "Impact of the Media on Adolescent Sexual Attitudes and Behaviors," *Journal of Pediatrics*, Vol. 116 No. 1 July 2005.

3   "Children, Adolescents, and Television," American Academy of Pediatrics' Committee on Public Education, February 2001.

4   David Hinckley, "Americans Spend 34 Hours a Week Watching TV," *New York Daily News*, September 19, 2012.

5   Gordon B. Hinckley, in Conference Report, April 1995, 117.

6   Spencer W. Kimball, in Conference Report, October 1976, 6.

7   Nickelodeon Survey, "The New Normal," *Associated Press*, November 20, 2005.

8   "Sex on TV," Kaiser Family Foundation Press Release, November 9, 2005.

9   "Generation M2: Media in the Lives of 8- to 18-Year-Olds," Kaiser Family Foundation Press Release, January 20, 2010.

10 Victor C. Strasburger, *Children, Adolescents, and the Media* (Thousand Oaks, CA: Sage Publications, 2009), 213.

11 David Kupelian, *How Evil Works: Understanding and Overcoming the Destructive Forces That Are Transforming America* (New York: Simon and Schuster, 2010), 30.

12 Ellen B. De Franco, *TV On–Off: Better Family Use of Television* (Santa Monica, CA: Goodyear Publishing, 1980) 5–6.

13 Marie Winn, *The Plug in Drug* (New York, NY: Viking Penguin, 1977), 141.

14 M. Russell Ballard, in Conference Report, April 1989, 98.

15 David Bauder, "Violence in Primetime Fades as an Issue," Associated Press, November 20, 2005.

16 Victor B. Cline ed., *Where Do You Draw the Line?* (Provo, UT: Brigham Young University Press, 1974), 165.

17 Brad J. Bushman, "Do Violent Video Games Increase Aggression?" *Psychology Today*, January 27, 2012.

18 D. A. Walsh, "A Validity Test of Movie, Television and Video Game Ratings," *Pediatrics*, Vol. 107, No. 6, June 2001, 1302–1308..

19 M. Russell Ballard, "O That Cunning Plan of the Evil One," *Ensign*, November 2010, 109–10.

20 *American Family Association Journal*, April 1988, 24.

21 M. Russell Ballard, "Let Our Voices Be Heard," *Ensign*, November 2003, 16.

MUSIC

MISTAKE: Failure to limit children's access to inappropriate music.

"My parents were totally uninformed about the music of our day. They not only allowed me to listen to anything I wanted to, they usually bought inappropriate CDs I would ask for. They were clueless about the connection between the questionable group of friends that I hung out with and the music that I listened to. Music had a huge negative influence on me at a critical time of my life."

Several years ago, I attended a CES symposium in Provo, Utah, and roomed with an early-morning seminary teacher from an eastern state. During the days we were together, we had several conversations on various topics. One night, he told me that all sixteen of his children's great-grandparents came from pioneer stock. I was amazed by this legacy. Then he told me that he was confused. Why, he asked, with such a rich heritage, would he have a seventeen-year-old son go inactive in the Church? He went on to explain that his son was heavily involved with drugs and had several brushes with the police. Not only did he not attend church, but he was also bitter toward all it symbolized. This father was confused by his son's behavior. He told me that in their family they prayed, read scriptures daily, and held weekly family home evenings. This man knew that I had graduate degrees in family studies and asked if I had any explanation for his son's rebellion. I asked a few questions about his son's dress and then told him I had an idea about what was happening. I wrote down "heavy metal music" on a piece of paper, and turned the paper over on the small desk that was in the room. He asked me what I had written on the paper. I then turned over the paper and showed him the words "heavy metal music." He became defensive and said, "Yes, you are right, but my wife and I decided a long time ago that we would pick our battles carefully. Music is not one that we were willing to fight with him over." I thought of a statement made by President Boyd K. Packer many years ago: "Young people, you cannot afford to fill your mind with the unworthy hard music of our day. It is not harmless. It can welcome onto the stage of your mind unworthy thoughts and set the tempo to which they dance and to which you may act."[1]

Shortly after that experience, I spoke at a youth conference in a southern state concerning the influence of inappropriate music. After the talk, a fifteen-year-old young woman came up to me and said that she had walked out in the middle of my talk because she was afraid I would say something about the type of music she listened to. I had a long conversation with her about various topics and found that she was from an active LDS home. As we talked, I was shocked by some of her views. Among other things, she said that she saw nothing wrong with drugs. In fact, she believed they were good for you because they are part of God's creations. She also told me she had no desire to ever marry or have children and that she saw nothing wrong with having sexual relations outside of marriage. I asked her how she felt about the Book of Mormon, which she easily dismissed as just a bunch of fairy tales. We then discussed, in detail, the kind of music she liked and who her favorite groups were. She described it like a who's who of the hardest groups at the time. My final question to her was, "Do you think that music affects you?" She loved the kind of unworthy hard music that President Packer warned about and listened to it constantly. I asked what her parents thought of her music, and she commented that they liked it too.

After working closely with youth for many years, may I make a suggestion? When you are choosing which battles to fight with your children, whatever you do, please *choose to fight the music battle!* And the earlier you fight this battle and the more consistently you fight it, the better your chances for winning. I have seen very few tools in Satan's bag of tricks that will destroy innocent lives more effectively than inappropriate music. If parents refuse to fight the battle or even delay the fight and let the destructive root take hold, it will be extremely difficult to pull children away from it.

Recognize Its Power

Music has been called the universal language because it speaks directly to our emotions. Our feelings can, in turn, actually influence our behavior. Music has a unique ability to inspire or to destroy. Realizing the power of music is nothing new. Over the ages many people have used it for various reasons. When Christ needed strength to face his terrible ordeal in the Garden of Gethsemane, he turned to music. The scriptures record, "And when they had sung an hymn, they went out into the Mount of Olives" (Matthew 26:30). Joseph and Hyrum Smith also turned to music before facing their deaths. One of the last things Joseph and Hyrum did in the Carthage Jail was to request John Taylor to sing "A Poor Wayfaring Man of Grief" to comfort them. And in our day, music plays a very important role in our church services and activities. Can you imagine a sacrament meeting or a general conference without music?

The business world and our school systems also recognize the power of music and use it to imbed their messages deep into our consciousness. Can you ever forget messages like, "Plop, Plop, Fizz, Fizz?" No. Once you hear these little jingles, you remember them, perhaps, for the rest of your life. The movie industry uses music to attract audiences. I'm confident that without music, many of Hollywood's biggest hits would be flops. For example, watching "Rocky" without music would be more like watching a boxing match on ESPN! Music brings excitement to the movies.

Characteristics of Music

There is no question that the adversary realizes the tremendous power of music and that he is using it for his evil purposes. He knows that everyone loves music, and he uses it to destroy the unsuspecting. Several characteristics of music make it extremely enticing.

Music Is Divisive

Have you considered the power of music to unite people in a common cause? Think back to athletic events you attended during your high school or college days. Was music played at the football games? Did you have a school fight song? Why? Schools use fight songs to build school pride and unite the student body in a common cause.

The Book of Mormon teaches a priceless lesson about unity in fourth Nephi. Imagine a society that goes two hundred years in total peace and happiness. We read, "There were no robbers, nor murders, neither were there Lamanites, nor any manner of -ites; but they were in one, the children of Christ, and heirs to the kingdom of God" (4 Nephi 1:17). Because of their total unity they were "blessed in all their doing" (4 Nephi 1:18). However, within a few short years there was a small group that left the church and took upon themselves the Lamanite name again. What a tragedy to see the division into groups again with wickedness soon to follow.

The adversary uses many devices to divide people into separate groups. Few tools he uses are more effective at dividing people than music. Ask any high school student if there are cliques in their school. They will tell you that every public school has cliques that dominate the high school scene. Many teenagers believe the only way to be recognized is to be affiliated with one of these groups. One common trait cliques share is their individual type of music. Equally, each clique or group tends to hate the music of other groups. Imagine, for example, a boy with cowboy boots, shirt, belt, and Wrangler jeans listening to heavy metal music. No, that does not usually happen. By the same token, imagine a kid in baggy pants, with back pockets so big you could put a kangaroo in them, and a ball cap turned sideways jamming to country western music. This won't happen either.

Cliques are a divisive factor in our society and help to destroy the unity that is needed. Evil, conspiring men know that with each new group created, there will be new markets to exploit. Every clique will need to attend the concerts of their groups and buy their latest music. Satan has many tools to destroy our children, and few are greater than inappropriate music.

Music Can Bring In or Kill the Spirit

Several years ago, I had a wonderful experience serving as the session director for BYU's Especially for Youth program held at Texas A&M University. Many lives changed as the youth and their leaders came closer to Christ. Many tears were shed during the testimony meetings, a special fireside, and classes held during the week. Perhaps the most memorable event, however, was the Thursday night musical fireside. The Spirit was especially strong during the musical performance that night. I realized more than ever before how powerful music can be in our lives. We had such a wonderful week that I think everyone dreaded boarding the buses the next day to take them back to the real world. I had been asked to ride a chartered bus back with the youth from one of the distant stakes. For about the first thirty minutes of the trip, everyone talked about the spiritual feelings they had experienced during the week. Some expressed that this had been the best week of their entire lives. It was rewarding to hear these teenagers talk about sacred things.

Then, one of the young men asked the bus driver if he would play a cassette tape over the stereo system. I assumed it would be the EFY music tape they had received. However, when the first song began, I realized that the music was from one of the popular artists of the day. The second song was very inappropriate and dealt entirely with immorality. It was the number one hit of the summer. As the song played, over fifty percent of the youth on the bus sang along word for word. The lyrics were a pathetic reminder of what our youth face in this permissive society. The superstar singing it included lines about how immorality is natural and fun and how they should participate. I sat there shocked at what had happened. The spiritual feeling enjoyed moments before was now totally gone. For the next two and a half hours, I never heard another word spoken about the spiritual week the youth experienced.

I learned for myself that day that beautiful music has an amazing ability to bring the Spirit into our lives while inappropriate music can quickly drive the Spirit out. No wonder President Ezra Taft Benson said, "The magnetism of television and radio is in the accessibility of their mediocrity. Lovely is not an adjective to describe most of their products. The inventors of these wonders were inspired by the Lord. But once their good works were introduced to the world, the powers of darkness began to employ them for our destruction."[2]

Addiction

Is music, especially rock music, addictive? I decided to offer a simple challenge to several groups of young people to determine the answer to this question. The challenge to go without any music for three days was given to hundreds of youth over several years' time. I quickly found that most would not even agree to try it for one day, much less three. Occasionally, however, a few brave souls accepted the challenge. Depending on their past involvement, those who attempted it would almost always experience severe withdrawal pains. Only a small percentage actually made it through the three-day experiment. Most of those were recently returned missionaries. The following is the summary of Stacey, a nineteen-year-old institute student. Her experience is very typical of the ones received.

> I discovered that I am very addicted to music! The first night, on the way home from Institute, I felt really strange and out of place without the radio on. I heard so many weird sounds—my tires screeching when I took off, my muffler, and all kinds of squeaks that I had never heard before. I had decided to do this, though, even if it killed me! It practically did! I concluded that I couldn't go to sleep at night without music. I don't function in the mornings without my radio. My car sounds like it's about to fall apart, and my mood and attitude change when there is no music! I seriously *had* to listen to meditation—ocean tapes—just to go to sleep. Then the last day, I really found myself depressed.
>
> These past three days have been really hard for me. But I found that I studied a lot more, and I talked to my parents more than I ever have. If there is such a thing as being addicted to music, then I am 100 percent. P.S. Thanks for three days of torment![3]

During research for my dissertation, we asked teenagers from several states how much money it would take for them to totally give up music for thirty days. The results were startling. The average youth said it would take over three thousand dollars for the month. Nearly 20 percent said it would take over a million dollars, with many saying no amount of money could entice them to give up music for a month.[4] With this kind of idolization of music, its dramatic impact on their lives should come as no surprise. To further complicate the situation, some choose their friends on the basis of a preferred music type. When this shared music type encourages immorality, a precarious situation may exist. Not only that, but inappropriate music can be addicting to its listeners. It is hard for the spirit to whisper to us if we never have any quiet time.

Influences Immorality

Listening to music is not just passive adolescent entertainment. Simply listening to or watching music videos can alter viewers' perceptions of the social world. And yet, we found that only 12 percent of the parents of these adolescents placed any kind of limits on time or content of their children's music. Sister Ardeth Kapp pointed out, "Music has a very powerful and wonderful influence in establishing feelings and moods that can lift and elevate your thoughts and your actions. But because it is so powerful, it is cleverly used by the adversary to stimulate your thoughts, feelings, and moods, to pollute and poison your mind and cause you to do things you would not otherwise consider doing."[5]

In 2006, a RAND Corporation study presented strong evidence that sexually degrading lyrics in music encourages adolescent sex. The study found that, "the more time adolescents spend listening to music with sexually degrading lyrics, the more likely they are to initiate intercourse and other sexual activities. This holds true for boys and girls as well as for whites and nonwhites, even after accounting for a wide range of other personal and social factors associated with adolescent sexual behavior."[6]

Music Television

Music can be even more potent when combined with visual images. Music Television (MTV), founded in 1981, was the first to demonstrate the tremendous appeal and power of combining video and music. In the early years, MTC played music videos twenty-four hours a day, seven days a week to its target audience of young adults. An early MTV slogan, "You'll never look at music the same way again," has definitely proven factual. The company has become a huge worldwide force that now targets adolescents while still appealing to its young adult demographic. The original MTV channel no longer plays music videos constantly, but several spin offs like MTV Jams and MTV Hits still do. What began as MTV now has numerous sister stations in the United States like VH1, CMT, and Comedy Central. They also have partner affiliate stations in most countries throughout the world.

Today's MTV programing includes series that focus on music, news, reality, competition, comedy, drama, and talk. One thing that seems to follow MTV since its inception is controversy regarding its program content. For example, the annual MTV Video Music Awards are often called the "Oscars for Youth" and are viewed by millions of adolescents and young adults. It seems that each new program tries to outdo the previous year's crudeness. Websites that host clips containing titles like "Top 10 Most Shocking Performances" from the Music Video Awards are common. Obviously these programs contain very objectionable material and are totally inappropriate. Unfortunately, some of the most controversial and sensual acts at the award ceremony have involved former stars from popular children's shows on television.

Many of the reality shows now produced by MTV have also drawn widespread criticism. The following press release is one example representing the concern that many parental groups have.

> The Parents Television Council™ today called on the chairmen of the U.S. Senate and House Judiciary Committees and the Department of Justice to immediately open an investigation regarding child pornography and exploitation on MTV's "Skins." *The New York Times* reported today that the network itself is concerned about violating child pornography laws. In addition to the sexual content on the show involving cast members as young as fifteen, PTC counted forty-two depictions and references to drugs and alcohol in the premiere episode. The run-time was only forty-one minutes excluding commercial breaks.[7]

Not only has research demonstrated a connection between watching sex-saturated programming on MTV and changes in sexual attitudes, but other areas of concerns have surfaced. Children who watch MTV are also being exposed to massive amounts of profanity, violence, and glamorized portrayals of alcohol and tobacco use, with a significant impact.

University of North Carolina–Chapel Hill professor Dr. Jane Brown observed, "If you believe Sesame Street taught your four-year-old something, then you better believe MTV is teaching your fourteen-year-old something, because the influence doesn't stop when we come to a certain age."[8]

Researchers from Emory University and the University of Alabama at Birmingham studied the behavior of females ages fourteen to eighteen and found those who watched fourteen plus hours of rap videos a week were far more likely than their peers to engage in violent behavior, get arrested, have sex with multiple partners, and acquire sexually transmitted diseases.[9]

For parents who are uninformed about MTV, perhaps a study conducted by the Parents Television Council (PTC) will serve as a wake-up call. MTV has, without a doubt, come to the forefront as a visual and vocal communicator of sexual messages to our youth. Researchers for the PTC group taped MTV's Spring Break coverage during the week of March 20, 2004 to March 27, 2004. Analysts recorded all instances of sexual content, profanity, and violence into the PTC's computerized Entertainment Tracking System (ETS). The following results were documented.

- In 171 hours of MTV programming, PTC analysts found 1,548 sexual scenes containing 3,056 depictions of sex or various forms of nudity and 2,881 verbal sexual references. That means children watching MTV view an average of 9 sexual scenes per hour with approximately 18 sexual depictions and 17 instances of sexual dialogue or innuendo.
- Analysts recorded 1,518 uses of unedited profanity and an additional 3,127 bleeped profanities on MTV programming. That means the young children watching MTV are subjected to roughly 8.9 un-bleeped profanities per hour, plus 18.3 bleeped profanities per hour.[10]

Without timely and appropriate sex education in the home, music television and other media will most likely become the leading sex educators of our children. The wanton sex and other filthy messages being poured into innocent children's minds and hearts through MTV is tragic. It is hard to imagine that any parent who is informed of the graphic content of MTV would allow their children access to it.

Ability to Hear Repeatedly

Over the years, I've noticed a few things about music that is quite remarkable. Have you ever noticed that regardless of what a song's message, if you like the rhythm and the beat, you can listen to it over and over again without tiring of it? In our church meetings, we sometimes hear stories, experiences, and even jokes more than once. How many times have we thought to ourselves, "Oh boy, hear we go again with a story I've already heard." Sometimes when we hear familiar words, we immediately turn the speaker off. Yet, when we put music to words, something almost magical happens. Instead of being bored or turned off at hearing the music over and over, we tend to enjoy it even more with repeated exposure. Have you ever heard a teenager call the radio station to ask that they not play a particular hit song again because they have already heard it? There is something inherent in music that makes the repeated exposure enjoyable. I don't believe, for the most part, that the spoken word can duplicate this feat. Unfortunately, because of this unique characteristic, inappropriate messages are repeated over and over, until the messages are recorded forever.

I've also observed that once we hear a song repeated over and over, the words remain with us for long periods of time, and perhaps for the rest of our lives. Recently, I spoke at BYU Education Week about the tremendous power of music. During the lecture, I asked the class members to fill in verbally the words to songs that had been popular many years before. As I read portions of the words to a song, almost every person in the room roared out the answers to the parts left out. See if you can fill in the blanks to the following song titles and phrases that were popular many years ago. If you can remember the words to these songs, then obviously your children will be able to remember the songs of their day.

"It was a one-eyed, one-horned, flying purple _____"
"You ain't nothing but a _____"
"Love me tender, love me _____"
"Yesterday, all my troubles seemed so _____"
"Rock around the _____"
"Twist and _____"
"I left my heart in _____"

Lyrics to songs are learned by repetition. Words that may be barely recognizable the first time they are heard become clear by the twentieth or hundredth time. Radio stations tend to play relatively few songs. The music and messages have changed dramatically over the years. Often when questionable lyrics are pointed out to our youth, they have a way out of feeling any responsibility. The standard answer for many is, "Yes, I know the words are bad, but I don't listen to the words; I just like the music and the beat." According to research in this area, this simply is not true. Our brains are very perceptive, and we actually pick up these messages whether we are consciously aware of it or not. It seems very improbable that we could listen to a song over and over without recording the messages in our minds. And as pointed out earlier, these messages do stay with us for long periods of time. Do you think the adversary is aware of this power?

Parents Beware

When we consider that the average American listens to almost 1,300 hours of music each year and the tremendous impact this music can have on our lives, it would seem wise to choose music that will build our spirits up rather than tear them down. I wonder if all parents are aware of the type of music with which their youth are involved? I'll never forget the surprise I received while trying to teach my own children the importance and influence that music can have in our lives. When I read that there was a famous hard rock group giving a concert at our local civic center, I decided to teach my children a lesson by observing the people expected to attend this concert. Our plan was to park our car close to the civic center and just watch the people who showed up. This particular performing group had been associated with the occult and Satanic worship by the press. I thought it would teach our family the effects of music by observing our preconceived notion of the fans as they arrived. We loaded up the kids and drove downtown to prove my point. I expected the fans to drive up on motorcycles, with knives and chains fastened to their belts, and that this would frighten our children into avoiding this type of music. Instead, I was startled as we saw mothers and fathers drive up in station wagons, vans, and cars full of young well-dressed teenagers, being dropped off at the concert.

Among the group, unfortunately, were several LDS youth. Although it wasn't the lesson I had planned my children learning, I gleaned something from the night's activities. Many of our good kids are involved with unworthy music, and many parents are not even aware of the danger that this inappropriate music produces.

Music can be one of the deadliest weapons the adversary has in his vast arsenal. With its power, he can create a sugarcoated poison that can slowly destroy our spirituality and that of our families. Somehow the adversary has been so successful with this tool that he has misled many into voluntarily inviting this temptation into their homes, and occasionally even into our church dances. Remember, Satan is very tricky. You can imagine his delight in discovering that through music, you can remember the messages and words to songs for extended periods of time and perhaps for life. What effect will these messages then have on us if they are negative or immoral?

Parents, can we sit back uninvolved as our youth are subjected to this terrible influence? I've found in my studies that many parents, including Latter-day Saints, not only allow this involvement but actually help pay for their youth to be influenced negatively. By providing money for youth to purchase degrading CDs, parents allow their youth not only to have these songs in their possession but also to play them in the home with no comments or concern whatsoever. Parents should be alarmed when they realize the messages of the songs.

Notes

1 Boyd K. Packer, in Conference Report, October 1973, 25.
2 Ezra Taft Benson, *Teachings of Ezra Taft Benson* (Salt Lake City, UT: Bookcraft, 1988), 326.
3 Personal correspondence in author's possession.
4 Randal A. Wright, "Family, Religious, Peer and Media Influence on Adolescence Willingness to Have Premarital Sex" (PhD dissertation), Brigham Young University, 1995, 113.
5 Ardeth Kapp, "Crickets Can Be Destroyed through Spirituality," *Ensign*, November 1990, 94.
6 Steven C. Martino, et al., "Exposure to Degrading Versus Nondegrading Music Lyrics and Sexual Behavior Among Youth," *Pediatrics*, Vol. 118 No. 2, August 1, 2006, 441.
7 Press Release, Parents Television Council, January 20, 2011.

8   Decency, Indecency and Community Standards, "Talk of the Nation," National Public Radio, February 9, 2004.

9   Gina M. Wingood, et al., "A Prospective Study of Exposure to Rap Music Videos and African American Females Adolescents' Health," *American Journal of Public Health,* March 2003, Vol. 93, No. 3, 437–39.

10 Casey Williams, "MTV Smut Peddlers: Targeting Kids with Sex, Drugs and Alcohol, A Report on MTV Programming March 20, 2004– March 27, 2004," Parents Television Council Publications, 2005.

MOVIES

MISTAKE: Failure to prevent children's exposure to inappropriate movies.

"As far as R-rated movies go, my parents rent them, my bishop's kids rent them, my stake presidency counselor's family rents them and watches them, so I figure it's no big deal. In my family, if I were to refuse to watch R-rated movies that my parents rent, they would be irritated at my being 'fanatical,' so to speak."

Many years ago, while working toward a master's degree, I focused on the impact of the electronic media (television, movies, and music) on the sexual attitudes of adolescents. The purpose was to determine if youth could recall inappropriate content in movies.

In my travels around the nation, one particular movie continued to be mentioned by LDS youth. Just for fun, I began asking adults in the same states to name their favorite movie. I was surprised when both youth and adults mentioned the same movie consistently. Equally surprising was the number of times many of those polled had seen this particular movie. It proved typical for many youth, and even adults, to have seen it four to six times at full theater price. I was intrigued by the drawing power of this movie, so I began asking more detailed questions about its content. A daughter of a local church leader told me she had seen the movie five times, and planned to see it again. Although I knew the answer, I asked her what the movie was rated.

"PG," she replied. I then quizzed her in detail about the movie's content. How much drug use? "None." Is there any nudity? "No." Are their any sexual scenes? "No." Are you sure? "I'm positive. I've seen it five times." Is vulgar language or profanity used in the movie? "That's what I liked about it. It only had one four-letter word."

Armed with this information and the recommendation of many other youth and adults, I purchased a ticket and sat in the theater and did a content analysis of the movie. Pencil and paper in hand, I recorded anything that was considered against traditional family values. It was difficult to do because the photography and action shots were fantastic; however, I did not go to be entertained.

Something that surprised me was how far my young friend was off in her profanity count. She had been emphatic about the movie having only one inappropriate word. Actually, she had the one right, she just forgot to add the one and zero to it. It in fact had 101 incidents of profanity and crude language, including 29 times the Lord's name was used in vain. I thought back on all the recommendations to see the movie and wondered why no one had mentioned the abundant use of profanity. Even more offensive was the graphic and controversial immoral scene involving the lead characters. I wondered how the movie had received a PG rating. Also included were seven incidents of crude sexual talk, and three episodes involving vulgar hand signs. I wasn't really expecting *Swiss Family Robinson Part 10*, but I was surprised at the content, given the recommendations I received from others. I also wondered how my young friend, who had seen the movie five times, missed the fact that the movie contained a vivid sexual scene and 101 uses of profanity, instead of just one. Social scientists call this process desensitization, a phenomenon that occurs when we see or hear something so often that it no longer consciously registers.

A couple of years after this incident, I used it as an example of desensitization in a talk I gave in a southwestern state. The movie had been released on VHS tape by that time, but I never told the audience the name of the movie. After the talk, several people came up and asked, "What was the name of the movie?" I hesitated but finally told them. Several looked startled. One of the sisters said, "We showed that to all of our *teachers* at our Primary in-service meeting." At first, I thought she was kidding. She wasn't.

Since then, I've thought a lot about this sister's comment, asking myself, "If I were the Primary president or the bishop of a ward, would I show to the Primary teachers a movie with a controversial sex scene, excessive profanity, and vulgarity?" Would you? Another question also came to mind, "If I were the director of Temple Square in Salt Lake City, would I permit this movie to be shown in the lower theaters at the north visitor's center?" Would you? Consequently, "If I were the Salt Lake Temple president, would I permit the movie to be shown to the temple workers inside the temple?" Would you? As I try to put myself in such situations, I cringe at the thought of showing this type of movie in these spiritual environments.

We have been told that even the elect will be deceived during the last days. Speaking of our day, the scriptures say, "For in those days there shall also arise false Christs, and false prophets, and shall show great signs and wonders, insomuch, that, if possible, they shall deceive the very elect, who are the *elect according to the covenant*" (Joseph Smith—Matthew 1:22; italics added). Who are these false prophets? Is it television evangelists? If so, we can all relax. All is well in Zion. However, what if these false prophets we are being warned about have nothing to do with religion. That would be the ultimate deception. I don't know of one youth we have lost to a TV evangelist in all the places I've traveled. One thing is certain, however, we are losing thousands of our youth, not to false religious teachers, but to the falsities of the world.

Now back to our questions. No committed Latter-day Saint would consciously choose to show this kind of movie at the church or in the visitor's center, certainly not at the temple. But remember, Satan is the master of deceit and will lead us carefully down to hell. His deceit is gradual; unsuspecting victims may not wake up until they are caught in his snare.

Of course, we wouldn't allow the movie in the Lord's holy temple. But what is a temple? Is there anything on earth that rivals a temple in sacredness? What about our chapels or our visitor's centers? The Bible dictionary gives the meaning of the word *temple:* "A place where the Lord may come, it is the most holy of any place of worship on the earth." It goes on to say, "*Only the home can compare with the temple in sacredness.*"[1] Now we must ask the final question: How many of us would allow the movie mentioned, or thousands like it, to be shown in our own temples (homes)? Isn't Satan sly? Each year our tolerance level endures a little more, and a little more, until we allow in our own sacred temples things that we would not even consider allowing in the Lord's house.

Of all the deceits of the last days, none are more successful and powerful than the popular entertainment of our day. We put dead-bolt locks on our doors to keep evil influences out yet invite them in through inappropriate entertainment. It is as if we totally let down our guard in this area. To be deceived is to be led down the wrong path without recognizing it. That is frightening!

In recent years, there has been a dramatic increase in the number of adolescents involved in illicit behavior. Many factors contribute to this epidemic. I have been particularly interested in how inappropriate movies are associated with this problem. It appears that the media industry is well aware of the strong basic human desires and impulses, and eagerly takes advantage of these desires with immoral scenes in order to increase audience size. These inappropriate scenes appeal to youth because of inexperience and their changing emotions. This makes them easy targets. Movies can conjure up inappropriate thoughts that can easily lead to improper behavior. The movie industry is bombarding our society with filth.

While doing research concerning the influence movies have on the attitudes and behaviors of adolescents, we asked high school students why they chose to watch R-rated movies. Following are a few of the justifications these young people used.

They Are Appealing

"I think the reason I see R-rated movies is because I hear they are good and worth the money. I feel like I am missing out when I don't see these movies."[2]

Movie promoters and advertisers use similar methods as those who make alcohol consumption look wholesome and fun. Elder Milton R. Hunter observed, "The world is in such a condition today that evil is oft-times presented on television and radio, in the movies, in books, magazines, and newspapers as if it were virtue and good."[3]

These products must appear so appealing that even Latter-day

Saints will go against modern prophets' warnings to become involved. Of course, movies are going to look enticing. How else would Satan convince anyone to take the risks involved? President Kimball said, "Whoever said that sin was not fun? Whoever claimed that Lucifer was not handsome, persuasive, easy, friendly?"[4]

We must always remember that during the last days Satan will use every trick he has ever learned through thousands of years of practice to ensnare people in sin. Inappropriate movies have invaded our culture and have been made to look very attractive. President Spencer W. Kimball again warned of this: "The attractiveness of sin is a lie. Have you seen a real mirage in the distance with lakes and trees and dwellings and castles and water, but as the thirsty traveler moves on and on and on through it, he finds it but an illusion, and when he has gone too far to return he stumbles choking in the desert of deception."[5]

Satan is very sly. He makes things appear attractive and inviting but are, in reality, a sugarcoated poison. Inappropriate movies of our day can be the source of great temptation to our families. The forces of evil have persuaded vast numbers to accept this temptation as something very desirable. Who would think that Satan could be so crafty, that he would persuade us to actually pay our own hard-earned money to be tempted! And yet, isn't this exactly what he has done? In many cases, parents are paying the bill for the very temptation that leads to youth immorality.

Everyone Is Doing It

"I guess the reason why I see R-rated movies is because every one else does, and it doesn't seem to be that big of a deal. It's also embarrassing to tell your friends that you don't watch them."[6]

When our youth use the excuse that everyone is watching R-rated movies, they are not far off. It is true that the vast majority of Americans, and many members of the Church, watch them. Perhaps we should think back to past civilizations that have rejected the prophets' call to repentance. Only eight people were preserved through the great flood while all others were drowned. I wonder if it was comforting to those who were drowning, that everyone else was drowning also? Sodom and Gomorrah were also destroyed because everyone was doing it. They, like countless other great civilizations, including the Nephites, were destroyed because the voice of the people chose iniquity. The prophets do not seek to find which way the winds of public opinion are blowing when they speak the will of the Lord. The consequences will remain the same for those who reject their teachings, regardless of the numbers involved.

While a student at BYU, I had a professor who said, "If you want to find truth, take what the world says about a subject, reverse it, and you will have the truth." Throughout much of the world's history, what has been popular with the masses has been in direct opposition to the teachings of the Lord. George Albert Smith said, "That a thing is popular is frequently justification for the Latter-day Saints to avoid it."[7]

As Latter-day Saints, our basis for making decisions should have nothing to do with whether everyone is doing it or not. The question is whether an issue is right or wrong. Elder Albert E. Bowen taught, "That which is right does not become wrong merely because it may be deserted by the majority, neither does that which is wrong today become right tomorrow by the chance circumstance that it has won the approval or been adopted by overwhelmingly predominant numbers."[8]

One of the subtlest forms of deceit is the gradual normalization of abnormality. Alexander Pope so cautioned:

Vice is a monster of so frightful mien,
As, to be hated, needs but to be seen;
Yet seen too oft, familiar with her face,
We first endure, then pity, then embrace.[9]

It Only Has One Bad Scene

"When movies are good except for one bad part, I'll close my eyes and sing a hymn."[10]

How often have you heard someone say, "It was a great movie except for the one bad scene," or "It has a good message, if you can get past the filthy language." Avoid such films. Think back on a movie you have seen with just one bad scene. Can you still see that scene in your mind? If so, then any temporary benefit you may have received from viewing it has been nullified.

Several years ago, I worked with a young lady named Teri. She often attended R-rated movies and saw nothing wrong with this practice, as long as they only had a few bad scenes. We often had discussions about the prophet's teachings on this subject, but she never changed her position. After a time, Teri decided to go on a mission for the Church. Eighteen months later she came by to see our family. We were excited to hear about her experiences. I was very surprised by her first words to me. She said, "You were right. I never should have attended those movies with one bad scene. Time after time, as I sat in homes giving the missionary discussions, I would have to turn the time over to my companion, because I was having flashbacks of those bad scenes that I thought I had forgotten."

Once inappropriate scenes have been recorded, it is hard to control the time and place when they come back into the conscious mind. President N. Eldon Tanner warned of this danger when he said,

> We are surrounded by the promotional literature of illicit sexual relations on the printed page and on the screen. For your own good, avoid it. Pornographic or erotic stories and pictures are worse than filthy or polluted food. The body has defenses to rid itself of unwholesome food, but the brain won't vomit back filth. Once recorded it will always remain subject to recall, flashing its perverted images across your mind, and drawing you away from the wholesome things in life.[11]

All Satan wants to do is open the door an inch at a time. He doesn't have to be a door crasher. We are too wise to become involved if he gives it all at once. Maybe an inch at a time cinematically means a scene at a time until he has led us from the purest white to black. Satan is only trying to get us to commit a little sin at first. Speaking of our day, the Lord warns us of this dangerous philosophy in the Book of Mormon, "And there shall also be many which shall say: Eat, drink, and be merry; nevertheless, fear God— he will justify in committing a little sin . . . Yea, and there shall be many which shall teach after this manner, false and vain and foolish doctrines" (2 Nephi 28:8).

It Only Has Violence

"If movies only have violence and not sex in them, I don't think they are bad to see."[12]

While serving as bishop, I had the opportunity to interview several eleven-year-old boys about their involvement with movies. I was shocked at the number of R-rated movies these young boys had viewed. Finally, I asked one of the boys, "What good things have you learned from the R-rated movies you have seen?" He began to laugh and said that he had not learned anything good. I pushed him to think of something. Finally he said, "The only thing I have learned from these movies is how to break arms and necks." As soon as he made these comments, he got out of his chair and grabbed my arm and began twisting it. He said, "This is how I would break your arm." He then put his hand under my chin and said, "And this is how I would break your neck." I wondered what the future held for this young LDS boy.

Many of our people think that a movie is OK if it doesn't have any sexual material included, although it is filled with violence. Something about this philosophy confuses me. We read in the scriptures that immorality is "abominable above all sins save it be the shedding of innocent blood or denying the Holy Ghost" (Alma 39:5). How did we get to the point that it is wrong to watch someone have sexual relations on the screen but not wrong to watch every perverted form of murder and violence?

Many indications show that as a nation we are spending tremendous amounts of time watching media with violent content. Many years ago, Dr. David Pearl of the National Institute of Mental Health conducted a study and reported on four identified effects of media violence on viewers that still applies today: (1) It provides how-to-do-it training for viewers inclined to imitate observed behavior; (2) it can trigger violence that the viewer might have otherwise repressed; (3) it desensitizes viewers to the occurrence of violence; (4) it increases viewer fearfulness."[13]

Ultimately, these findings may be the greatest dangers of media violence. Jesus said that loving our neighbor was the second great commandment. He also said, "A new commandment I give unto you, that ye love one another; as I have loved you, that ye also love one another" (John 13:34). How frightening to think that something as critical to our salvation as obedience to this commandment could actually be nullified because of repeated exposure to violence in the media.

Around Inappropriate Things Everyday

"I suppose the reason that I see R-rated movies is that I am around all the stuff that these movies contain, so it really doesn't matter where I hear it or see it."[14]

This is one of the most common reasons youth give for watching inappropriate movies. Many parents who hear this excuse are unable to come up with a suitable response and allow it into their homes. Is it a valid excuse when we see or hear inappropriate things in real life to voluntarily bring them into our lives? Or is this just another insidious deception of the adversary?

What would you do if you went to work every day and someone much larger and stronger than you slapped you in the face each time they saw you? There are several ways to handle this situation. Maybe the best way is just to avoid the person who slapped you. How much sense would it make to go home and pay someone to beat you with a baseball bat, since you had already been slapped at work? We hear profanity out in society, and then we pay to rent movies to hear the same thing?

I'm sure terrible things happen in our high schools, but I don't think that it happens to the extent of a single, typical movie. This fallacy can be demonstrated in the following illustrations.

In a recent year, there were 128 R-rated movies released in America. Movies are approximately two hours in length. Therefore, the total time we would spend if we watched all of the releases for the year is about 250 hours. The average time spent in most public schools is seven hours a day for approximately 180 days per year. That means the average student spends about 1,260 hours per year in school or about five times the amount of time it would take to watch every R-rated movie released. To compare our high schools to R-rated movies, we should be able to take the movie content for a year and multiply it by five.

Does a typical high school student really see 960 nude people in the halls of the schools each year? Are there really 1,180 incidents of people having sexual relations each year in the halls of their schools? Is it possible that they are seeing 2,380 graphic deaths at their schools each year? Or is this whole argument just another slick rationalization? We cannot continue to use these worldly rationalizations to justify our involvement with inappropriate media without suffering consequences. President Benson warned us of this danger when he said, "We counsel you, young men, not to pollute your minds with such degrading matter, for the mind through which this filth passes is never the same afterwards. Don't see R-rated movies or vulgar videos or participate in any entertainment that is immoral, suggestive, or pornographic."[15]

R-Rated Movies Don't Affect Me

"I justify going to rated R movies by thinking that I am above what is being shown on the screen. I go to church, home teach, have a calling and read my scriptures. I don't believe the material in these movies will affect me or cause me to be tempted."[16]

For years we have been warned about the dangers of tobacco by our prophets and more recently by medical research. Hundreds of thousands die each year because of the effects of this loathsome habit. And yet, in spite of the overwhelming evidence, tobacco companies and even some smokers continue to claim that the research results are inconclusive and that smoking has no effects. Most of us would agree that smoking is very dangerous.

Likewise, we have also been warned about the influence of inappropriate movies by prophets and more recently by media researchers. And yet, do we give the same heed to these warnings as we do on other matters? Satan is obviously whispering that these movies have no effects even though prophets and researchers say they do. Someone once said, "Tell a lie, make it big, repeat it often, and the majority of the people will believe you." For those who question the effect of inappropriate movies, let's look at some statistics from media research to show that the belief that movies have no effect is not true.

The following data shows the results of a survey conducted among high school students in various states. As you examine the charts, keep in mind that the research represents correlation only and is not meant to show cause and effect. Sexual attitudes of youth are influenced by many factors. The correlation, however, between the number of R-rated movies a student sees and permissive attitudes is too strong to simply ignore. The students were given several questions and statements and asked to express their opinions on the matter. They were also given a list of every movie released for the year and asked to check off the ones they had seen. The students were then placed in five groups based on the number of R-rated movies they had viewed for the year. The five groups were approximately equal in size. Their responses to the questions and statements concerning sexual attitudes were then analyzed against the number of R-rated movies the students viewed for the year.

Willingness to Have Premarital Sex Based on
Number of R-Rated Movies Per Year

0–4: 20%
5–15: 51%
16–29: 65%
30–49: 73%
50+: 93%[17]

A Beautiful Love Story

One day, a brother came to the institute where I taught and talked to me about raising the level of gospel scholarship in our area. During the conversation, he changed the subject to movies and told me how much he loved a current popular movie. He called it a beautiful love story. I had checked out the movie on an Internet research site and was familiar with its content. I said, "Let me see if I have the story right. We have an irresponsible, unemployed artist who has been painting nude prostitutes in France who goes back to England, gambles for and wins a passage on a ship to America. When he gets on the ship, he meets a suicidal girl who is engaged. Within two days, he has sexual relations with her, paints her nude, and has her smoking and drinking with him. Then the ship sinks, and he drowns. Is that the beautiful love story?" He told me that I had left out a lot of detail. I admitted that I didn't talk about the beautiful Hollywood stars or the enticing music and love story romance. But that is not a beautiful love story!

A beautiful love story is when President Hinckley said this about Marjorie: "As I looked at her across the table, I noted a few wrinkles in her face and hands. But are they less beautiful than before? No, in fact, they are more so."[18] The so-called beautiful love stories of our modern movies are repeated every night at singles bars around the nation. A couple meets, and within a few hours they are at one of their houses for a long time, and then they never see each other again. This is a corrupted love story.

It is time we seriously consider the counsel of President Gordon B. Hinckley in our homes. He said, "No good will come of going to movies that are designed to take from you your money and give you in exchange only weakened wills and base desires."[19]

Notes

1 LDS Bible Dictionary, 781.
2 Personal correspondence in author's possession.
3 Milton R. Hunter, in Conference Report, October 1966, 39.
4 Spencer W. Kimball, in Conference Report, April 1967, 66.
5 Edward L. Kimball, ed., *Teachings of Spencer Kimball* (Salt Lake City, UT: Deseret Book, 1982), 153.
6 Personal correspondence in author's possession.
7 George Albert Smith, in Conference Report, April 1933, 71.
8 Albert E. Bowen, in Conference Report, April 1941, 85.
9 Alexander Pope, "An Essay on Man," epistle 2, lines 217–21.
10 Personal correspondence in author's possession.
11 N. Eldon Tanner, in Conference Report, October 1973, 124.
12 Personal correspondence in author's possession.
13 Engage/Social Action, July/August 1985, 13.
14 Personal correspondence in author's possession.
15 Ezra Taft Benson, "To the 'Youth of the Noble Birthright,'" *Ensign*, May 1986, 43.
16 Personal correspondence in author's possession.
17 Randal A. Wright, "Family, Religious, Peer and Media Influence on Adolescence Willingness to Have Premarital Sex" (PhD dissertation), Brigham Young University, 1995, 119.
18 Gordon B. Hinckley, "This I Believe," Brigham Young University Speeches, March 1, 1992.
19 Gordon B. Hinckley, "Four B's for Boys," *Ensign*, November 1981, 41.

PARENTAL
EXAMPLE

MISTAKE: Failure to set a proper example for their children to follow.

"I lost a lot of respect for my parents because of their double standards. They would teach the gospel and then not live it. This fostered an attitude of distrust for what they said. For example, they would teach morality and then watch R-rated movies on a regular basis and think that nothing was wrong with it. My dad was a church leader, yet he had a terrible temper, and you never knew when it would blow. My mom was, and still is, always right even when she's dead wrong and knows it. You shouldn't preach one thing then do another and expect to be believable."

A few years ago, I was watching a men's basketball game between two wards playing for the stake championship. With a few seconds to go in the game, ward A scored a basket, but they were still behind by one point. Matt, a senior in high school, was on ward B's team. He was playing with the men because he was on the varsity team at high school and could not play on the young men's team. After ward A scored, Mark was to in-bound the ball to one of his teammates. Of course, they would then try to pass the ball around and dribble around for a few seconds to run out the clock and win the game. However, a member of team A, who was one of Matt's teachers at church, called for a "check ball," which is used when you play a "pick up game" without a referee. With a check ball a player throws it to a member of the opposing team before actually in-bounding the ball to his own team. When the opposing player receives the ball, he looks around to make sure his team is ready and then throws it back. Matt threw the ball to his church teacher who had called for the check ball, assuming he would throw it right back to him. What happened next stunned me. Instead of throwing the ball back to Matt, the man dribbled the ball once, and went up for a layup since he was right under the basket. After much confusion, the referee ruled it a live ball once Matt threw it to his teacher, counted the two points, and ward A won the game by one point. Matt looked bewildered at what just happened since he had trusted his teacher to be honest when he called for a check ball. His teacher actually laughed at him for his mistake. After the game, I heard the man justify his actions by saying, "If he is dumb enough to throw the ball to an opposing team member, he needs to learn a lesson and be a smarter player."

Thinking back on that experience, I am still shocked at what happened that day. I heard some of the youth in Matt's ward say that he, along with many others, had lost respect for this church teacher. I wonder what the man's wife and children thought of his winning basket, since they were all in attendance that day. Jacob said to the fathers of his day, "Ye have broken the hearts of your tender wives, and lost the confidence of your children, because of the bad examples before them" (Jacob 2:35).

It is no secret that children follow the examples set by their parents. Sandra was speaking at church on parental example and mentioned an experience she had with her three-year-old son. She had asked him to do something for her, and he put his hands on his hips and said, "I don't think so!" She was shocked at his response and wondered where he had picked up that defiant line and what to do with him. That night when her husband came home, she discussed the problem with him. He said, "Well you know where he got it from, don't you?" Sandra replied, "No I don't." He then said, "He got it from you!" She was shocked at his comment and promptly put her hands on her hips and boldly replied, "I don't think so." Her reply had been so impulsive that she didn't realize what she was saying until it was out. Terribly embarrassed, Sandra learned a valuable lesson that day.

The example we set for our family members is every bit as important as our word and, most likely, even more so. Years ago when I was an undergraduate in college, my class discussed research conducted with preschool children. Parents were given two bowls of candy. With the first bowl, they ate a piece of the candy and commented on how good it tasted while making facial expressions that explicitly showed that the candy tasted terrible. When the candy from the next bowl was tasted, they used facial expressions indicating that the candy was delicious while stating the candy tasted awful. The parents then let their children choose a piece from one of the two bowls as researchers observed. A vast majority of the children chose the candy based on parents' facial expressions, not their words. Even though this is a very simple experiment, the implications are tremendous! Actions of the parents had far more impact than their actual words.

Walt Whitman once said, "A child went forth and became what he saw." One day, our five-year-old daughter asked my brother if he ever went anywhere without telling his kids. He told her that he didn't think so. She went on to say, "My dad does. He went to McDonalds and didn't tell us. We found the bags!" I was again reminded how closely our children watch us.

In too many cases, parents are not setting proper examples for their children. Many have learned the sad lesson mentioned by Richard L. Evans, "Parents who indulge themselves 'in moderation' may have children who indulge themselves to excess."[1] In a survey, we asked high school students what type of movies they and their parents enjoyed watching. A large percentage of the youth said their parents enjoyed watching R-rated movies. One young man said, "My parents watch R-rated movies with abundant sex and violence because they 'reached maturity.' So have I." In a majority of cases, when parents watched inappropriate movies, their children followed their example and watched them also.

A very small percentage of this high school sample had never watched an R-rated movie. We asked these students why they chose to avoid these movies when so many of their peers watched them. The following comment is typical of those who fit into this category: "I have never even seen an R-rated movie. It's not something I care to support. It's really not something that has been hard to avoid either. I guess it's just the way my parents raised me."

The example set by parents, whether good or bad, can have a huge influence on children. Many years ago, President George Q. Cannon stated, "Where parents set proper examples to their children, and with those examples join good precepts, the influence is felt throughout the lives of their children. There may be some who will forget or disregard that which is shown and taught them, but they will be the exceptions. As the children grow in years, they will think about the examples and precepts of their parents. Increasing years will add weight to all that they have said and done."[2]

A few years ago I was asked to speak at a *Know Your Religion* series (KYR) in Mesa, Arizona, on a Friday night. Earlier that same day, I spoke to the Dobson High School seminary classes in Chandler. My topic was the importance of being a good example. That night after the KYR talk, I decided to go see a movie that several LDS friends had highly recommended. I checked a local newspaper and found that it was playing at a theater in Tempe. As I pulled up to the theater, I noticed most of the movies were R-rated along with the PG-rated one that I had come to see. As I walked up to the ticket booth, I saw a poster for a well-advertised, highly acclaimed R-rated movie. For a split second, the thought passed through my mind, "You are in Tempe, Arizona, and don't know one person here. No one would ever know which movie you went to see." Immediately, another thought came to mind. "Yes, at least two people would know—Heavenly Father and me." I walked up to the ticket booth and told the teenage worker that I wanted one ticket to the PG-rated movie. When I said that, the young man started to smile, as if pleased with my choice. I wondered why he cared which movie I saw. As he handed me my ticket, he said, "Thanks, Brother Wright." Startled, I asked him how he knew who I was. He said he was at the talk I had given to the seminary students earlier that day on being a good example. A tremendous feeling of relief rushed through me. I thanked my Heavenly Father for helping me have the courage to resist temptation. I then imagined what the result would have been if I had made the wrong choice that night.

Later, as I drove to the motel, I thought of another experience when I spoke to a group of LDS high school students about the influence of electronic media in our lives. I quoted this statement by Elder Gene R. Cook:

> I am not surprised that President Benson would counsel us, as members of the Church, to avoid . . . R-rated movies. Yet there are still many

who are going to R-rated movies. I guess they have not really believed the President of the Church, and that is risky business. To me, some of the PG and PG-13 movies are even questionable.

I have had some adults say to me, "Well, I'm an adult. I can see an R-rated movie. Of course I don't let my children see them, but I do." The scriptures tell us to become like little children, and we ought not go where we can't take our children. If it's not good enough for your children, it's not good enough for you. We ought not have double standards. There is one standard and it's the Lord's standard and we ought to abide by it whether we're old or young.[3]

After the talk, a handsome, muscular seventeen-year-old came up to me. I could tell he was an outstanding young man and a good example of what a Latter-day Saint youth should be. He told me about a Sunday School teacher that he and his friends from the ward had greatly admired. One Sunday, she read a statement to the class from President Ezra Taft Benson about not attending R-rated movies. She then challenged the class to make a vow to never see an R-rated movie. The young man then said, "Because I loved and respected this teacher so much, I made a vow that day that I would never watch one of these movies." He said that later, the class was discussing prejudice one Sunday, when the teacher recommended seeing a movie depicting the atrocities of the holocaust. She went on to tell them how good the movie was and what great lessons it had taught her. One of the class members raised his hand and asked if this particular movie was R-rated. The teacher replied that it was R-rated, but it was okay to see since it was historically based. He then asked her if it contained nudity and immorality. She said it did, but the nudity was not meant to be sexual. As the young man was sharing this experience, he made a statement that I don't think I will ever forget. He said, "I still love my teacher, but I don't respect her!" This teacher had said one thing and done another. Because of the teacher's inconsistent words and actions, the young student lost the respect he once had for her. Of course, it could have been much worse! The teacher could have been the young man's mother or father.

In a world with so few positive role models, it seems imperative for parents to set a consistent, positive example for youth. If parents and teachers want our youth to be good, we must be good ourselves! Youth are looking for those they can pattern their lives after. Sometimes it only takes one mistake to lose the respect others have for you. Elder H. Burke Peterson spoke truly when he said: "If our words are not consistent with our actions, they will never be heard above the thunder of our deeds."[4]

A few years ago, I served in the presidency of the San Antonio Mission with President Kent Richards. I was greatly surprised and impressed when he told me that he was a fifth-generation mission president. Think about that unique distinction. Five consecutive generations of mission presidents! Even today with millions of members worldwide, we still only have around 360 mission presidents. Who started this unparalleled tradition of service in the Richards family?

Interested in his heritage, I read the story of President Richards' ancestors and the example they set for their posterity. It began when thirty-one-year-old Willard Richards opened a Book of Mormon at random and read, "Adam fell that men might be; and men are that they might have joy" (2 Nephi 2:25). He came to the conclusion that, "Either God or the devil had had a hand in that book, for man never wrote it."[5] He then read through the book two times in ten days, and knew it was true. His cousin, Brigham Young, then baptized him on December 31, 1836. He went on a mission with Heber C. Kimball and Orson Hyde to England in 1837. One of the early converts was the daughter of a protestant minister by the name of Jenetta Richards. On the day she was baptized, Heber met Willard and prophetically said, "Willard, I baptized your wife today."[6]

Eight months later, Willard escorted Jenetta and another young woman to a church meeting. He commented that Richards was a good name and then remarked, "I never want to change it; do you Jenetta?" She replied "No, I do not, and I think I never will."[7] They were married on September 24, 1839. He learned of his call to be a member of the Twelve while in England and was ordained April 14, 1840. He served as private secretary to the Prophet Joseph Smith. Later, he crossed the Mississippi River with Joseph and accompanied the Prophet and Hyrum to the Carthage jail.

By the afternoon of June 27, 1844, most had been sent to take care of certain matters of business, leaving only John Taylor and Willard Richards with the Prophet and his brother. That afternoon following dinner, the jailer, knowing that a mob had gathered outside, suggested that the prisoners would be safer in the cell of the jail. Turning to Willard Richards, Joseph asked, "If we go into the cell will you go with us?" To this Elder Richards responded, "Brother Joseph, you did not ask me to cross the river with you . . . you did not ask me to come to Carthage . . . you did not ask me to come to jail with you. And do you think I would forsake you now? But I will tell you what I will do; if you are condemned to be hung for 'treason,' I will be hung in your stead, and you shall go free."[8]

Willard arrived in the Salt Lake Valley in 1847 and served as Second Counselor in the First Presidency from 1847 to 1854. He died of dropsy at age 49 on March 11, 1854. Brigham Young said, "He was as true and unwavering in his course as the sun is to the earth. There is not a shade of deviation from the principles of righteousness."[9]

As I thought about the example set by Willard Richards, I was not as surprised that he had posterity as committed to the gospel as he was. What a legacy he left behind!

Book of Mormon Examples

When parents are as unwavering in their course as the sun is to the earth, then they often produce children who are the same in their commitment. I asked an institute class who they felt the two most influential teachers were in the Book of Mormon, excluding Jesus Christ. Someone named King Benjamin first and he was soon followed by a variety of names that included Alma, Ammon, Moroni, Mormon, and Abinadi. We then discussed each of these names and why they would be considered the "most influential." I pointed out that perhaps Moroni and Mormon were much more influential in our day than in Book of Mormon days. And Abinadi had a huge impact indirectly on the whole civilization because of a convert named Alma. Consider the influence of Abinadi as you think about the "mission presidents" produced among Alma's descendants.

However, I am personally of the opinion there are two men who are even more influential than any of the names mentioned. How could anyone have been any more influential than Nephi? Once the Lord softened his heart (1 Nephi 2:16), then he always went and did as the Lord commanded (1 Nephi 3:7). What influence did he have? For one thousand years people were still calling themselves Nephites in his honor. Think of those who identified themselves as his descendants:

Mosiah: "And now all the people of Zarahemla were numbered with the Nephites, and this because the kingdom had been conferred upon none but those who were descendants of Nephi" (Mosiah 25:13). That means that Benjamin; Mosiah; and his four sons, Ammon, Aaron, Omner, Himni were also his descendants.

Alma: "But there was one among them whose name was Alma, he also being a descendant of Nephi" (Mosiah 17:2). That means Alma the younger, Helaman, Helaman, Nephi, Nephi, Nephi, Amos, and Ammaron were also his descendants.

Amulek: A descendant of "Aminadi was a descendant of Nephi, who was the son of Lehi" (Alma 10:3).

Mormon: "And I, Mormon, being a descendant of Nephi . . ." (Mormon 1:4). That means Moroni is also one of his descendants.

Think of the heritage of faith Nephi left behind because of his willingness to always go and do as the Lord commanded.

Who is the other most influential leader in the Book of Mormon? In my opinion, there is only one more obvious choice besides Nephi, and that is Laman. The influence of his bad example on his children and his descendants is staggering. "And thus they have taught their children that they should hate them, and that they should murder them, and that they should rob and plunder them, and do all they could to destroy them; therefore they have an eternal hatred toward the children of Nephi" (Mosiah 10:17). Laman felt he was robbed of his birthright and wronged by his younger brother.

He taught this to his children and they taught it to their children, and so on, until almost a thousand years passed. Ultimately, the Lamanites carried our exactly what Laman attempted numerous times almost a thousand years earlier. They destroyed the Nephites. And thus we see that improper parental example has an incalculable impact on their children. N. Eldon Tanner once said, "Improper parental example in the home is a leading cause of the wandering of youth from the principles as taught in the gospel of Jesus Christ."[10]

From the Book of Mormon we learn of the tremendous influence that righteous or wicked parents can have on their posterity. No wonder President Howard W. Hunter stated, "The greatest training that can be given to a child is that which comes from the example of parents. Parents need to set the example for young people to follow. Great strength comes from the home where righteous principles are taught, where there is love and respect for each other, where prayer has been an influence in the family life, and where there is respect for those things that pertain to God."[11]

Many think teaching the gospel in the home is all that is needed to produce righteous children. Good parental teaching in the home combined with bad parental example seldom leads to obedient children. Jacob points out the consequences of parents setting a bad example. He said to the members of the Church in his day: "Ye have . . . lost the confidence of your children, because of your bad examples before them; and the sobbings of their hearts ascend up to God against you" (Jacob 2:35).

Good teaching, however, mixed with good parental example has proven to be the most effective and essential way to entice children to do well. Paul gives us these guidelines, "Be thou an example of the believers, in word, in conversation, in charity, in spirit, in faith, in purity" (1 Timothy 4:12).

We Can Change

Some parents have made mistakes and have been poor examples to their children. To those who are in this situation, the Savior's message is clear: We can change! When my grandmother died in childbirth, my mother was forced to drop out of school to care for her three younger siblings. They lived in a rural area of Alabama, and it was a very difficult time period for the family.

My grandfather was working long hours in the fields to support his children. My great-grandmother Nelia Thompson lived in Oklahoma during that time, but would sometimes come and stay for months at a time to help her son and grandchildren. My mother had many long talks with her during these visits and developed a great love and respect for her grandmother. Following is an experience that can teach us we can change when we have done wrong. My mother records:

"She said that a short time after she and Grandpa had joined the

Church, they moved to another little farming town, for Grandpa was a farmer. They had no nice chapel to hold church in, as we enjoy—in fact, they had nothing, except for a little magazine that came once a month and through this they kept contact with the Church. Every now and then the missionaries would come through." You can see how hard it would be to grow in the gospel. Not only that, but they were the only LDS family for miles. She continued,

> It was customary in those days for the women in the community to get together in the afternoons to visit on their front porches and dip snuff. They'd take a little piece of sweet gum stick, chew the end until it looked like a little brush, stick that brush down into the snuff, put it into their mouths, and then spit off the porch when enough saliva had accumulated. It looked awfully nasty to Grandma, but all the women kept encouraging her. This was really a big decision for her, being new in the community. She wanted so much to be accepted, so one evening she got her a little stick, made her little brush and took her first dip of snuff. It tasted terrible, but determined to be accepted, she did not complain. On her way home that evening, she stopped by her mail box and there, inside, was her church magazine. Immediately her eyes fell to the words that seemed to jump out at her as if they'd been written just for her. It said, "Any mother who would take the filth called snuff into her mouth and then kiss her darling baby is not worthy of being a mother." She went home and fell on her knees and begged the Lord to forgive her. She never again partook of the filthy stuff called snuff.[12]

When I first heard that experience, I got emotional thinking about how unusual my great grandmother was. How many people make a mistake and then never repeat that mistake again for the rest of their lives? Yet, that opportunity is open to all of us. A story is told of a Bible scholar who was asked which of all the translations of the Bible he liked the best. His reply was that he liked his mother's translation best for she had translated it into her own life.

Be an Example of Good Behavior

We need to commit today to be a better example to our family. One little boy riding with his mother asked a thought-provoking question, "Mom, why do all the idiots come out when Daddy drives?" The father was teaching his boy through his driving habits. Brigham Young said, "We must first learn to control ourselves before we can think to control our fellow creatures."[13]

If we want our children to live pure and worthy lives, we must be willing to set the example. President N. Eldon Tanner stated, "Parents must realize that every word they speak, every act, every response, attitude, and even appearance and manner of dress will affect the lives of their children and the whole family."[14]

Notes

1   Richard L. Evans , in Conference Report, April 1969, 75.

2   George Q. Cannon, *Juvenile Instructor*, January 1, 1892, 27:28.

3   Gene R. Cook, *13 Lines of Defense: Living the Law of Chastity*, audio tape, Deseret Book.

4   H. Burke Peterson, "Prepare the Heart of Your Son," *Ensign*, November 1982, 43.

5   Claire Noall, *Intimate Disciple: A Portrait of Willard Richards* (Salt Lake City, UT: University of Utah Press, 1957), 104.

6   Ibid.

7   Lawrence R. Flake, *Prophets and Apostles of the Last Dispensation* (Salt Lake City, UT: Deseret Book, 2001), 247–49.

8   B. H. Roberts, *A Comprehensive History of the Church of Jesus Christ of Latter-day Saints, Century One, 6 vols.* (Provo, Utah: Corporation of the President, 1965), 2:283.

9   Preston Nibley, *Brigham Young: The Man and His Works* (Salt Lake City, UT: Deseret Book, 1974), 212.

10   N. Eldon Tanner, "Why Is My Boy Wandering Tonight?" *Ensign*, November 1974, 84.

11   Clyde J. Williams, ed., *The Teachings of Howard W. Hunter* (Salt Lake City, UT: Deseret Book, 1997), 146.

12   Personal correspondence in author's possession.

13   Brigham Young, "Design of the Lord in Gathering Together His People," *Journal of Discourses*, Vol. 10: 30, June 8, 1862.

14   N. Eldon Tanner, in Area Conference Report, August 1974, 63.

EXPRESSING LOVE
VERBALLY

MISTAKE: Failure to express love verbally to family members daily.

"One thing that did not occur in our home was our parents saying the words 'I love you' to any of the children. I don't remember ever saying it myself until my first phone call home during my freshman year at BYU. It was my first experience away from home and I was homesick. I told them 'I love you' over the phone for the first time. After my marriage, my sister was shocked to hear me tell my mom that I loved her. She said that she wasn't used to hearing anyone saying that to each other in our family."

On Sunday, June 25, 2000, I spoke at the gathering for the one-hundredth anniversary of my great-grandparents' baptism into the Church of Jesus Christ of Latter-day Saints. Beforehand, I was at a loss as to know what I should say to the large crowd of descendants and friends who would gather at the stake center. To seek the Spirit, I went to the country cemetery where both of my great-grandparents are buried. It was very peaceful looking at their old tombstones. As I stared at the fifteen names of their children, I felt great sorrow for those of the eight who died in their youth. I imagined the pain the parents must have felt. I walked over, sat on a bench, and pondered what to say at the meeting. As I looked up, I saw a laminated poem hanging in a tree near the tombstone of Billy Wayne Ezell, December 7, 1972–February 26, 1994. His mother wrote the poem. I felt sad as I read the following words:

If Only I Had Known (By his mom)

If I'd only known it would be the last time,
That I'd see you walk out the door,
I'd give you a bigger hug and kiss
And called you back for one more
If I'd only known it would be the last time,
I'd hear your laughter and playful way,
I'd tape each action and word,
So I could play them back every day

If I'd only known it would be the last time
We would have an extra minute or two,
I'd been sure to have said once again,
"Son, please know how much I love you!"

If I'd only known it would be the last time,
I'd be there to share your day
Believing there would always be more,
I wouldn't have let it just slip away.

If I'd only known it would be the last time
That I'd see you fall asleep
I'd pray, take me Lord, but please,
Give my son his life to keep.

If only I had known.

As I read this poem, I thought about the fact that things would be different had this mother only known. However, the point is, she didn't know. No one knows when it will be the last opportunity to express love to family members.

Children have an innate need to verbally hear that their parents love them. Although many do not have a problem expressing love, others struggle to say the words "I love you" regularly. When children do not feel loved, they frequently search for that love in the wrong places. Often, the problem has been passed on from previous generations. Fathers generally have a harder time expressing love to family members than do mothers.

Many years ago, Paul Popenoe conducted a study with teenagers. He said, "In a study, several thousand HS students were asked what they would most like to hear from their parents. The survey found that 50 percent of the students said they wanted most to know if their parents loved them."[1] Perhaps you are thinking that things have changed since the sixties and that this study is rather outdated. In recent research conducted with high school students, I found that the problem is lingering. High school students from various regions of the United States were asked

Q. *How often do your parents tell you that they love you?* This is what they said.

How Often Parents Say "I Love You"
Father; Mother

Never; 27%; 9%
Once or so a month; 25%; 14%
Several times a month; 19%; 21%
Daily; 29%; 56%[2]

It appears that parents still have a problem telling their children they are loved on a daily basis. Fathers in this study are three times less likely to never tell children they love them than mothers are. Fathers are also almost half as likely as mothers to tell children daily that they love them. This tendency in parents is heartbreaking when you consider the consequences of such neglect. Often the simple expressed "I love you" works miracles. Elder H. Burke Peterson said, "Among the tragedies we see around us every day are the countless children and adults who are literally starving, because they are not being fed a daily portion of love. We have in our midst thousands who would give anything to hear the words and feel the warmth of this expression."[3]

A friend shared an excerpt from her grandfather's journal, which emphasizes the neglect that some parents, and especially fathers, make when not expressing love. As a young man, he had a strong desire to leave his native Norway and come to America. In this illustration, it proves true that the father had not expressed love to his son and created such a tradition. He recorded,

In the fall of 1922, four other boys in the neighborhood and I decided to go to America. It took several months to get our papers ready.

In January 1923, we were ready to leave home. On the morning I was to leave, my mother came upstairs at 4:00 am to wake me up. As I lay there, she knelt by my bed and put her arm around me with her cheek against my cheek, and told me how she loved me and how she would miss me. She told me to be a good boy. She felt that she would not see me again in this life.

I had been *taught never to cry or show emotion*, but at that moment I wanted to put my arms around her. Unfortunately, I let them lie still by my side under the covers. I didn't say or do anything, because I was a man. How could I be so soft to put my arms around my mother, or maybe cry and tell her how I loved her? I couldn't do that. It wasn't manly. How I have regretted that moment all these years!

I got up, and she walked me 2 miles in the knee-deep snow to the bus stop. She helped me carry my suitcase. When I got on the bus, I shook hands with my mother and said goodbye. Now for 52 years I have regretted all this.

Thirty-eight years after I came over to this country, I had a chance to go back to Norway for a visit. My mother had died eighteen years before. The first thing I did the first day I was there was to go to the graveyard. I didn't know where the graves were located. I searched up and down the rows till I finally came to the graves of my mother and father. I stood there and looked at them for a minute, and all my past days were going through my mind, especially the last day I saw my mother.

I knelt down and put my arms around the marker. I put my cheek against her name, and those tears that I should have shed 38 years earlier were shed there. I was not such a big man after all.[4]

How unfortunate that this young man had been taught to never cry or show emotion. I wonder who taught him that it wasn't manly to show emotion or say the words I love you? Obviously, it could not have been his mother. I can picture this good brother with his arms around his mother's tombstone expressing his love for her.

We can learn a valuable lesson from this story. As parents and as sons and daughters, we need to continually learn to express love and affection to family members. This can be a great protection against temptation. Research has shown that youth who have love communicated to them daily by their parents are much less willing to engage in illicit activities than those who never hear those words. And yet, far too many parents (especially fathers) are either never telling their children they love them or they only do so occasionally. Perhaps some may think that their children, particularly teenagers, do not want to be told they are loved. Past research states this is not the case. It may be that some do not want to be told in public—in front of their friends—but they do want and need to be told in the family realm.

Why Does This Problem Exist?

I have often wondered why so many parents have trouble expressing love to members of their own family. Clearly, there are many reasons for this behavior. While some are probably very complex, a few of the following reasons may apply.

Appearance of Weakness

Over the years we have been socialized to believe that we are to take on certain roles. Men are the providers, and women are the nurturers. Perhaps for some, like my friend's grandfather, it is not a masculine trait for fathers to express outward love. In some way, those who fit into this category think they appear weak if they express love for others.

Not Expressed in the Home

Growing up, I didn't notice that my father never told me he loved me. Although he did many things to demonstrate his love, the verbal words never came. Maybe the reason he struggled saying it was because his mother or father never once told him that he was loved. His parents were from the old school that did not express those feelings. If the truth were known, they probably never heard the words themselves.

"It Goes without Saying"

Frequently, there is the assumption that our family members know they are loved, and consequently there is no need to express it. When love is left unexpressed, family members are left to wonder. In a very frightening world, the one thing no one needs to wonder about is whether they are genuinely loved. Some parents believe that since they do so much for their children, there is no need to express love verbally. After all, they provide food, shelter, and clothing and put gas in the car. I'm not sure that a typical teenager comes into the house and says, "Wow, my parents really love me—we have a home to live in." Someone once said, "Children couldn't care less what you do for them. They care a whole lot how you make them feel."

John Powell wrote of a significant experience he had the day his father passed away. He writes:

> It was the day my father died. . . . In the small hospital room, I was supporting him in my arms, when . . . my father slumped back, and I lowered his head gently onto the pillow. I . . . told my mother . . . "It's all over, Mom. Dad is dead." She startled me. I will never know why these were her first words to me after his death. My mother said: "Oh, he was so proud of you. He loved you so much."
>
> Somehow I knew . . . that these words were saying something very important to me. They were like a sudden shaft of light, like a startling thought I had never before absorbed. Yet there was a definite edge of pain, as though I were going to know my father better in death than I had ever known him in life.
>
> Later, while a doctor was verifying death, I was leaning against the wall in the far corner of the room, crying softly. A nurse came over to me and put a comforting arm around me. I couldn't talk through my tears. I wanted to tell her:
>
> "I'm not crying because my father is dead. I'm crying because my father never told me that he was proud of me. He never told me that he loved me. Of course, I was expected to know these things. I was expected to know the great part I played in his life and the great part I occupied of his heart, but he never told me."[5]

The Consequences

There is no question that a lack of expressed love in families is associated with various forms of delinquent behavior. Of great concern are those who seek to find love through inappropriate friends and immoral behavior.

A few years ago my friend Mark, a family therapist, was in a counseling session with a couple and Mary, their teenage daughter. The father was terribly unaffectionate with his children and never expressed love verbally to them. Mary was very rebellious and involved in immoral behavior that greatly alarmed her parents. Trying to get their daughter help for her problem, they brought her in for counseling. During the counseling session the father had several negative things to say about Mary and her behavior. Finally, Mark asked the teenage girl what she felt her father was trying to say to her. The young woman looked directly at Mark but did not respond to his question. He then told her to ask her father a question. He said, "Mary, ask him if he thinks you are a loser." Mary turned to him and said: "So, do you think I'm a loser, Dad?" There was a long pause before he said, "Mary, what I'm really afraid of is that I'm going to lose you." When he said those words, she began to sob. Mary seemed to finally realize that her father really did love her even though he did not express it. That scenario is repeated daily in various forms and situations.

The Solution

The solution to this problem is a simple one that only involves three words, "I love you." The Savior, His prophets, and apostles have repeatedly taught us by word and example to openly share with those around us how we feel about them. For example, Jesus Christ expressed His love to the Twelve Apostles with these words: "As the Father hath loved me, so have I loved you: continue ye in my love"(John 15:10). And in our day, President Gordon B. Hinckley expressed his love to the saints by saying, "I have a confession to make, my brothers and sisters. It is simply this: I love you. I love the people of this Church."[6]

Many benefits come into our homes when we express love meaningfully. While I was serving as a bishop, one of the fathers in our ward was bearing his testimony. In closing he said, "I just want to tell my family how much I love them." Immediately after he said those words, his little three-year-old girl sitting with her mother in the back of the chapel stood up in her chair, put her hands up to her mouth, and yelled energetically, "I love you too, Dad." A very special feeling entered the chapel. Almost the entire congregation, including the father, got teary eyed. The effect that those words had on the audience was remarkable. By hearing the words "I love you" expressed sincerely by this young girl, we found ourselves surrounded by love.

I have experienced the closeness that comes with openly expressing feelings of love, within my own family and with friends. We had moved from Utah to Texas, and my teenage daughter quickly became friends with a young woman named Melinda. Her parents were divorced, so she and her brother went to church alone. After a few years, her brother stopped going, so she would come alone to church. Melinda visited our home regularly over the years. One day, I was sitting at our kitchen table talking to her and said, "Melinda, out of all Natalie's friends, I like you the best." She smiled and said, "I bet you say that to all her friends." I said, "Actually, you are the first one I have ever told that." She made no reply. When I looked at her, I saw her lip quivering and her eyes fill with tears. Melinda, like every one of us, needed to be told she was loved. Do you think that Melinda and I were even closer friends after that experience? When feelings are expressed, it tends to bond people together. If our children's friends need to be told verbally that they are cared for, then how much greater are our own family members' needs? If we want our children to know that they are loved, then we need to tell them every day.

Notes

1   Paul Popenoe, "Do Your Children Know You Love Them?" *Parents and Better Homemaking*, 40, December 1965, 43–45.
2   Randal A. Wright, "Family, Religious, Peer and Media Influence on Adolescence Willingness to Have Premarital Sex" (PhD dissertation), Brigham Young University, 1995, 115–16.
3   H. Burke Peterson, "The Daily Portion of Love," *Ensign*, May 1977, 68.
4   Personal correspondence in author's possession.
5   John Joseph Powell, *The Secret of Staying in Love* (Allen, TX: Tabor Publishing, 1974), 68.
6   Gordon B. Hinckley, "Latter-day Saints in Very Deed," *Ensign*, November 1997, 85.

PHYSICAL
AFFECTION

MISTAKE: Failure to give appropriate physical affection to family members.

"Never once did I see my mom or dad show any physical affection toward each other. There was no hand holding or kissing in front of the family. Neither did my father ever once hug or kiss me or tell me he loved me. I think it was the same for my siblings. The only time I remember my mother giving me a brief hug was when I was leaving for college. I think we were all starved for affection and went seeking it outside the home."

A few years ago, I attended a talk given to approximately 350 LDS teenagers by a very popular youth speaker. The message was well presented, and the youth seemed to respond positively. However, the speaker's strongest points were not his words. I noticed he had a unique ability to radiate love for his entire audience. After the class ended, something happened that puzzled me a great deal. I watched as several teenagers went to the front of the room to talk to this man. I noticed that instead of the traditional handshake, the speaker hugged each of the youth, patted them on the back, and told them how special they were. At first, only a small group of teens got this special attention.

Then something very unusual happened. Those leaving the building noticed what was happening at the front of the room. Most turned and went to stand in line for their opportunity to talk to the speaker. A long line, which extended along the wall to the back of the room, began to form. Each youth waited for a turn to get a hug and uplifting words from this dynamic teacher. Many of the teenagers actually burst into tears after their short embrace. Puzzled, I asked myself why these youth wanted to meet the speaker and why so many were emotional after a short embrace. Was it the talk he had given? While it was very good, I had heard many similar talks with no such outcome.

As one young man walked away from his embrace in tears, I decided to ask him about his experience. He had a fake earring and bleached blond hair that stuck out about eight inches in the front. By all outward appearances, he seemed to struggle with his self-worth. I asked him why he was so emotional. Though choked with emotion, he replied, "I don't know. I guess I have never felt love like that before in my life. I think I knew that guy in the preexistence!" I wondered to myself if this young man was an orphan. How could a five-second hug from an unknown brother make him feel love like never before? Where do his parents fit into this story?

It was obvious that it wasn't just the talk that had such a dramatic effect on the youth that day. It was the physical embrace and the words of encouragement from the speaker that got to their emotions. After talking to many of the youth, I think I have a better idea of what happened that day. Those who were most visibly affected by the speaker's emanating love were those not getting enough physical affection in their own homes. Could there be a connection between little or no affection in a youth's home and the high rates of immorality in our society? Perhaps youth who don't get appropriate affection from their parents seek affection outside the home.

Trying Times

We live in a very challenging time. Our children face temptations and trials that many of us would never have imagined in our day. It is not just the drugs, alcohol, gambling, pornography, and inappropriate media that they must deal with daily. Think also about the fear of rejection, weight issues, peer pressure, homework, future education plans, career choices, and dating. More than ever they need a friend. But in an effort to improve our children, we often point out their faults.

A university research study reported many years ago estimated a typical teenager hears ten negative comments for every positive one. One of my friends told me that on her son's fourteenth birthday, she was pointing out a few things he needed to work on to become a better person. He finally stopped her and asked, "Mom, is there anything you do like about me?" Of course, there is great danger in all of this. If children are getting bombarded with worldly pressures, the last thing they need is to question whether they have a friend at home, or even if they are really loved.

All of us have a basic human need to feel loved and appreciated. One powerful way to express love is through appropriate physical affection. When children are given this affection, they often feel secure, loved, and worthwhile. When family members do not get affection in the home, they often seek it from friends. And of course, there is usually someone who will gladly give them physical affection. Unfortunately, it is almost always an inappropriate type of affection that will damage them instead of protect them.

Few Are Shown Affection

Unfortunately, many have trouble showing love and affection. This problem is especially true of fathers. In unpublished research among high school students, I posed the following question: "How often does your father/mother show you physical affection (kisses, hugs, etc.)?" The results of this survey were disturbing. "Only 24 percent of fathers showed their children physical affection on a daily basis. Mothers were better but still only 49 percent gave daily physical affection to their children."

Often this lack of affection is passed on to the next generation, which creates a vicious cycle that is extremely hard to break. After a presentation on the power of love and affection, I received the following note from one of the participants.

> I am 80 years old, born in Utah into a good pioneer family. My grand-mother was the daughter of a prominent bishop, but I never heard grandma say the word love. My mother was the second of eight children. I was the second of three. I never saw my mother and father hug or kiss. I was raised during the depression. My father was a traveling salesman. He would sign his letters, "oodles of love" but that was the only time I ever heard or read that word.

My mother died at 97. I visited her every day the last seven years. She never said, "I love you" once, and I never said it to her. Mother had never ever hugged or kissed me. I kissed her casket—first time. I am the mother of five sons and one mentally handicapped daughter. She is the only one I can hug and kiss.

My husband was very starved for any physical affection too—*he took his own life*. All of this I now realize that I was starved for some physical affection. Keep teaching this message. Thank you!"[1]

This sister and her husband were both in need of affection. The consequences in this home are tragic. This sister, who had no affection from her parents, gave none to her own family members. In this short message, we see that the lack of affection became a tradition carried on for at least four generations. I hope that her posterity is able to break the cycle and show affection to their children.

The Consequences

The results from failure to give family members appropriate physical affection are many. One consequence of great concern is the tendency to be sexually immoral. President Ezra Taft Benson commented on this by saying, "I recognize that most people fall into sexual sin in a misguided attempt to fulfill basic human needs. We all have a need to feel loved and worthwhile. We all seek to have joy and happiness in our lives. Knowing this, Satan often lures people into immorality by playing on their basic needs."[2]

The following statement by a thirteen-year-old girl is chilling: "When my father stopped hugging me, I decided I could either tear up the beautiful book he had given me for Christmas, or I could kill myself, or I could try to get hugs from someone else," says Janie, thirteen, who recently had her first sexual encounter. "I finally decided to get a boyfriend."[3] Why do you think her father stopped hugging her? This young girl obviously felt that her father no longer loved her when he stopped hugging her. I have a feeling that her assumption was completely misinterpreted.

I read Janie's statement to a group attending a *Know Your Religion* lecture a few years ago. After the talk, a beautiful, young teenage girl approached me. She began, "Every night since I was born, my father came into my room, laid on the bed beside me, and talked to me. We laughed and shared meaningful experiences together every night. He often counseled me and encouraged me to live the gospel. Before leaving, he always hugged me, gave me a kiss, and told me how much he loved me. Sometimes, he would bear his testimony to me." Then she said, "Last year he quit coming into my room, and he has not come back in once." I asked her how old she was. She replied that she was fourteen. Then this young LDS girl said, "Sometimes, I just want to take him by the shirt and shake him and tell him that I still need that." Is this young girl in danger?

Dr. Elizabeth R. McAnarney, director of Adolescent Medicine at the University of Rochester Medical School, said, "Adolescents need touch to facilitate communication and convey caring. When children are no longer held and comforted by their parents, they may turn to their peers instead. There is almost no data on this, but I wonder if the increase in very young teenage pregnancy comes from the need to be held. They may be using sex for a nonsexual purpose."[4]

Personally, I believe that in both cases mentioned above, the fathers quit hugging their daughters for the same reason. After all, what would people think of a father hugging his teenage girl, who has become a young woman? They may think that there is something inappropriate going on. In reality, *not* expressing appropriate affection may be related to the very thing they were trying to avoid.

After a youth conference, I visited with several youth and their leaders while waiting for my ride to arrive. I met two Mia Maid–aged girls who had been in attendance at the conference. Knowing I would probably never see them again, I expressed to them how much I enjoyed being at their conference, gave them a brief hug, and told them I loved them.

Shortly after returning home, I received a letter from one of these young girls.

> I thought you might want to know how much it meant to Misty and me when you talked to us after youth conference. It really made us feel good that you cared enough about the youth of the Church to talk to us when you really needed to leave. And whether you knew it or not, we were touched so much when right before you left, you hugged us and then on top of that you said, "I love you." That meant a lot to both of us—thank you so very much.

When I got into the car, my father was angry about something, and he started degrading the Church, its leaders and members. He didn't want to hear about youth conference or anything that had happened. This really upset me, as I love the Church and its leaders. It hurt me so much that I couldn't stop crying from 12:30 to 3:00.[5]

She went on to describe her dad as a very good man, but one who had a bad temper and was very emotionally cold, showing her little love and affection. She doubted if he even loved her. My heart went out to this fine young sister, and I realized why a simple hug and saying "I love you" meant so much to her. I fear for her and all young women in similar situations if a young man comes along and shows inappropriate affection.

Before we are quick to judge this father, let's ask ourselves if our own children really know they are loved. Oh sure, we can say they know, but I have a strong feeling that my young friend's father truly loves her and simply has a hard time showing it. He probably isn't even aware of her doubts. When we do not express love to family members, they may question our feelings for them. Children need love, affection, and kindness from their parents.

The Solution

The solution, of course, to all of this is to follow the example of Jesus Christ and His church. Even though we do not have a detailed description of the Savior's daily ministry, we do have insights about Him in our limited account. For example, we read the following about His visit to the Americas, "And it came to pass that when Jesus had made an end of these sayings, he touched with his hand the disciples whom he had chosen one by one, even until he had touched them all, and spake unto them as he touched them" (3 Nephi 18:6).

Why did Jesus touch them as He talked to them? Of all the ways of showing love, physical touch is perhaps the most powerful. Why is touch used so much in the Church today? When called to a Church position, hands are laid on your head to set you apart. Why? If you think about it, we use physical touch with handshakes, blessings, anointings, sealings, ordinations, confirmations, baptisms, temple ordinances, and so on. There are significant reasons, of course.

The Benefits

In a landmark study by Kunz and Dyer on effective LDS families, they asked parents: *How do you express love in your family?* They found the following.

Ways Effective Families Express Love

Telling them we love them 97%
Do things for them 96%
Hugging 94%
Tell by writing or phoning 91%
Kissing 85%[6]

A few years ago, I attended a high school basketball game between two powerhouses vying for the championship of an important tournament. Lincoln High had won five Texas State Championships in the 1980s and was the number-one team in the state at the time. Their opponent was Beaumont West Brook, led by Lukie Jackson, son of former Olympic and NBA All-Star Luke Jackson. Both teams gave it everything they had. West Brook held the lead from the beginning of the game, thanks to the 27 points accumulated by Lukie Jackson. Then, with just a few seconds left in regulation play, Lincoln tied the score, and the game went into overtime. The West Brook team was able to gain a one-point advantage over their opponents. It appeared they would hold the lead and win the game. However, with less than 30 seconds to go, a Lincoln player drove to the basket and was fouled by Lukie. He made both free throws, and Lincoln won the game by one point. Lukie was visibly upset. To have played so hard, scored so many points, but then to make a foul that cost his team the game against the defending state champions was devastating.

I wondered what his dad was thinking. Would he yell at his boy for making a mistake that cost them the game? Then I turned around to see a huge man coming down the arena's aisles toward the dejected player. It was Luke Jackson. Surely Lukie would get the tongue lashing that so many sons receive in similar situations. When they met, Luke threw his arms around his son, and in front of thousands of people, held him tightly, patting him on the back and quietly talking to him. I watched this touching scene, wondering what I would have done had he been my own son. After the long embrace ended, Lukie's countenance changed. He looked as if his team had just won the state championship. He was smiling and happy as he went over to congratulate the winning team. I don't think I've ever witnessed such a change in attitude in such a short time. Maybe this incident confirms a statement made by Dr. Harold Voth, a psychiatrist with the Menninger Foundation, who said, "Hugging can lift depression. It breathes fresh life into a tired body and makes you feel younger and more vibrant."[7]

Do you think Lukie loves and respects his father? Do you think he was more inclined to listen to his father's counsel after that game? Lukie went on to stardom at Syracuse University. Our children can go on to stardom also in whatever they choose to do if they truly feel that they are loved.

From these simple acts, many remarkable benefits will occur. Our children will have added self-confidence that is desperately needed to be successful. Elder H. Burke Peterson said, "Impossible mountains are climbed by those who have the self-confidence that comes from truly being loved. Prisons and other institutions, even some of our own homes, are filled with those who have been starved for affection."[8]

Several years ago I was fortunate to be the session director of the first Especially for Youth program ever held in Texas. It was a great experience and I was able to meet many wonderful administrators, counselors, and participants. One of the coordinators that week was named Mark, and he shared an experience he had in Hawaii that I will never forget. This is his experience:

> "I seem to be at rock bottom in my life. I'm so depressed." That was my journal entry for February of 1981. I was nineteen years old, attending school at the Brigham Young University, Hawaii campus in Laie, Hawaii. I lacked direction and purpose and felt that my life was floundering. My reason for coming to Hawaii seemed clear: my family was experiencing some serious problems, and I wanted to get away from them. Upon arriving in Hawaii, I found that I was not any happier. Surfing, swimming, playing on the beach, none of these activities seemed to fill the emptiness I felt. With time I learned that it was not my family I was trying to get away from. I was really running away from myself.
>
> I had fought off all pressures of going on a mission. My testimony

had weakened over the years and it became increasingly difficult to understand the role the Church played in my life. At BYU Hawaii I was slow to make friends. I had a chip on my shoulder and people could detect it. My countenance and appearance seemed to underscore the fact. I kept my hair down to my shoulders and because I was in violation of the standards code, I would tuck my hair into a baseball cap whenever going to class. No one was going to make me get a haircut. My hair had become a symbol of my rebellion and unhappiness.

Although I had closed myself off to family and friends, deep down I wanted to change. I wanted to be loved. But because of family problems, because of past mistakes I'd made, and because of my feelings of inadequacy, I would not open myself up, nor did I know how to. I did not love myself and therefore I concluded that no one else loved me either. What was there to love?

One day I heard that President Spencer W. Kimball was coming to Hawaii and was to speak on campus to a gathering of members in the newly constructed sports arena. I had never seen the Prophet before. The Sunday he was to speak, I dressed, walked over to the arena and took a seat on the back row. I was very moved by President Kimball's remarks and expressions of love.

After arriving back at my dorm room, I laid on my bed thinking about the wonderful words that had been spoken and how I felt during the talks. I was restless and wanted to get away to think about my life and try to understand myself. I walked to the Hawaii Temple located near campus and sat on a stone bench in front of the entrance. I sat there for some time pouring over my life, wondering why I had elected to take certain pathways.

I suddenly noticed that a small number of people were excitedly gathering around the entrance of the Temple. Moments later, President Kimball and some of the other General Authorities emerged from the building. As they shook his hand and embraced him, I watched from a distance away, too frightened to approach him. I feared that he, as a prophet of God, would be able to discern the present state of my spirit and would peer into my eyes seeing the mistakes I had made. I also feared he would see my long hair, chastise me for breaking the rules and possibly have me kicked out of school. And so I quietly watched as he proceeded down the walkway across from where I stood.

The image of what then happened will always remain with me. President Kimball stopped and gazed into my frightened eyes. I prayed he would not come toward me. And yet he left the group he was traveling with and walked directly toward me. The feeling of shame that engulfed my soul made me want to get up and run from him. When he reached me, he threw his arms around my neck, kissed my cheek, and whispered in my ear, "I love you." I shall never forget the warmth and love that I felt. I could not dispute it he loved me. I actually felt his love for me. I then did something I hadn't done for a long, long time I cried. I couldn't control myself and I went behind the temple and continued to sob. That pure love had melted away my anger and bitterness and made me realize that I did have worth. I felt that I was loved, and that if my Father in Heaven had been there, he would have told me the same thing that he truly loved me.[9]

When children know they are loved, they will be better able to withstand the tremendous moral temptations that they will surely face. Who better than President Kimball to ask parents this question: "How long has it been since you took your children, whatever their size, in your arms and told them that you love them and are glad that they can be yours forever?"[10] Make a commitment today to show family members that you love them by giving them appropriate physical affection.

Notes

1 Personal correspondence in author's possession.
2 Ezra Taft Benson, "The Law of Chastity," *New Era*, January 1988, 4.
3 Kathleen McCoy, "Is Your Child Flirting With Sex?" *Reader's Digest*, September 1989, 114.
4 Elizabeth R. McAnarney, "Hugs and Kisses," *Parents*, November 1984, 77.
5 Personal correspondence in author's possession.
6 William G. Dyer and Phillip R. Kunz, *Effective Mormon Families* (Salt Lake City, UT: Deseret Book, 1986), 109–10.
7 Leo F. Buscaglia, *Loving Each Other* (New York, NY: Random House, 1984), 139.
8 H. Burke Peterson, in Conference Report, April 1977, 103.
9 Personal correspondence in the author's possession.
10 Edward L. Kimball, ed., *Teachings of Spencer W. Kimball* (Salt Lake City, UT: Deseret Book, 1982), 248.

SUPPORT

MISTAKE: Failure to support each other's events, games, and activities.

"My parents did not support us in the activities we were involved in. When I was grown, I asked my mom why she never came to any of my games in high school. I played volleyball, basketball, tennis, track, softball, and was on the dance team. She said that I never invited her. I never once saw my dad at anything I did. They were detached emotionally and did not care about the activities we were involved in. That was disappointing."

braham Lincoln once gave a powerful insight into his success: "I am a success today because I had a friend who believed in me and I didn't have the heart to let him down." Unfortunately not everyone has someone who believes in them. Lack of support is a huge problem in our society. Our daughter Naomi once worked for an organization called Support Kids. The company has one main purpose—to track down deadbeat dads and get them to financially support their children. This lack of support has grown to an epidemic stage. *USA Today* reported, "While only 3 percent of all Americans default on car payments, 49 percent default on child support, and 97 percent of the defaulters are fathers."[1] Some apparently fail to realize children are more important than cars. Lack of support, of course, is one of the characteristics of the adversary. Korihor, an anti-Christ in the Book of Mormon, learned this lesson after being deceived by the adversary. After his encounter with Alma, he was struck dumb and forced to go from house to house begging for food. Finally, he was run down and killed. Mormon teaches us a great lesson from this experience. He said: "and thus we see that the devil will not support his children" (Alma 30:60). When my daughter and those she worked with tracked down these non-supportive fathers and legally forced them to start paying what they owed, an amazing thing often happened. Many fathers got involved in their children's lives in more ways than just financially.

In many new subdivisions, we often see small trees planted in the front yards. Usually, they have two metal rods driven into the ground on either side of the tree with a wire attached for support. Our children are a lot like those small trees. They need support to hold them up. This support is especially needed when they are young. Our responsibility as parents is to be the steel support rods. Without the support rods attached, these small trees would be uprooted when the first strong wind comes. Children are in a highly dangerous situation until they develop their own strong roots. The word support has several meanings: 1. to bear or hold up; 2. to sustain or withstand weight, pressure, strain, etc. without giving way; and 3. to maintain a person with the necessities of existence.

It is obvious that supporting our families has far deeper meaning than just providing for them financially. Family support means to attend their games, performances, talks, ordinations, ordinances, awards, and so on. It also means to lift them when they are down and cheer them up when they are sad. Our role is to be a support to family members to keep them from falling. When parents do not support their children before their roots are deep, many negative consequences may follow. Consider the feelings of a young high school basketball player who did not feel support from his parents:

> I'm the star player on the school basketball team, but never once has either parent come to see me play. They're either too busy, too tired or can't get a baby-sitter for my younger sister. The crowds cheer for me, the girls hang around my locker, some kids even ask me for my autograph. But it doesn't mean anything if the two most important people in my life don't care.[2]

In this case, the young man did not feel supported because his parents did not attend his basketball games. He, therefore, interpreted this lack of support to mean his parents did not care about him. Surely he was incorrect in his assumption; however, that is how he perceived it. King Benjamin said, "And ye will not suffer your children that they go hungry" (Mosiah 4:14). Children can suffer from more than just physical hunger. There is an emotional hunger that they crave. Children often long for support from parents, siblings and friends. When this need is not met, serious consequences can follow.

Those who don't feel support from family and friends can develop feelings of resentment. For example, a good friend was not having much luck giving away a new litter of kittens. Knowing I would personally decline her offer, she gave our four-year-old son Nathan a kitten as a gift. We thanked her and went on our way with a new, unwanted pet to care for.

Nathan, on the other hand, loved his new kitten and named her "Miss Mormon." When I witnessed how much fun Nathan and his younger brother, Nolan, had with the kitten, I began to enjoy watching them play together. Then one day, Nathan couldn't find Miss Mormon anywhere. We looked all over the neighborhood. After several days, my wife was coming home from a meeting and saw our cat on the side of the road—dead. A car had apparently hit her.

I gently told Nathan what had happened and that we needed to go pick her up so we could bury her. He went into the house, got a plastic garbage sack, and bravely took my hand as we walked down the road in the direction my wife pointed out. When we found our cat, she was stiff and bloated from the heat of summer. Her tongue was hanging loosely, and her tail was sticking straight into the air.

I said, "Son, it's your cat. You put her in the bag." But the cat was so stiff, that he couldn't do it. I tried to use my foot to help him out a little, but we didn't have much luck. Finally, we saw it was no use. The cat was so bloated and stiff that Nathan just wrapped the bag around the cat and carried it home. It was quite a sight—our small son, carrying a huge, stiff cat, with its tail sticking straight out from under the bag.

Making our way down the road was tiring, and Nathan had a hard time carrying the cat. As we passed by our neighbor's home, Mrs. Cooper waved at us from her yard. She took one look at Nathan's bundle and began laughing hard. I looked down at that big, stiff cat that he'd loved so much—it seemed almost as big as he was right then—and I almost laughed myself. Then I saw the big tears rolling down Nathan's cheeks.

We finally arrived home and buried the cat in the backyard. Several months later, the Cooper's moved from our neighborhood. Three years went by, and one day Nathan, now eight, was told Mrs. Cooper was coming for a visit. He said, "I don't like Mrs. Cooper." I asked him why he didn't like her, since she was probably the best neighbor we'd ever had. He said, "Because she laughed at me when Miss Mormon got killed." He had remembered that incident vividly for three years even though he was just a little boy.

When people go through the everyday trials of life, they need support from their family and friends. When they don't get that support, resentment can develop toward those who fail to give it. What would have happened if family members had laughed at him when he needed their support? Do you think he still would have felt resentment?

My father grew up with ten siblings in a logging camp in Louisiana. His father was an abusive alcoholic. Because of these circumstances, my father never really knew what it was like to feel support. Consequently, he never really learned to support his own children, other than financially.

In small Texas towns, like the one I grew up in, Friday night football is almost sacred, because football in Texas is extremely popular. Fans from the community usually pack the stadiums for every game, whether the team is good or bad. There is excitement in the air as cheerleaders, marching bands, and fans join together to support the home team. My brother, Jack, played football from the seventh grade through his senior year of high school. During those six years, my dad went to one of his games. Through the years, I played in hundreds of baseball games. My dad never came to one of those games. I don't mention these things to criticize. I know now without a doubt that my father loved us, but he struggled to know how to show us support. I think his way of showing support was to work extremely hard from daylight until dark every day.

Most of my dad's ten siblings also struggled to be supportive to their children. My cousin, Dan, was an all-state football player at my high school and received a football scholarship to BYU after graduation.

My aunt and uncle went to one game during his entire football career because as they explained, "We just didn't understand it." This lack of support may have led to a lack of closeness between Dan and his parents.

Many years ago, I was asked to speak at Education Week on the BYU campus. It was very exciting until I saw the class schedule. Speaking at the same time were several of the most popular speakers in the Church. In the weeks leading up to the event, I got more nervous and less confident. What if no one came to my classes? What if a few people came the first day and then no one came back? I distinctly remember praying that I would have at least six people in each of my classes. I really thought there was a strong possibility not one person would show up. I talked like a country hick and had less education than almost anyone else on the program, which didn't exactly help alleviate my fears.

When I walked into the first class on Tuesday morning, I was shocked to see the classroom full. I almost got openly emotional because of the support I felt. It was a wonderful feeling. I told the class I had been nervous because it was my first time ever to speak at the program, and I was afraid that no one would show up. Attending were four young mothers from California, who were students that every teacher dreams of. They seemed to enjoy everything taught. I realize now they must have felt sorry for me and were just trying to build me up. Afterwards, these young ladies approached me and spoke kind words and then stayed for my next class. The next morning, I feared no one would be back. When I walked into class that second morning, the same four California sisters were in attendance with big smiles. I asked them before class what they were doing back, and one enthusiastically said, "We are your California cheering section." After class, they came up and spoke with me again. The next two days, they returned, sitting in the same place with big smiles on their faces. I'm sure these sisters had no idea how much they helped me that week. Sometimes when I read the following scripture, I think of these sisters. "Wherefore, be faithful; stand in the office which I have appointed unto you; succor the weak, lift up the hands which hang down, and strengthen the feeble knees" (D&C 81:5). I realized that week how much we all need to feel support from others.

Be Supportive

King Benjamin pointed out an important characteristic of our Heavenly Father when he said, "I say unto you that if ye should serve him who has created you from the beginning, and is preserving you from day to day, by lending you breath, that ye may live and move and do according to your own will, and even *supporting you from one moment to another*" (Mosiah 2:21). There is a valuable lesson in that verse for parents. Do we support our children from one moment to another? When family members don't receive support in the home, they may seek it outside the home.

Several years ago, I watched a large, musically gifted family perform at a ward talent show. They were extremely talented and had won numerous awards for their musical abilities. However, that night everything that could go wrong, went wrong. The microphones were not working properly. They had trouble with the minus track of the music and when they began singing, they were horribly off-key. Many people felt uncomfortable and put their heads down or looked away. I wondered what their parents were feeling at that moment. I looked around and saw their father at the back of the room. What was he doing? He was looking directly at his children with a big smile on his face, giving his children a big "thumbs up" sign. A warm feeling came over me as I watched this supportive father lift up hands that hang down. I wonder if it is a coincidence that every one of his children turned out to be highly accomplished and committed Church leaders.

A few years ago, our youngest son, Nolan, was a member of his junior high school football team. Being the smallest player on the team didn't give him much playing opportunity. He was a wide receiver on a team that never threw the ball. I attended every game of the season except the last one. My brother also had a son on the team, so I volunteered to work for him while he attended. I thought to myself, as my family drove off, that Nolan would probably have a ball thrown to him in the one game I couldn't attend. Sure enough, when the family returned home, our ten-year-old daughter, Naomi, excitedly ran up to me. "Dad, you should have been there! Nolan almost made a touchdown. It was so close!" I felt sick I had missed my son's big moment. "What happened?" Again she exclaimed proudly, "It was so close!" I pictured my son's great feat—all seventy-five pounds of him dragging defenders toward the goal line. "What happened?" I asked again. She replied, "Well, he went out for a pass. The quarterback threw the ball toward him, but a boy on the other team was a lot taller than Nolan, so he caught it." I said, "Do you mean it was an interception?" She replied, "Yeah, that's what it was." I countered, "I thought you said it was almost a touchdown." She acknowledged, "Well, if Nolan would have caught it and run with it, then it would have been." I had never thought of an interception as "almost" a touchdown. From a proud sister's point of view, however, that's just what it was. The support of his sister meant a lot to my son. They are still very close friends.

Naomi found that she too needed support at times during her school years. We made a vow early on that we would attend any event our children were involved in, if at all possible. We were excited when she tried out for junior high cheerleader. The excitement, however, was short lived because she didn't make the squad. She then tried out for the drill team, and again, we got excited, but she didn't make that either. Then she tried out for the basketball and volleyball teams, but didn't make either one. With those disappointments, we tried to steer her away from school athletics and into student government. When she decided to run for student council, we knew she had found her niche. She had a great campaign strategy playing on her "Wright" name and had lots of help from family and friends. When Election Day came, everyone was very excited for her, until she came home and informed us she hadn't won. I have been amazed at how Naomi could laugh at all of those rejections. Now, don't feel too sorry for Naomi, because she made the Church basketball team every year! We had a wonderful time going to all the games on Saturday mornings. We never had to worry about finding a seat at the games because we were often the only parents who attended.

The Challenge

Our children often face rejection and feel a lack of support in the world. Wouldn't it be a terrible thing if they didn't feel support from their family? When a family member takes part in any school, community, or Church function outside the family circle, it should be

153

considered an event for the whole family. Everyone should go, if at all possible, to talks, plays, sporting events, dance or music recitals, and so on. Family members should be taught that the accomplishment of one family member reflects positively on the whole. "Children don't care how much you do for them; they care about how you make them feel." When you support them, they feel that special bond with you.

President James E. Faust said, "Some parents have difficulty expressing their love physically or vocally. I do not ever recall my own father using the words, 'Son, I love you,' but he showed it in a thousand ways which were more eloquent than words. He rarely missed a practice, a game, a race, or any activity in which his sons participated."[3] We can also show our children that we love them by supporting the activities in which they are involved, in addition to expressing our love physically and verbally.

Notes

1   *USA Today*, Thursday, March 9, 1995, 11A.
2   F. Philip Rice, *The Adolescent: Development, Relationships and Culture* (Boston, MA: Allyn & Bacon, 1975), 476.
3   James E. Faust, "Enriching Family Life," *Ensign*, May 1983, 41.

MARRIAGE

MISTAKE: Failure to work on building a strong marriage and to set a good example of how a marriage works.

"The one thing I wish my parents had done better was to have gotten along with each other. I would have liked to see them nurture their own relationship more. I couldn't tell if they were in love or not! When they argued, they would be so loud that we could be upstairs in our rooms with the doors shut and still hear them. They would also argue about personal matters in front of us and would often drag us into the argument. It was awful and we worried about divorce all the time."

A few years ago, I drove my daughter Naomi back to college after the holidays. We had a great time singing and laughing. As we drove into a Dairy Queen parking lot for a quick bite to eat, a lady pulled up beside us. Within a short time period, a man drove up with three children. We watched as two of the kids got out of the car and walked toward the woman. However, a boy about nine years old refused to get out of the car. His dad finally convinced him to get out, but the little boy was crying uncontrollably. The lady then took him by the arm and led him toward her car. The boy was sobbing saying over and over again, "I want to stay with my daddy." It didn't take a rocket scientist to figure out what was happening. Here was a divorced couple, meeting at a neutral site to give the kids back to mom after a weekend visit with Dad. I had a sick feeling in my stomach as I witnessed this pitiful sight. I wondered what led to the divorce and if it could have been prevented. Did the divorce solve the problems the parents had with each other or create even more misery for the family?

President Gordon B. Hinckley said, "Marriage is in serious trouble in much of the world. With the disintegration of the marriage comes the breakdown of the family unit. Lawrence Stone, the noted Princeton University family historian, says: 'The scale of marital breakdowns in the West since 1960 has no historical precedent that I know of, and seems unique . . . There has been nothing like it for the last 2,000 years and probably longer.' You are familiar with the fruits of broken homes. I think the home is the answer to most of our basic social problems, and if we take care of things there, other things will take care of themselves."[2]

When President Hinckley came to Texas to dedicate the San Antonio temple, my wife and I were fortunate to hear him speak. He explained to the audience what he felt was the hardest thing he had to do as President of the Church. I was curious to know the most difficult thing a prophet dealt with in this day of trouble and turmoil. He said that it occurred every Wednesday morning in a meeting with only him and his secretary. What is it? This meeting is the time he must make the decision to cancel temple sealings that people had requested. I did not realize that only the Prophet made those decisions and that even his counselors in the First Presidency are not involved. What an added heart wrenching burden for our Prophet to deal with as he not only witnesses the break down of marriage in our society but also those who have made sacred promises in the house of the Lord.

Many years ago, an LDS couple living in our area announced they were getting a divorce. This came as a great shock to all who knew them. The father was a highly successful businessman, and they lived in a beautiful home with seven children. All the children were talented and well-respected in the community. I was hoping my children wouldn't hear about it and ask the "why" questions that always come. That was not to be. Our ten-year-old daughter asked why the couple was divorcing. I told her I didn't know the real answer, but the couple said they just didn't love each other any more. She then asked if they were married in the temple. I said they were. She then concluded, "Then that means they lied to that guy at the temple." I asked her what she meant. She said, "I thought when you went to the temple, you told the guy you would be married forever." Children have a way of putting things into perspective. While this little girl had no idea what takes place during the temple ceremony, she knew eternal covenants were made.

Our society does not treat marriage with the sacred respect it deserves. Cohabitation is skyrocketing in America. *USA Today* reported, "The number of unmarried couples living together increased tenfold from 1960 to 2000, the U.S. Census says; about 10 million people are living with a partner of the opposite sex." In the years following that report, the number of couples living together rose even higher.

Number of Couples Cohabitating, by Year

1960: 440,000
1970: 520,000
1980: 1,600,000
1990: 2,900,000
2000: 4,700,000
2010: 7,650,000[3]

Many seem convinced the marriage certificate is nothing more than a piece of paper—it has no real meaning. I think back to a time in my life when I was trying to finish my doctorate at Brigham Young University. I was teaching full-time, while taking a full load of classes myself. I had speaking assignments almost every weekend, with one son on a mission, one getting ready to leave, and three daughters still in school. My wife was also going to school full-time and teaching piano lessons in our home. During this time of extreme stress, the stake president invited my wife and me into his office and called me to be the bishop of a home ward in Orem, Utah. There were many days when I thought I could not possibly finish my doctorate program. I cannot describe the feelings of relief when I defended my dissertation and the committee told me I had successfully completed all the requirements for my degree. What do you think they gave me after all of my work, sacrifice, and money? They gave me a piece of paper with my name on it, the name of the university, and a couple of signatures on it.

Are those pieces of paper that say BS, MS, PhD, MD, JD all without meaning? No, with those pieces of paper, certain doors open because of what they represent. What a ridiculous argument that a marriage certificate is just a piece of paper. It is a legal document that has extensive meaning because of the commitments made at marriage, even outside the temple. Following are the actual words used in a state marriage ceremony. Look closely at what the couple agrees to do, even in a civil marriage: "Those who enter into this relationship must learn to cherish, esteem and love; to bear with each other's strengths and weaknesses; to comfort each other in sickness, trouble, and sorrow: With honesty to provide for each other, and to live together as heirs of the grace of life."

Once we say, "I do" or "I will," we commit ourselves to esteem, love, bear with, and comfort each other in all situations, on our sacred honor. If we are not willing to do that, then we should never commit to begin with. It is not that the piece of paper is meaningless. It is a legal, binding agreement between two parties. What is becoming meaningless is the integrity of many people who sign marriage documents. To say we will comfort each other in sickness, trouble, and sorrow and then fail to honor that commitment, our word, not the legal document, becomes meaningless. Of course, once a marriage partner breaks the agreement, then sometimes there may be valid reasons to seek divorce.

In our survey about the strengths and weaknesses of their parental upbringing, a vast number commented on marriage. The following are mistakes active LDS members felt their parents made while they were growing up. They are in no particular order.

Selfishness

"I think my parents had one problem in their marriage and that was selfishness. They were unbending in their opinions and refused to change no matter what the consequences. They seldom thought about the other person. Special occasions were seldom celebrated and sometimes forgotten altogether."

Selfishness is a widespread problem in marriages. President Spencer W. Kimball stated, "Every divorce is the result of selfishness on the part of one or the other or both parties to a marriage contract."[4]

Recently, I was talking with a single returned missionary about marriage. He had grown up in Switzerland but was going to school here in America and had dual citizenship. He was telling me about the girl he would one day marry. He became very passionate about not marrying a Western girl who "wants to live close to her family, so she could be home for Sunday dinner every week." He said, "That drives me crazy." He explained he considered that to be a very selfish thing for girls to do in a marriage. He went on to say, "The girl I marry has to be very adventuresome and willing to live abroad." I then asked if he meant to move back to Switzerland one day. He said, "Yes" and explained that is why he needed to marry a girl who was the adventurous type. I said, "Let me see if I understand what you want. You don't want a typical Western girl who wants to live close to her family and be over there every Sunday for dinner. What you do want is an adventurous girl who will move to Switzerland so you can be close to home for Sunday dinners with your family." He stuttered a bit and then said that wasn't what he meant.

Too often we think of our own self-interest instead of what is best for our marriage. President Gordon B. Hinckley warned, "Selfishness is the canker that drives out peace and love. Selfishness is the root on which grow argument, anger, disrespect, infidelity, and divorce."[5]

I don't think any of us desire to be selfish. However, it is one of those natural-man tendencies we consistently have to work on. There is no place like marriage to expose this weakness. It would be nice to have a formula that would help put things in their proper perspective. President Hinckley gave us that formula when he said, "If you will make your first concern the comfort, the well-being, and the happiness of your companion, sublimating any personal concern to that loftier goal, you will be happy, and you will go on throughout eternity."[6]

While driving home one day, I turned on the radio and listened to the Paul Harvey news broadcast. He described a lady who called her husband at work, and asked him the question that all men dread, "Honey, do you remember what today is?" After a long pause, he replied, "Of course, I remember what today is." She said, "Okay, I was just checking to see if you remembered." That evening she was surprised when he brought home a dozen red roses. He then took her out to her favorite restaurant. He treated her like a queen for the whole evening. That night as they prepared for bed, she said, "Honey, I just want you to know that this is the best Groundhog Day that I have ever had."

We should have the comfort, well-being, and happiness of our spouse as our first concern at all times, regardless of what day it is. How many unhappy marriages or divorces would we have if we would simply follow this counsel from our prophet?

Affection

"Very seldom did my parents show affection toward one another. There was always a cold, distant feeling between the two of them and there still is."

One of our LDS marriage experts asked this thought-provoking question: "If you were accused of being married, would there be enough evidence to convict you?" Looking at couples, even in the Church, you have to wonder if they have ever even kissed. Not only do you seldom see couples holding hands, many do not even sit beside each other at church. It would be nice to see more husbands sit by their wives, perhaps holding hands or with his arm around her. We are not talking about public displays of affection here. We are talking about showing you care about each other.

Too many couples seem clueless as to the affectionate needs of their spouses. An old story tells of a newly married man and wife having serious marriage problems. The wife demanded they go to a marriage counselor or else she would file for divorce. The husband reluctantly went, and the counselor asked him what the problem was. He couldn't think of one problem in the marriage. Everything seemed fine to him. The wife, however, had a list of about forty problems in the marriage. Her biggest concern was that her husband showed her no affection. Suddenly, the counselor stood up and gave the wife a kiss right on the lips. She and her husband were shocked at this. The counselor said, "What your wife needs is for that to happen at least two times a week." The young husband said, "Okay, I'll try to have her here on Tuesdays and Thursdays at about 3:00."

Disloyalty

"Both my mother and father would talk to all of the children about their spouse's weaknesses while they were not around. I know my mother also talked often about my dad's faults with her friends. They were not loyal to each other."

I have been surprised over the years to hear so many people speak of their spouse's faults. I would be very upset if I knew my wife talked about my weaknesses to her friends. Loyalty to each other implies that you defend your spouse, not disparage them. There is no doubt in my mind that once a marriage partner discusses their partner's weaknesses outside the home, the marriage has been damaged. President Thomas S. Monson said, "When you are married, be fiercely loyal one to another."[7] Loyalty implies that you lock your heart and are totally faithful to your spouse.

The Lord tells us there are two people we should love with all of our heart. First of all, "Ye love the Lord your God *with all your heart* and with all your soul" (Deuteronomy 13:3). And also "Thou shalt love thy wife *with all thy heart*, and shalt cleave unto her and none else" (D&C 42:22).

Insensitivity

"My mother and father were not very sensitive to each other's feelings. Usually we could expect one of them to be sulking at least once a week because of some insensitive remark that the other made to them. They never have learned what to say and what not to say."

My wife, Wendy, grew up in a home where her mother did all the cooking for the family. I grew up in a home where either my dad cooked or I cooked for myself. When we first married, my wife didn't really know how to cook and was self-conscious about the fact. One day, she warmed up a can of corn in a cheap Teflon pan we had received for a wedding gift. Stirring the corn with a metal spoon, the Teflon began flaking off into the corn. I made a big deal of it and refused to eat "Teflon corn." I embarrassed her in an area she felt very inadequate. I was insensitive and, of course, hurt her feelings.

Not long after the Teflon corn incident, Wendy ironed some

clothes for me, trying to be helpful. She grew up in a home where she never had to iron. My parents usually worked fourteen-hour days, six days a week. They paid me to iron clothes for our family. I preferred to have my clothes ironed to take the wrinkles out. When Wendy handed me my shirt, I put it on and commented, "It looks like I just got out of the washing machine!" What did my words do? Did they help her want to do better? No, it only hurt her feelings. As a result, I have done much of the ironing in our family since that day.

The words of Elder W. Eugene Hansen should be considered daily. He said, "Be considerate. Be sensitive to the thoughts and feelings of others, always careful not to demean or belittle by either word or act. Be encouraging, uplifting, careful not to break down a person's confidence."[8]

Criticism

"If there is one major mistake that my parents made, it was constantly criticizing each other about trivial matters. My mother could not even put the keys in the car ignition without my dad telling her she was doing it wrong. She would do the same kind of things to him. Their constant criticism of each other destroyed our respect for them."

Overly critical marriage partners damage relationships and destroy the respect couples should have for each other. A good friend named Barbara told me of a conversation she had with her husband, Hal, when they first got married. He said, "Barbara, about 80 percent of me is good and about 20 percent of me is not so good, and needs some work. If you will concentrate on the 80 percent and help me with the 20 percent, we are going to have a great marriage. However, if you concentrate on the 20 percent and criticize me constantly, then we will have a terrible marriage." Barbara took his advice, concentrated on the good, and gently helped him with his weaknesses. He became a saint because of it. Elder Joe J. Christensen said, "Generally, each of us is painfully aware of our weaknesses, and we don't need frequent reminders. Few people have ever changed for the better as a result of constant criticism or nagging. If we are not careful, some of what we offer as constructive criticism is actually destructive."[9]

Perhaps we can learn a lesson from the story of a sister who had to choose between two young men when it was time for marriage. The man she married later became the CEO of a major company while the other became a garbage man. One day, the CEO turned to his wife and asked, "How do you feel about being married to a CEO instead of to the guy who became a garbage man?" She replied, "If I would have married him, he would have become a CEO, and you would have been the garbage man!" I believe the old saying "Behind every good man is an astonished woman" is not true. With praise and encouragement, we can expect our spouse to reach new heights. Criticism, on the other hand, kills not only motivation but also kills love.

Sister Ardeth Kapp would often have the sister missionaries in the Vancouver, British Columbia Mission ask her how she found a "man like that." Of course, they were referring to her husband Heber, their mission president. She would say, "I didn't find him like that. And he didn't find me like this either. We have been working on each other for years!" Our responsibility as marriage partners is to build, love, and support.

Poor Communication

"My parents couldn't communicate, and we saw the results of this on a daily basis. They argued about money and other issues all the time in front of us. This was very unnerving for us. It was always so tense around them, whenever they were arguing."

Finances are often mentioned as the number one cause of divorce in America. I have never really believed that to be the case. Otherwise, the rich Hollywood stars should be the happiest couples in America. A huge factor in happy marriages, or miserable marriages, is the ability to communicate. So many couples never truly learn to do this. They just keep repeating the same mistakes over and over again. When two people grow up in totally different homes, they won't always see things exactly the same every time. Feelings must be suppressed at times and words left unsaid. President Gordon B. Hinckley stated, "If every husband and every wife would constantly do whatever might be possible to ensure the comfort and happiness of his or her companion, there would be very little, if any, divorce. Argument would never be heard. Accusations would never be leveled. Angry explosions would not occur. Rather, love and concern would replace abuse and meanness."[10]

Communication is an important topic—one that cannot be covered in a few paragraphs. Perhaps one valuable lesson we can learn is to keep our comments to ourselves if they are not uplifting. I have always enjoyed a lesson taught by the young couple who moved into a little home after their honeymoon. The wife took a little box, put it under their bed, and told her husband that he must promise her to never look into it. The husband agreed to her request. He was, however, dying to know what the box contained. The first year, he kept his promise even though he was tempted to look several times. Twenty years later, he had still not looked at the contents of the box. One night, after twenty-two years of marriage, his wife went to Relief Society, and he just couldn't stand it any more. He pulled out the box, looked in, and found three potholders and $21,000 in cash. That night he felt so guilty, he confessed to his wife what he had done. She, of course, was shocked and exclaimed, "You didn't!" He said, "Yes, I'm very sorry. But now that I have looked, can I ask you where you got the $21,000, and why three potholders?" She replied, "I made a vow when I disagreed with you, I would not say anything but would just go in and make a potholder." He said, "Wow, you only disagreed with me three times in twenty-two years?" She said, "No, that was the number of times I thought you were right." He then asked, "Where did the $21,000 come from?" She answered, "That's the profits I made from selling the potholders I made!"

Too many couples have never learned the valuable lesson to resist saying critical or angry words that come when couples disagree. President Gordon B. Hinckley said,

> I constantly deal with those cases of members of the Church who have been married in the temple and who later divorce and then apply for a cancellation of their temple sealing. When first married, they are full of great expectations, with a wonderful spirit of happiness. But the flower of love fades in an atmosphere of criticism and carping, of mean words and uncontrolled anger. Love flies out the window as contention enters. I repeat, my brethren, if any of you young men have trouble controlling your temper, I plead with you to begin the work of making that correction now. Otherwise you will bring only tears and sorrow into the homes which you will someday establish.[11]

Building a Strong Marriage

While hundreds of suggestions could be offered to build stronger marriages, I offer two very helpful ideas.

First, Elder M. Russell Ballard stated,

> When a couple comes to me for counsel relative to various struggles in their marriage, one of the first questions I ask them is, "Do you kneel together at the end of the day and hold hands and say your prayers?" Interestingly, not once—not once—has the answer to that question been positive. Then I suggest, "Will you please go home and do that for the next thirty days? Then you can return and we will talk again." Almost always the couples come back and, with tears in their eyes, share with me the sweet feelings that have returned to their marriage and how they think, at last, that they are going to make it.[12]

Second, President Gordon B. Hinckley stated,

> If every man in this church who has been ordained to the Melchizedek Priesthood would qualify himself to hold a temple recommend, and then go to the house of the Lord and renew his covenants in solemnity before God and witnesses, we would be a better people. There would be little or no infidelity among us. Divorce would almost entirely disappear. So much heartache and heartbreak would be avoided. There would be a greater measure of peace and love and happiness in our homes. There would be fewer weeping wives and weeping children. There would be a greater measure of appreciation and of mutual respect among us. And I am confident the Lord would smile with greater favor upon us.[13]

Notes

1   Quoted by David Popenoe, "A World without Father," *The Wilson Quarterly*, Spring 1996, 13.

2   Gordon B. Hinckley, *Teachings of Gordon B. Hinckley* (Salt Lake City, UT: Deseret Book, 1997), 209–10.

3   The United States Census Bureau

4   Spencer W. Kimball, "Marriage and Divorce," BYU Devotional Address, September 7, 1976.

5   Gordon B. Hinckley, "Five Million Members—A Milestone and Not a Summit," *Ensign*, May 1982, 44.

6   Gordon B. Hinckley, "Graduates Receive Challenge from Prophet," *Church News*, May 6, 1995, 11.

7 Thomas S. Monson, "Priesthood Power," *Ensign*, April 2011, 68.

8 W. Eugene Hansen, "Love," *Ensign*, November 1989, 23.

9 Joe J. Christensen, "Marriage and the Great Plan of Happiness," *Ensign*, May 1995, 46.

10 Gordon B. Hinckley, "The Women in Our Lives," *Ensign*, November 2004, 82.

11 Gordon B. Hinckley, in Conference Report, April 1998, 49.

12 M. Russell Ballard, *When Thou Art Converted: Continuing the Search For Happiness* (Salt Lake City, UT: Deseret Book, 2001), 200.

13 Gordon B. Hinckley, "Of Missions, Temples, and Stewardship," *Ensign*, November 1995, 53.

FAMILY FUN

MISTAKE: Failure to make the home a place of fun and laughter.

"I think, by far the biggest mistake that my parents made, is that we did not have fun together as a family. A normal Saturday for instance, at my house included lots of cleaning. I know that it is important to have a clean house and nice yard, but I wish we could have spent just a few hours every Saturday going to a movie, or having a picnic, playing games, going to a park or even going on a walk. We just didn't have fun as a family. If the gospel is supposed to be fun, I think my parents missed that point."

During my early-morning seminary years, we had a teacher who was quite stern. Her philosophy seemed to be that the gospel was serious and seminary was not a place to have fun. One day, a few class members were talking quietly among themselves during her lesson. Obviously irritated, she raised her voice and said, "Let's have a little order in here." My cousin Chris blurted out, "I'll take a hamburger, an order of fries, and a large root beer." I thought that was the funniest and most clever thing I had ever heard! Everyone in the class laughed hysterically. The teacher never cracked a smile. She appeared to be furious with this outburst. We were studying the Old Testament that year, but she must not have been familiar with the verse, which states that there is "a time to laugh" (Ecclesiastes 3:4). She scolded us about our inappropriate behavior. I don't think the teacher enjoyed our class very much that year. And of course, the feelings were mutual since we didn't enjoy her very much either. I wonder if things could have been different if she would have loosened up and had a little fun with us. Maybe a statement by President Hugh B. Brown applies to this situation, when he said, "A wholesome sense of humor will be a safety valve that will enable you to apply the lighter touch to heavy problems and to learn some lessons in problem solving that 'sweat and tears' often fail to dissolve."[1]

I contrast that teacher with a close friend who is an extremely successful father of thirteen children. I've often thought about the secret of this family's success. Many things they've done stand out, but the most prominent is they have fun as a family. They believe our homes should be the center of fun. Parties were often held for their teenagers at their spacious home. Youth from church and friends from school were always invited, along with several adults to chaperone. These parties would draw up to two hundred youth. Strict Church standards were requested, expected, and observed. Many youth joined the Church because of these activities. The children of appropriate dating age would bring dates to their own home to play games. Most times, they would invite their parents to join in. One popular date game was to play Hide and Seek in their darkened home. I remember one Sunday hearing this father, a stake president and successful attorney, talking to Todd, a Priest in his ward. Todd had been over the night before playing Hide and Seek with friends. The smiling leader exclaimed, "Todd, I thought for sure you were going to see me! You passed right by me. I was hiding on top of the refrigerator!" I wondered what others would think had they seen this father hiding on top of the fridge as his teenagers and those visiting his home scurried through the house trying to find him. Do you think the youth in the area loved this family? Do you think the children loved their parents and each other?

Think about those families you greatly admire and respect. How many of them take time to have fun together? Extensive research backs up the fact that highly effective families are fun. When you laugh and play together, special bonds are formed and unity is created that help family members make it through hard times. In President Gordon B. Hinckley's biography, we read,

Home was a refuge where Gordon was rejuvenated to handle the increasingly heavy load he carried, though his children weren't always aware of the obligations he was balancing. Said Clark, "Even when Dad was stake president and working in the Missionary Department and helping with the opening of new temples, I never got the sense that there was a great deal of pressure on him. He had a good sense of humor, and he would come home from the office and repeat jokes he had heard that made him laugh so hard he couldn't catch his breath." Marjorie agreed, adding, "Gordon's sense of humor got us through all of the crises in our lives."[2]

If you think about it, President Hinckley was a model to the entire world that the gospel is fun and this life is to be enjoyed.

Over the years, I have had the opportunity to direct twenty-seven different sessions for the Especially for Youth program, in various parts of the country. I have learned many lessons from these experiences. One EFY I remember well was held at Cornell University, in Ithaca, New York. The schedule called for a service project with mentally impaired children out in a large open area of the campus. Unfortunately, the agency was not able to bring the children to the campus. We went to Plan B, which involved bringing in a group of Primary-aged children from a local ward. I watched as the EFY participants played Ring around the Roses, Red Rover, and other games with these children. The children, and the teenagers, were having a great time together. A Cornell linguistics professor walking by stopped and asked what was going on. I briefly explained to her a little about the program and how we had high school students from throughout the East attending. Before I could say anything else, she commented in a derogatory tone, "I lived in Europe for many years. At about age eight we learned to put away childish games and do something constructive." I thought, "Lady, you have no idea who these youth really are! We have student body presidents, valedictorians, star athletes, outstanding musicians, and so on, in this group. And no, they have not fallen for the message of the world that you need a bottle in your hand to have fun!" I don't know if she was married or not, but I imagined being one of her children as she walked away. I have a feeling that her home would not be the most fun place to grow up.

A couple of years later, I was the director of an EFY session in Anchorage, Alaska. On the last night, the participants had a dance in the basketball arena. My wife and I were standing in the bleachers, watching hundreds of LDS youth having as much fun as ever. At one point, they all participated in a line dance that they had been taught. I didn't see one person on the sideline. As I heard the cheers and laughter for a brief moment, I saw in my mind's eye the prophet Joseph Smith, with a huge smile on his face, watching the youth dance. It appeared to me as if he wanted to be down on the dance floor with them. I know it was just my imagination, but it was as if he were giving his approval of the fun they were having. I thought back to how he loved to have fun with his family and friends. The following journal entries give us a small view of how the Prophet Joseph Smith interacted with those he loved:

"In the morning I took my children on a pleasure ride in the carriage."[3]

"At four in the afternoon, I went out with my little Frederick, to exercise myself by sliding on the ice."[4]

"Rode out in the afternoon . . . and afterwards played ball with the boys."[5]

"The man was eager to have a tussle with the Prophet, so Joseph stepped forward and took hold of the man. The first pass he made Joseph whirled him around and took him by the collar and seat of his trousers and walked out to a ditch and threw him in it. Then, taking him by the arm, he helped him up and patted him on the back and said, 'You must not mind this. When I am with the boys I make all the fun I can for them.'"[6]

"When with us, there was no lack of amusement; for with jokes, games, etc., he was ready to provoke merriment."[7]

Choice Theory

One of America's most well-known and respected psychiatrists is Dr. William Glasser. He is the author of numerous books on counseling, mental health, and teacher improvement. The term "Choice Theory" is closely associated with his work and is the culmination of some fifty years of research into the theory and practice of psychology and counseling. His theory posits that behavior is central to our existence and that it is driven by five basic human needs we are continually attempting to satisfy:

1. Survival—includes hunger, thirst, shelter, and sexual drive
2. Love/Belonging—to love and be loved, to belong and have friends
3. Power—feeling worthwhile; achievement and winning
4. Freedom—ability to choose how we live our lives free from the control of others, having autonomy, and having your own space
5. Fun—includes pleasure and enjoyment

When I first saw number five on the list, I was a little surprised. Why would this well-respected researcher of human behavior refer to fun as one of our five basic human needs? In my opinion, Dr. Glasser is spot on with his observation. I believe that all people have an inborn desire for fun placed in us by a loving Heavenly Father. I also believe that Glasser uses the word *fun* to represent several other terms that we are very familiar with. In scriptural language, this need is probably illustrated with two familiar scriptures: "Men are, that they might have *joy*" (2 Nephi 2:25) and "The great plan of *happiness*" (Alma 42:8).

These words represent the same meanings that Glasser found in his vast research. Since all of the five basic human needs are represented by one word in his theory, he simply chose the word 'fun' to represent the need for joy and happiness. Prophets have chosen different words to say the same thing. When we have fun, we are happy and enjoy life. When we have fun, we feel relaxed and can temporarily forget about some of our challenges. In fact, worries, cares, or concerns that we experience seem to fade into the background, and we feel rejuvenated when we are having fun.

If these five areas are truly basic human needs, just think what implications this knowledge has for individuals and families? First, the adversary would use these needs for our destruction. Also, businesses would use them to take advantage of us financially. In addition, peers would use these to tempt us to follow the crowd. So, if these needs are not met in the home, we will go outside the home to seek them. But of course, if these needs are met in our families, we can be happy, content, and safe.

Have you noticed that almost every beer ad shows people having fun? Of course, what most people don't realize is the situations depicted would be just as fun if people were drinking orange juice, milk, or water. Anytime you go to the beach with close friends, there is a very good chance you will have fun. Watching a football game with close friends is fun whatever you drink. It has nothing to do with the beer! The Lord warned of these men when he said, "In consequence of evils and designs which do and will exist in the hearts of conspiring men in the last days. . ." (D&C 89:4). Most ads for alcohol do, in fact, appeal to all five basic needs pointed out by Glasser. However, they focus heavily on our need for fun, then associate it with beer.

Think about some of the slick ads that play upon our need for fun:

"Happy hour 5:00–7:00" —Alcohol ad.
"Your passport to pleasure" —Cigarette ad.
"Happiness is a cigar called . . ." —Cigar ad.
"Don't live a little, live a lotto" —Gambling ad.
"It's fun to play together" —Video game ad.
"The joy of . . ." —Caffeinated drink ad.

Advertisers have done a good job convincing our society of their evil designs. In this nation, a vast majority of teenagers and adults feel as if they can't have fun if they don't drink alcoholic beverages. Most are shocked when they hear that someone does not drink. Even with the vast research connecting alcohol to various social and health problems, it is those who don't drink that are a little weird.

The alcohol advertising industry has done an incredible job of fulfilling one of Isaiah's prophecies, which states, "Woe unto them that call evil good, and good evil; that put darkness for light, and light for darkness; that put bitter for sweet, and sweet for bitter!" (Isaiah 5:20).

Satan has done such an unbelievable job of stealing the word *fun* from us, that even our LDS kids are confused. At Especially for Youth, I have often heard the youth comment, "I never knew I could have so much fun and not do anything wrong!" The point is, if we don't have fun in our families, our children are likely to go seeking it in the world since they are being bombarded with messages from the adversary about what fun should consist of. Children from families that do not have fun together seem especially vulnerable to alcohol. Perhaps some feel that if their parents are faithful members of the Church and fail to have fun in life, then the gospel must not be fun. If that is the case, they may reason the gospel does not meet their needs, so they need to look elsewhere.

Having fun has many benefits for families and individuals. The following are a few of those benefits.

Healing Influence

Years ago, Elder Carlos E. Asay was very ill and in the intensive care unit at the hospital. During this time, his bishop snuck in the hospital with a box of cards and drawings from the Primary children in his home ward. Elder Asay described one of the cards this way: "One young lad drew a picture of me stretched out on a coffin. Protruding out of my chest was a single rose. Off to the side of the sketch were these words: 'Please get well, but if not, have fun!' I laughed so loud and hard that the nurses came rushing into the room, wondering what was wrong. Those moments of humor were lifting to my spirits and, I believe, healing to my body."[8]

Relieves Tension

We live in a very stressful, fast-paced world. All of us need ways to relieve that stress. Elder Gene R. Cook told us how to do that when he said, "Activities are a real blessing to a family. They provide a way to have fun together, relieve tensions, and develop relationships on new levels with one another."[9]

Righteous and Happy

One of our main goals in life is to be righteous. That does not mean that we are solemn at all times. In fact, it is usually the opposite. President James E. Faust taught, "Don't forget to laugh at the silly things that happen. Humor . . . is a powerful force for good when used with discretion. Its physical expression, laughter, is highly therapeutic."[10]

Develops Closeness

When Elder David A. Bednar was a stake president in Arkansas, he was interviewed for an article about family fun by the *Church News*. He commented, "It's tough for parents to talk to children about heavy-weight topics such as peer pressure, drugs and morality if they don't already have a closeness. A parent can't just all of a sudden pick out an hour and talk to a son about being morally clean, if the parent and child haven't spent much time together for three or four years. I think closeness is developed more quickly by having fun together."[11]

Solution

We don't have to go to Disney World or other costly places to have fun as a family. Parents should plan activities that involve the entire family and not leave it to chance when it comes to enjoying each other. As we look back on our own childhoods, when were our families the happiest? Chances are, we will recall the happy memories of having fun together. When family members get together after being apart, they often talk about the fun memories they had growing up. I challenge you to make fun a priority in your family. Almost everyone wants to be around people who are fun. If parents are fun, then their children will most likely want to stay close to them. Bishop Victor L. Brown made this suggestion for having a balanced life when he said, "First, may I suggest that you have fun. Now, it isn't really necessary for me to make this suggestion, is it? The Lord, himself, said 'Man is that he might have joy.'"[12]

Notes

1   Hugh B. Brown, in Conference Report, April 1968, 100.

2   Sheri L. Dew, *Go Forward with Faith: The Biography of Gordon B. Hinckley* (Salt Lake City, UT: Deseret Book, 1996), 192.

3   Joseph Smith, *History of the Church of Jesus Christ of Latter-day Saints, Vol. 5* (Salt Lake City, UT: Deseret Book, 1902), 369.

4   Ibid., 5:265.

5   Ibid., 5:307.

6   Hyrum Leslie Andrus, *They Knew the Prophet* (Salt Lake City, UT: Bookcraft, 1974), 80.

7   Benjamin F. Johnson, *My Life's Review* (Independence, MO: Zion's Printing & Publishing, 1947), 92–93.

8   Carlos E. Asay, *Family Pecan Trees: Planting a Legacy of Faith at Home* (Salt Lake City, UT: Deseret Book, 1992), 100.

9   Gene R. Cook, *Raising Up a Family to the Lord* (Salt Lake City, UT: Deseret Book, 1993), 278.

10 James E. Faust, "Learning for Eternity," *Brigham Young University Speeches* (Provo: Brigham Young University, 1998), 78.

11 David A. Bednar, "Getting Serious about Family Fun," *Church News*, September 30, 1989.

12 Victor L. Brown, "Is There Balance in Our Lives?" Brigham Young University Speeches (Provo: Brigham Young University, 1964), 3.

DISCIPLINE

MISTAKE: Use inconsistent, harsh, or lax discipline with children.

"My parents spoiled me! I always got almost everything I wanted and seldom had to deal with doing without or being told no. There were a few rules, and when the rules that existed were broken there were no consequences for the misbehavior. I made far too many mistakes in my youth that I partly feel was due to a lack of discipline. I had friends whose parents were either harsh or inconsistent. It didn't seem that any of us had proper discipline."

A friend of mine recently summed up what he felt to be the root problem of our society's moral problems. He said, "Randal, do you know why our moral values are so low in America?" Although a few ideas came to mind, I politely said, "No." He said, "Teachers." He then paused just long enough for me to mentally agree and then continued, "Do you know what's wrong with teachers? They are afraid of the principals." He had my curiosity piqued by now. "And the problem with principals is they're afraid of the superintendents." I felt I knew what he'd say next. "And the superintendent is afraid of the school board. And the school board—they are afraid of the parents." He would pause just long enough between each parallel to allow a mental calculation to occur. He continued, "And the parents are afraid of their kids." He finally concluded by saying, "And the kids—well, they ain't afraid of no one! And that's why we are in the moral shape we are in."

There are too many families where we have the tail wagging the dog. Elder Robert D. Hales has observed, "Sometimes we are afraid of our children—afraid to counsel with them for fear of offending them."[1] And Elder Larry R. Lawrence put it this way: "Imagine for a moment that your daughter was sitting on the railroad tracks and you heard the train whistle blowing. Would you warn her to get off the tracks? Or would you hesitate, worried that she might think you were being overprotective?"[2] There is wisdom in the fortune cookie proverb that says, "Parents who are afraid to put their foot down usually have children who step on their toes."

Once, I was walking through the parking lot of a fast food restaurant. A mother and her preteen son passed by in a car. I heard the young boy shout at me in an obnoxious way, "Hey man, how do you like to pick up trash?" I asked him to repeat what he had said. He again said, "How do you like to pick up trash?" I didn't respond because I was unsure what he was talking about. He then took a sack full of trash and threw it out in front of me onto the parking lot. I expected his mother to make him get out and pick it up, but she just drove on, telling him he shouldn't do that. Obviously, this young man lacked discipline in his life. If we could speculate about his future, what may happen when peer pressure comes in later years? Do you think this young man will be taught proper discipline and be able to resist temptation? Will he have the self-discipline required to control his impulses, desires, and moral behavior during his dating years? From my observation of youth who have not experienced proper discipline in their lives, he probably won't. We must discipline our children while they are in our homes so they will have the self-discipline to live a clean life when they are away from home.

Many of us do too much for our children without requiring enough of them. A father of five young children was given a small toy at work. When he arrived home, he called his kids together and asked them some questions to determine who to give the present to. "Who never talks back to mother?" No one answered. "Who always does everything mother says to do?" Again there was silence. Finally, five small voices answered in unison. "You play with it, Daddy." Elder Neal A. Maxwell pointed out, "Those who do too much for their children will soon find they can do nothing with their children. So many children have had so much done for them they are . . . done in."[3]

Raising obedient and self-disciplined children is a challenge for all parents. All children are unique individuals with their own ideas and goals. It can be a real trial to teach youth to stay loyal to family, Church, and Heavenly Father. Of course, it is good that we are individuals, but sometimes there is only one right way. One of our main duties as parents is to teach our children right from wrong so they can make correct choices as they mature. This requires discipline.

In order to keep families and society strong, appropriate discipline is essential. President Gordon B. Hinckley pointed out, "No system can long command the loyalties of man that does not expect of them certain measures of discipline, and particularly of self-discipline."[4] We have witnessed the truth of this statement in both families and society. Discipline is a must if these systems are to survive intact.

Some people have misconceptions about discipline. Unfortunately, in our society, the terms *discipline* and *punishment* are used synonymously. The terms actually have different meanings. Punishment is to impose a penalty for an offense. The word *discipline* derives from the stem word *disciple*, meaning one who accepts the teachings of a master and often assists in spreading them. The definition of discipline is training that develops self-control and efficiency. When the word is used in this context, a discipline system should imply teaching and guidance, with the particular methods of restraint or punishment used only as one component of that system.

To determine the appropriate amount of supervision is not an easy job. It takes our best efforts to determine the best system for our individual families and each individual child. Some in our society teach that parents should let their children do anything they want to. "Don't take away their agency," some say. Even some in the Church fall for this argument. The problem usually starts early with a child saying something like:

Child: "I don't want to go to the primary party."

Parent: "Please go. They are going to have red punch and cookies."

Child: "I hate red punch and cookies."

Parent: "Okay, baby, I'm not going to force you to go."

Child: "I don't want to go to Scouts."

Parent: "Please, they are going to tie knots."

Child: "I hate tying knots."

Parent: "Well, it is your choice. You are old enough to decide for yourself."

Child: "I don't want to go to youth conference."

Parent: "Please, they are going to pull weeds at the cemetery."

Child: "I hate pulling weeds at the cemetery."

Parents: "Well, it is your agency if that is how you choose to use it."

Agency is a gift from God. Just because parents set rules and expectations, children are not left without their agency. While it is true that children need to learn to make their own decisions, we would have less straight A students, Eagle Scouts, seminary graduates, and even virtuous children without guidance and limits set on behavior. Effective parents do not take away agency by setting limits. We should all remember that no one can take away our agency. It is a gift from God (see 2 Nephi 2:16).

The responsibility of parents is to discipline their own children. Too many parents expect church and seminary teachers, school teachers, and others to teach their children proper discipline. Many times over the years I have heard parents say something to the effect of, "I hope you can do something with him! We never have been able to." When dress standards and other such rules are not properly taught in the home, their enforcement becomes very difficult for leaders.

Four Types of Family Control

During the maturing process, children may not fully comprehend the consequences of certain actions. Part of the teaching process includes certain limits placed on their behavior. Researchers have found four basic types or patterns of family control. The type used in our families will play a major role in whether our children grow into responsible adults.

1. Permissive

In the Permissive type of family, the child has more control in making decisions for himself than his parents do. The effects of this system may vary somewhat, but often the child becomes tyrannical, self-centered, and selfish. In later life, this child often has conflicts with those who will not pamper him the way his parents have. Without limits placed on his behavior, the child often feels insecure, bewildered, and uncertain. These children have never known self-control.

When children are given too much freedom, the world's temptations become very appealing. While visiting in a distant stake, I met a young man who came from an active LDS family. During our conversation, I asked how much freedom his parents gave him. He replied, "I'll put it this way: if I were given any more freedom, I would be on my own." I made a mental note to check on this young man's progress if I ever had an opportunity to visit his area again. Five years passed, when I happened to meet the boy's seminary teacher. I found out the young man had gone on a mission, but had been sent home for moral transgressions. Later, he married a young girl he had impregnated. Elder A. Theodore Tuttle made the following observation regarding permissive parents, "Only the unwise foolishly indulge their sons and withhold proper discipline."[5]

Youth seldom fully see the dangers and consequences of decisions. They live in a world of here and now. Many studies prove that the youth believe they are not vulnerable to the things of the world. Nothing could be further from the truth. Permissive parents dramatically increase the chances their youth will fall to immorality and other deviant behavior. Research shows that the lack of discipline associated with the permissive family type often leads to delinquency and teen pregnancy. In addition, we surveyed youth and asked if their parents placed any restrictions on the time or content of the media they were involved with. We then compared their responses with their willingness to have premarital sex and found these results:

Percent Willing to Have Premarital Sex Based on Number of Media Rules

3 Rules; 33%
2 Rules; 37%
1 Rule; 52%
0 Rules; 71% [6]

---

2. Autocratic

In the autocratic discipline system, the parents make any and all decisions relevant to their children. Little concern is given to their children's feelings or desires. These parents are the opposite of permissive parents. Many of the children who grow up in autocratic homes are resentful of parental domination and rebel against them. Others tend to exhibit an over-dependency on their parents and have a difficult time making any decisions on their own. Both groups often show distress and have emotional problems. Elder Richard G. Scott has taught, "Forced obedience yields no blessings."[7]

During a speaking assignment, I met an autocratic father. He refused to let his teenage daughter go to seminary, even though she had pleaded with him. His reason was that "it is too early in the morning." She had absolutely no say in the matter. He refused to allow her to attend youth conference because the leaders didn't show him "an exact schedule of events."

One of the problems with the autocratic approach is that coercion often comes across as a lack of love and trust. Some fathers think the power of the priesthood is a doubled-up fist. This approach may have limited success while a child is young, but it will have less and less as the years roll by. Early obedience may turn to open rebellion in later years.

3. Erratic

Another type of family control is called *erratic*. In this type of system, control is inconsistent. Sometimes the parents are authoritarian, sometimes democratic, and sometimes permissive. Lacking clear, definite, and consistent guidelines, children often become confused and insecure. Such youth have been correlated in research with antisocial, delinquent behavior. Many times erratic discipline comes when parents are not united. The father may be a strict authoritarian, while the mother thinks she has to balance out the discipline by being very permissive. One of the most important elements of being a successful parent is to remain consistent in handling discipline issues.

4. Democratic

In a democratic home, decisions are made jointly by parents and children. This approach has been demonstrated to have the most positive effect on youth. It encourages individual responsibility, decision-making, initiative, and autonomy. This type of home—where there is warmth, fairness, and trust—is often associated with conforming, trouble-free, non-delinquent behavior. The fact that many decisions are made jointly does not mean there are no rules or laws. A democracy is defined as having equality of rights, opportunity, and treatment. The United States is a democracy. We have a voice in our government. But within this system of freedom, there exist certain rules of conduct that must be followed. These do not take away our agency; they simply place limits on certain freedoms for our protection. The same method holds true in effective families. Children have input and freedoms within the bounds of certain rules.

Of course, any system of discipline brings challenges and trials. Even in the most democratic families, questions constantly get asked, such as, "Why can't I do that?" or "Everyone else gets to do it," or "Why are you so strict?" or "Why don't you trust me?" Some youth will openly defy any family rules or test parental resolve to enforce them. The temptation to give in and be inconsistent is ever-present. One mother, after a particularly trying day, said to her disobedient children, "Okay, do as you darn well please. Now let's see you go against that!" While this short-term approach may be tempting at times, it certainly is not the best solution in the long run.

If you were to place yourself in one of the four categories of family discipline listed above, which would it be? The discipline we use in our homes will affect the behavior of our children. Most successful LDS families have what we would call a *strict democratic system.* In the study of successful families by Dyer and Kunz, they found 71 percent viewed themselves as stricter than other families they know, 17 percent about the same, while only 12 percent saw themselves as less strict than other families.[8] Strict should not be confused with autocratic. A strict family, by this definition, is one that always applies discipline for an infraction. A less strict family would be one that would overlook infractions much of the time and occasionally apply discipline.

We should always keep in mind that rules without relationships lead to rebellion. With these thoughts in mind, let's look at some suggestions that may help with discipline in our homes. No matter how much we try or how much we love our children, mistakes will be made.

Misbehavior is a part of every child's development. But how we handle these situations is very important.

Clearly Spell Out Family Rules

While an undergraduate student at Brigham Young University, I took a child development class. After all these years, I can still remember one particular lecture my professor presented. He told our class that all children need to have a circle drawn around them. This circle denotes family rules and what is expected of each family member. These expectations should be well defined and clearly understood by every member of the family. This circle should not be drawn so closely that we stifle them or so wide that they feel there are no boundaries. He said almost all children will step to the edge of the line at times to see how far they can go without suffering consequences. Some will even cross over the line, but if the rules have been well defined, almost all will jump back to the safety of the circle when danger appears. Those who have no rules often struggle with self-discipline throughout their lives.

Don't confuse setting rules with being an autocratic parent. President Spencer W. Kimball commented, "Setting limits to what a child can do means to that child that you love him and respect him. If you permit the child to do all the things he would like to do without any limits, that means to him that you do not care much about him."[9]

Parents should also teach family members the reasons behind the rules. When children are small, parents may be able to get by with simply saying, "No, because I said so." However, with time, children will want more of an explanation. This should not be a shock to parents, since adolescents are maturing and need to be treated more like adults. If we are going to establish a rule, surely we have a good reason to do so and can back it up with facts and logic. Someone has said, "He who is convinced against his will is of the same opinion still." In our homes, discipline should mean mostly teaching correct principles.

Teach Accountability

One of Satan's best tactics is to imply that there are no negative consequences for sin. Cigarette ads depict happy people smoking, not people on oxygen suffering from lung cancer. Alcohol ads show happiness and fun times, not divorce, loss of self-esteem, car accidents, and destroyed health. By our letting children suffer certain consequences, they can better relate when we teach them the terrible cost of sin. We help them understand that while they can choose their actions, they cannot choose the results of those actions. If you decide to jump off a building, the laws of gravity require you to hit the ground regardless of what you want.

I remember receiving a call from our Scoutmaster. He said our twelve-year-old son, Nathan, had been irreverent during merit badge training by an invited guest. He said while Nathan was not alone in this, nor the instigator, he had participated in an irreverent manner while the skills of a merit badge were being taught. How could I let Nathan experience some logical consequences? I called him in and asked him about his behavior. He quickly admitted his role; although, he pointed out, "everyone was doing it." I asked him if he knew that his Scoutmaster was attending college while working to support his family, along with trying to be a good Scoutmaster. He wasn't aware of all that. I then told him that on top of these responsibilities, he was an early-morning seminary teacher. With these duties and time commitments, he deserved some respect. When the moment was right, I decided it was time he experienced consequences for his behavior. "Don't you think you should call your Scoutmaster?" He agreed that he should. "Good!" I said. "Go call him and tell him you want to come over." Nathan looked like he had seen a ghost, but he knew it was right.

We drove to the Scoutmaster's house. Nathan got out of the car and meekly knocked on his door. It was a touching scene to watch this Scoutmaster and his Scout walking around the yard talking. When they came back, both were crying. Nathan got back in the car a more humble boy, one who had learned the pain of consequences and the joy of repentance. If our children are allowed to experience consequences as they grow up, they will believe when they are taught that there is a penalty to be paid for misbehavior.

Pick a Soft Spot and Be Consistent

Admonitions and threats without supporting actions teach children that parents do not mean what they say. I heard a young boy say to a friend, "They yell and scream a lot, but they are all bluff." This is compatible with recent studies. In our survey of high school students, we found that only 17 percent said their parents were very consistent with their discipline. These students were only half as likely to be willing to have premarital sex as those who came from homes with inconsistent discipline. Once we set our family rules, we must be completely consistent in enforcing them. If, for example, we have a rule that a child never be allowed to speak to his parents or brothers and sisters in a disrespectful manner, immediate action should be taken any time the opposite behavior occurs. If this rule is enforced every time, the problem is usually solved before it becomes an issue. Disobedience should be treated like a weed—nipped in the bud before it gets out of control. Once the rule breaking is allowed or inconsistently checked, the behavior becomes very difficult to control. As Elder Ted E. Brewerton said, "If we do not obey, the power to obey is lessened. Our capability to recognize good is weakened."[10]

John Wooden was the most successful college basketball coach in history. He coached 180 players during his career at UCLA. At age ninety, he was still in contact with 172 of those who played for him. He was very strict, yet when one of his players was asked by a reporter to describe his coach in one word, he replied, "Saint." Coach Wooden won ten national championships in twelve years, including seven in a row. At one point, they won eighty-eight games in a row. They had a team rule of no beards and no long hair during the hippie days of college rebellion. He told reporters, with a twinkle in his eye, that he didn't want his players to have long hair and a beard because he was afraid they would catch a cold after taking a shower.

One of the greatest players during the John Wooden era was a six foot, eleven inch center named Bill Walton. Bill had scored forty-four points in a national championship game and was one of the great All-Americans in college basketball history. The following experience demonstrates a coach who knew how to motivate his players. "Coach Wooden forbade his players to grow facial hair. One day All-American center, Bill Walton, the seven-foot-tall most coveted player in the nation, showed up with a full beard. 'It's my right,' he announced. Wooden asked if he really believed that. Walton said he did. 'That's good, Bill,' Coach said. 'I admire people who have strong beliefs and stick by them, I really do. We're going to miss you.' Before day's end, Walton had shaved off his beard. That was more than three decades ago. Walton still telephones the coach once a week to tell him that he loves him."[11]

Don't Overreact

Parents need to be very careful to suppress their anger during teaching times. Elder Elray L. Christiansen warned us of this danger when he said, "To make decisions while infuriated is as unwise and foolish as it is for a captain to put out to sea in a raging storm."[12]

A study done in the restaurant industry illustrates this point. Every waiter in this study had broken dishes at some point in their employment. When asked to describe their supervisor's reaction to these accidents, it was found that when their boss yelled at them or made them feel foolish, there was added pressure to the pressure they already felt. A high percentage of these employees resented their bosses. However, when supervisors were understanding and compassionate after the mishaps, a high percent of the employees loved them. Many times our teenagers, out of ignorance or inexperience, do things they did not mean to. When this happens, do we add pressure or take pressure away?

Someone said that children are like a bar of wet soap. To hang on to them, we must apply just the right amount of pressure. If you try too squeeze them too hard, they slip away. If you don't squeeze them enough, they also slip away.

Correct Misbehavior Immediately

Over the years, I have heard many parents say things like, "We pick our battles very carefully," and, "We don't fire the big cannons until we have big problems with our children." I have just the opposite philosophy. I view misbehavior as one link of a chain that the adversary is trying to wrap around our children. If we fail to correct the behavior when it begins, then the individual links turn into chains, wrapping around our children to the point where it is very difficult to get them off. For example, if a poster of an inappropriate rock star goes up on the walls of our child's bedroom, the time to fire the big cannons is the same day it goes up. If you wait until the walls are covered with worldly images and time has passed, you will most likely have an all-out war on your hands to get them removed. On the first day the poster goes up, the child might feel a little guilty anyway. If they are confronted and taught why those things do not belong in their rooms, there is far less chance of it becoming a major issue. We can diligently follow the verse that states, "Train up a child in the way he should go: and when he is old, he will not depart from it" (Proverbs 22:6).

Correct Misbehavior with Love

At times, every youth needs correcting. Any correction should be administered within the context of love and respect. Parents should attempt to remain as objective as possible and refrain from venting their own anger at the child's expense. If the parent stays calm and focuses on the behavior of the child, instead of the child himself, the child's self-respect will not be damaged in the process of facilitating acceptable behavior.

My friend Frank was the star running back on his junior high school's football team. One Sunday, he became ill and didn't feel well enough to return to school until Thursday. A football game was sched-uled that night, and Frank asked his parents if he could play. They both reminded him how sick he had been and that if he was too sick to go to school, then he was too sick to play football. He didn't argue but asked if it would be okay if he just stood on the sidelines and watched the game. After making a promise that he would not play, they agreed to let him go.

While he was standing there, several boys on the team tried to persuade him to suit up and play, but he politely declined, remem-bering the promise made to his parents. That promise held up until the team fell behind. His friends played on the fact that they needed him in the game. Finally, the temptation was too great, and he ran to the locker room and put on his uniform. The coach immediately put him in the game. He was given the ball a few times for good gains, and he felt excited to be helping his team. Then he noticed a lone figure standing on the side of the hill watching the game. A sick feeling came over Frank as he realized that it was his father. Slowly, he walked to the sideline, pulled off his uniform and started the long walk toward his waiting father. He was sure he was going to yell at him. But instead, his father only commented, "Are you going home, son?" Frank replied, "Yes, sir," and they turned and walked off together. There was a long silence, and then his father said, "Did you get a little too close to the temptation, son?" The reply came, "Yes sir." They continued to walk. After another long pause, his father asked, "Did you learn a lesson from it?" His son answered. "Yes, sir." That was all his father ever said about the incident. While relating this story, Frank recalled, "Years later, when all the other boys were sowing their wild oats, I never participated."

We need to rely on the Spirit to guide us in raising our families. Sometimes there are no textbook answers to the specific challenges we face. The Lord gave a wonderful guideline for parents to use when disciplining children. "No power or influence can or ought to be maintained by virtue of the priesthood, only by persuasion, by long-suffering, by gentleness and meekness, and by love unfeigned" (D&C 121:41).

Notes

1   Robert D. Hales, "With All the Feeling of a Tender Parent: A Message of Hope to Families," *Ensign,* May 2004, 90.

2   Larry R. Lawrence, "Courageous Parenting," *Ensign*, November 2010, 98.

3   Neal A. Maxwell, in Conference Report, April 1975, 150.

4   Gordon B. Hinckley, in Conference Report, April 1973, 73.

5   A. Theodore Tuttle, in Conference Report, October 1973, 88.

6   Randal A. Wright, "Family, Religious, Peer and Media Influence on Adolescence Willingness to Have Premarital Sex" (PhD dissertation), Brigham Young University, 1995, 112.

7   Richard G. Scott, "To Help a Loved One in Need," *Ensign*, May 1988, 59.

8   William G. Dyer and Phillip R. Kunz, *Effective Mormon Families* (Salt Lake City, UT: Deseret Book, 1986), 59.

9   Edward L. Kimball, ed., *The Teachings of Spencer W. Kimball* (Salt Lake City, UT: Deseret Book, 1982), 340.

10 Ted E. Brewerton, "Our Capacity to Recognize Good," *Ensign*, May 1981, 68.

11 Rick Reilly, "The Back Page," *Sports Illustrated*, March 20, 2000, 59.

12 Elray L. Christiansen, in Conference Report, April 1971, 27.

WORLDLY
HEROES

MISTAKE: Allow or encourage children to become too involved with worldly heroes.

"I was allowed to have worldly heroes from the time I was very small. I was not only allowed to have them but actually encouraged having them by my parents. They would allow me to spend countless hours watching super hero television programs and movies and then buy me their action figures to play with. Later, I had posters of rock stars and movie stars all over the walls of my bedroom, most of which they bought for me. In high school, they would also allow me to go to their concerts and buy their products. It seems strange to me now but I think they were shocked when I began to act like the heroes they allowed me to be exposed to."

Many years ago, a popular sports drink company ran a very successful ad campaign with the slogan, "Be Like Mike." The celebrity pitchman for the product was the great basketball player, Michael Jordan. We personally witnessed how powerful the message had been accepted by children and teenagers alike. One day, my teenage son, Nathan, was outside shooting baskets when he noticed our four-year-old neighbor, Nate, at his side. Nate was very blond, blue eyed, and light skinned. After talking for a few minutes, the young boy announced to my son, "When I get big, I'm going to be Michael Jordan." After a short pause, he said, "And I'm going to be black!" This young boy sincerely idolized one of the greatest basketball players of all time. But it is not just children who are affected. During Michael Jordan's last year with the Chicago Bulls, he was paid the equivalent of $428,571 per game. At the height of his popularity, he left basketball to try his hand at baseball. When that did not work out, he considered coming back to basketball. Shortly thereafter, a headline in *USA Today* read, "The Two Billion Dollar Rumor." The article described the incredible financial impact this basketball star had on the products he endorsed: "Michael Jordan is scoring big points on Wall Street. Since rumors surfaced Thursday the ex-NBA superstar might return to the Chicago Bulls, stocks of the companies whose products he endorses have surged . . . The combined stock market value of the five [companies he endorses] has jumped $2.3 billion."[1]

If the game of basketball didn't exist, would Michael Jordan or any of the current NBA stars still be considered heroes? What makes Michael Jordan or other celebrities giving their best any different from athletes in the Special Olympics giving their best? Are basketball stars heroes because they do something well? My auto mechanic is very good at what he does, but he doesn't get paid much at all. There must be hundreds of thousands of talented Americans working as cashiers, waiters, service station attendants, teachers, and policemen who receive no praise and little pay, yet are very good at what they do. Something else is happening here with the idols of our society.

All of us have an inborn yearning to look up to someone (or something) greater than ourselves. The Greeks had a word for it—*heros*, an idolized super man. A hero is, by definition, "a man of distinguished courage or ability, admired for his brave deeds and noble qualities." Do our children's heroes qualify by this definition? Hero worship has existed throughout history. In heroes, people have their values and dreams realized and their innermost hopes fulfilled vicariously. President Spencer W. Kimball describes these feelings and the confusion that they can bring when he said, "Man is naturally a religious being. His heart instinctively seeks for God whether he reverences the sacred cow or prays to the sun or moon; whether he kneels before wood and stone images, or prays in secret to his Heavenly Father, he is satisfying an inborn urge."[2] This inborn urge is lovingly placed within each of us by Heavenly Father so that we will turn to Him. However, these feelings can easily be misdirected and manipulated by evil, conspiring men in the last days.

At the turn of the twentieth century, the heroes of America's youth were dominated by historical figures such as Abraham Lincoln and George Washington.

Heroes of Youth in 1900

78% historical figures
12% literary
10% relatives/acquaintances [3]

Things began to change drastically after that time. In 1923, advertising genius Albert Lasker, of the Lord and Thomas advertising agency, was hired by the American Tobacco Company to boost sales. His campaign focused on trying to convince women to smoke, thereby doubling their potential market, if successful. To accomplish this, the agency hired female silent movie stars and opera singers to endorse Lucky Strike Cigarettes. This campaign also focused on making women weight conscious and the slogan, "Reach for a Lucky instead of a sweet," was coined. "Sales of Lucky Strike cigarettes increased by 312 percent during the following year."[4] This campaign demonstrated that celebrity heroes could do an amazing job of selling products. This discovery has had a huge impact on modern families and society as a whole. No wonder Clare Barnes said, "Advertising has done more to cause the social unrest of the twentieth century than any other single factor."[5]

By 1950, advertisers had totally distorted the traditional hero of the past. This new celebrity hero often had little to do with the traditional definition of brave deeds and noble qualities. The new hero fits much better with the term *idol*, which by definition is "a person or thing which is excessively admired." Let's look at the difference in the heroes of 1900 and 1950.

Heroes of Youth in 1950

33% historical figures
0% literary
10% relatives and acquaintances
57% sports, radio, and movie stars[6]

Heroes such as Marilyn Monroe and James Dean came to represent fame, good looks, individualism, wealth, notoriety, talent, and everything else a person dreams of possessing. This barrage especially influences teenagers searching for role models to follow.

We conducted a survey among American high school students to see how much the heroes of our youth had changed since the 1950s. We found the following information in 2001.

Heroes of Youth in 2000

2% historical figures
0% literary
12% relatives and acquaintances
86% sports, radio, television and movie stars[7]

But what does all this talk of celebrity heroes or teen idols have to do with our families? One thing is apparent. Today's heroes have one more characteristic in common than just fame, fortune, and good looks. What commonality do they share? The companies they represent are all selling something. It may be high-priced athletic shoes, digital downloads, CDs, DVDs, movie or concert tickets, immodest clothes, or teen magazines. They are all selling something, and we, as a public, are buying. But do they sell more than just products?

Speaking of our day, the Savior gave this chilling warning: "For in those days there shall also arise false Christs, and false prophets, and shall show great signs and wonders" (Matthew 1:22). What if the false Christs and prophets of our day have nothing to do with traditional religion? What if the adversary took our natural yearning for God, mixed those feelings with hero worship, and then turned it to idol worship? Since we are inclined to follow those we most admire, all the adversary would need to do is corrupt the heroes of our society.

The celebrity-hero-idols of our day share another thing in common. The media creates them and places them at the top. "Celebrities have become the Gods of our social system because our success-oriented culture has placed them at the top."[8]

What evidence do we have that our celebrity heroes have actually become idols? Let us consider just a few examples. Suppose that a visitor came to see you from outer space and asked you a few questions about the society in which we lived. Consider these questions and their answers.

Q. About how much do you pay a beginning school teacher per year?

A. $25,000

Q. How much do you pay a movie star to act like a teacher?

A. $15,000,000 for about three months of work

Q. About how much do you pay a rookie policeman to protect you per year?

A. $25,000

Q. How much do you pay a movie star to act like a policeman?

A. $15,000,000 for about 3 months of work

Q. How much do you pay a grocery bagger to put food in bags?

A. $12,000

Q. How much do you pay a top NBA player *to try* to put a ball through a hoop?

A. $20,000,000 for about eight months per year

How would you explain the outrageous fact that a movie star is paid eighty times more than the real President of the United States to act like him for a few months? President Spencer W. Kimball simply states, "We are on the whole an idolatrous people."[9]

In a nation starved for real heroes, almost anything can be used in their place. Imaginary superheroes can be created with names like Batman, Spiderman, He-Man, Power Rangers, Superman, or Teenage Mutant Ninja Turtles. Of course these imaginary heroes, like their real celebrity counterparts, share one goal—sell products. Cool camels can do a remarkable job of selling cigarettes to our youth. Celebrity frogs and lizards can sell beer in record numbers, and talking dogs can sell tacos. The parade of idols to worship and to sell products never seems to end. Charlotte Baecher said, "Barraged by hundreds of sales messages daily, kids are having trouble handling powerful celebrity sells, peer pressure, status products, exciting novelties dangling in front of them, and promises of everything from popularity to coolness, provided they buy the right things."[10] These pitchmen and the companies behind them have learned that what P.T. Barnum said many years ago is, in fact, true today, "A sucker is born every minute."

However, in 1982, another enormous discovery was made that has had even more extensive consequences for our families. A little creature from outer space named ET became a national hero. People went to see him in record numbers. This made his creators very wealthy. Everyone involved seemed a little surprised with the huge success of the movie; however, that was not the important discovery. You may remember that during the movie, ET was shown eating the candy Reese's Pieces. In the months that followed, the sales of this candy skyrocketed. With that breakthrough discovery, a whole new industry, called product placement, was created. Media executives realized that they could now sell products without advertisements if they showed a celebrity using them. This discovery also has enormous implications for families. Think about this: if the hero of one of your children acts a certain way, then your child tends to act similarly. Let's look at a few examples of what has occurred since *ET.*

In 1986, a movie called *Top Gun* was released. Tom Cruise made elite Navy fighter pilots look very appealing. After the movie, the number of applicants to the Navy fighter pilot program increased dramatically.

In 1993, *Jurassic Park* was released. Immediately following, the number of visitors and donations to dinosaur museums increased dramatically.

In 1996, *Twister* was released. Shortly after the movie came out, the number of teenagers and young single adults chasing twisters increased dramatically.

In 1999, *Fight Club* was released. Following its release, a massive number of fight clubs were formed around the nation.

In 2001, a movie called *The Fast and the Furious* was released. It became a series with others released in 2003, 2006, 2009, 2011 and 2013. According to multiple news reports, accident rates from illegal street racing always go up when another movie in the series is released.

Now reflect on the economic impact that movies like *Titanic* have had on our society. Hundreds of millions of dollars in movie tickets and other products are sold. It is a proven fact that popular movies can create idols, and that idols can sell products. Far more frightening is the discovery that these idols can sell attitudes and behavior. What happens, for example, when these heroes parade illicit sex before young people? That should be easy to test. If our youth follow their idols, then something dramatic should have happened in the late 1960s. In 1968, the Motion Picture Association of America adopted a rating system for its movies. Before that time, illicit sexual scenes were forbidden by code. After that time, movie producers could show anything they wanted, but the movies would then be rated. In 1965, before the new guidelines were adopted, the movie of the year was *The Sound of Music*. In 1969, the movie of the year was an X-rated movie called *Midnight Cowboy*.

As the movie industry began to change, television and music began to glorify immoral behavior. The number of stars who began to cohabitate skyrocketed. For the first time in American history, immorality was being shown to the masses by the very people who were most admired. If this idolatry theory is true, then immorality would show signs of a dramatic increase in the late sixties. That is exactly what happened. Consider the following statistics and their implications for your family.

Births Out of Wedlock: Year; Percent of All Births

1950; 4.0%
1960; 5.3%
1970; 10.7%
1980; 18.4%
1990; 28.0%
2000; 33.2%
2010; 41.0% [11]

The significance of what is documented here cannot be understated. Remember that our children's idols and heroes will have a significant influence on their attitudes and behavior. Whatever values their heroes have will be reflected in your children. If their idols are rock stars, don't be surprised if they begin to act like rock stars. If your girls look up to idols who wear immodest, mid-drift-baring clothes, then expect them to pressure you to allow them to do the same. If their heroes are immoral, don't be surprised if your children are tempted to follow in their footsteps and fail to understand why it is wrong. If their heroes smoke, use drugs, have bad attitudes, gamble, or are immoral, expect problems in those areas. It is critical that we are aware of those who our children admire. Most children will choose heroes from those to whom they are most exposed. If they listen to rock music and watch MTV constantly, then the chances that their heroes are rock stars will be higher. If they love professional basketball, then of course their heroes will most likely be basketball players. As parents, we can have a huge influence on those our children think highly of. The key is what we allow them to be exposed to.

In our study, we also asked high school students: *If you could change places with anyone, who would it be?* We then correlated their answers with the number of R-rated movies they had seen in the last year.

Willingness to Change Places with a Media Star Based on Number of R-rated Movies Viewed in One Year

0–5: 13%

6–15: 28%

16–25: 37%

26+: 45%[12]

What is the message here? The more R-rated movies these youth saw during the year, the more likely they would want to change places with a media star modeling inappropriate behavior. Ultimately, the more they watched filthy movies, the more they wanted to be like the people in those movies.

It, therefore, becomes critical to know whom our kids look up to, since research consistently shows that we tend to imitate those whom we most admire. President Thomas S. Monson said, "We tend to become like those whom we admire. Just as in Nathaniel Hawthorne's classic account 'The Great Stone Face,' we adopt the mannerisms, the attitudes, even the conduct of those whom we admire."[13] The heroes may have a huge impact upon their behavior—perhaps in some cases even more influence on their attitudes and behavior than their parents.

How can we find out whom our children admire? The following may be helpful.

Talk and Listen to Them

A good way for parents to find out whom their children really admire is to simply ask them. There are various ways to do this. For example, ask your children if they could trade places with anyone ,who would it be. If you have teenagers, you could ask, "If everyone in the world were LDS, single, and available, who would you most like to date?" Their answers, if sincere, could be extremely revealing. Be sure to listen closely as your children talk about their favorite TV and movie stars. Why it is that they are so impressed with them? Listen as they quote lines from movies, to find out who they are quoting.

Where Do They Spend Their Money?

A tour of our teenagers' bedrooms may be extremely helpful too. Are posters on the walls? Let your children explain who or what the posters are about and why they have chosen to look at these pictures every day. Ask them in a loving way to share with you the music they enjoy. What about their magazines and books? What kind of clothes do they buy or ask for. In the early days of our society, clothes had no brand names on them. As time passed, companies began putting their brand names on an inside label. Now, the brand names are on the outside. These labels tell us a lot about children's heroes. Who else wears them? Who advertises for these specific brands? What movie tickets do your children want to buy? What concerts do they want to attend? If you do this with a non-threatening attitude and a spirit of love, you will be able to determine your own children's idols and heroes.

Be a Role Model

Several years ago, I listened to a college student, who is now a recognized attorney, speak about his parents' influence on him. He stated, "Everything I have ever done well in life was because I listened to the counsel of my parents. Everything I did wrong was because I went against that counsel." Are you a hero figure for your children? I believe that all children want parents they can admire. I have never heard a teenager say, "My dad is awesome! He sits in his La-Z-Boy and watches television for eight hours straight, with no breaks. And my mother is such a dedicated worker. She is so involved in the community that I never even see her." Those are not the kind of parents children respect. Be a role model to your children. If they have no respect for you, then they will not value your counsel.

Expose Them to Good Role Models

Make sure that you let your children spend time with those who will have a good influence on them. Watch all the sessions of general conference together, and teach them to love and respect our modern prophets and apostles. Let them attend programs like Especially for Youth so they can be exposed to counselors and speakers who will have a positive influence. Read the scriptures together, and talk about the great examples set by the spiritual heroes whose stories are told.

President Spencer W. Kimball said, "We all need heroes to honor and admire; we need people after whom we can pattern our lives. For us Christ is the chiefest of these."[14] Let's make sure that we do everything in our power to teach our children about the greatest hero who has ever lived. This will be the best protection of all against the influences of the worldly heroes of our day.

Notes

1 *USA Today*, March 14, 1995, 1A.
2 Edward L. Kimball, ed., *Teachings of Spencer W. Kimball* (Salt Lake City, UT: Deseret Book, 1982), 2.
3 Dorothy Barclay, "Youth's Heroes and Hero Worship," *The New York Times Magazine*, November 4, 1951, 42.
4 US News and World Report, March 7, 1994, 21.
5 Laurence J. Peter, *Peter's Quotations* (New York, NY: Morrow, 1977), 43.
6 Dorothy Barclay, "Youth's Heroes and Hero Worship," *The New York Times Magazine*, November 4, 1951, 42.
7 Randal A. Wright, "Family, Religious, Peer and Media Influence on Adolescence Willingness to Have Premarital Sex" (PhD dissertation), Brigham Young University, 1995, 115.
8 "Fantasy Friends Fill a Gap in People's Lives," A Conversation with John Caughey, *U.S. News and World Report*, July 16, 1984, 106.
9 Spencer W. Kimball, "The False Gods We Worship," *Ensign*, June 1976, 6.
10 Carma Wadley, "Selling It to Kids," *Deseret News*, March 1, 1993, 1C.

11 The United States Census Bureau.

12 Randal A. Wright, "Family, Religious, Peer and Media Influence on
    Adolescence Willingness to Have Premarital Sex" (PhD dissertation),
    Brigham Young University, 1995, 115.

13 Thomas S. Monson, "Decisions Determine Destiny," CES Fireside for
    Young Adults, November 6, 2005.

14 Spencer W. Kimball, "Preparing for Service in the Church," *Ensign*, May
    1979, 47.

TEACHING CORRECT
PRINCIPLES

MISTAKE: Assumption that the Church, school, and society will teach children correct principles.

"My parents always allowed us to make our own decisions. I never felt pressured in one direction or the other. The problem is they never taught us the positive or negative consequences of the decisions that we were faced with. In fact, they didn't teach us much of anything. They let us choose and then delight or suffer in it."

One day in my early-morning seminary class, Diane and Linda were talking to other class members about a rape seminar they had attended the night before. Held at the city civic center, the event was sponsored by the police department and social experts in the field. The girls were taught several frightening statistics about rape and given safety tips on protecting themselves. They had become so frightened that they didn't want to walk to their car. Not knowing what to do, they stayed on the steps of the civic center refusing to leave. As they stood there totally alone, an unknown man walked up to them and asked what was wrong. Diane told him that they were afraid to walk to their car because of what they'd just learned at the rape seminar. The man was sympathetic and kindly offered to take them to their car. Todd, one of our athletic students, blurted out, "You didn't get in the car with him, did you?" Both girls said that they did voluntarily and that he was a very nice man.

Apparently the presenters at the rape seminar had done a great job frightening the audience, but forgot to teach them how to act or conduct themselves properly. John Taylor, while writing about the history of the Church, recorded a statement made by the Prophet Joseph Smith when asked how he led the members of the Church so successfully. The Prophet replied, "I teach them correct principles, and they govern themselves."[1]

With a smile, a visiting General Authority told our stake priesthood leadership that what the Prophet really said was, "I teach, and I teach, and I teach, and I teach the people correct principles and then they govern themselves." If we read the Prophet's statement carefully, we see that he didn't say, "I *tell* the people correct principles, and they govern themselves." He said *teach*. There is an immeasurable difference. To tell is simply to recount with words. To teach is to cause to learn by example or experience.

Teaching is one of the most challenging assignments parents have been given. Joseph F. Smith said, "The parents in Zion will be held responsible for the acts of their children, not only until they become eight years old but, perhaps, throughout all the lives of their children, provided they have neglected their duty to their children while they were under their care and guidance, and the parents were responsible for them."[2] This is an alarming thought, and yet, there comes a tremendous promise from the Lord: "Train up a child in the way he should go: and when he is old, he will not depart from it" (Proverbs 22:6). I learned early on that there is a vast difference between *telling* children correct principles and truly *training* them.

Several years ago, the *Ensign* magazine published my experience of teaching my children a lesson about reverence. In the process of trying to help them be more reverent, I learned a significant lesson about teaching.

> After a recent stake assignment in a neighboring city, I came home to find my wife, Wendy, upset and frustrated. When I asked her how the children had behaved at church, she told me that they had been irreverent in sacrament meeting. Irreverence is usually not a problem in our family, so I gave my four children a quick lecture and sent them on about their Sabbath-day activities. Wendy felt that the subject needed more attention than it had been given, so we decided to

devote our family home evening to reverence. The lesson began in the usual manner—another message on why we should be reverent and what would happen the next time the children chose not to be reverent in church meetings. Our children didn't seem particularly interested. They began to fidget and look away—until the lesson took on a new twist our family will never forget.

I asked Nathan, our eight-year-old, to go into another room for a few minutes, then return when called to tell the family a story he liked. Nathan loved to tell stories and was excitedly deciding which story he'd relate. The children thought we were going to play a game, as we often do during family home evening. While Nathan was out, my wife and I told the other three children that when he returned and began to tell his story, we would all talk, giggle, and fidget. We were not to look at him.

Nathan returned and began. An excellent storyteller with contest ribbons for his talent, he thought this would be an easy assignment, until he realized that no one was listening to him. Without his audience's attention, he began fumbling for words and leaving out portions of the story. Frustrated, he finally sat down—without even finishing his tale.

I asked him how this experience had made him feel. Hanging his head, he replied, "Really bad!"

We next asked our second son, aged seven, to leave the room. When Nolan was invited back to tell us his story, he said, "I don't know any stories." Knowing what was about to happen and how it had made his brother feel, he wanted no part of it.

When he tried to tell his story and we didn't pay attention, he became upset and said, "I can't do it! I can't talk when other people are talking!"

Here was the teaching moment I had hoped for. I explained, "Now you know how your teachers feel in your classes at church and school, and how it makes the speakers feel when the rest of the congregation or class is irreverent. They feel bad inside, just as you do now. They would like to just sit down and quit, too." Our children understood. They had learned an important lesson.

So that we could experience the positive side of this lesson, we asked our children to sit up straight, fold their arms, and look at Nathan as he told his story again. This time there was a dramatic difference. He did an excellent job, using facial expressions and hand gestures without stumbling on one word.

After our children had gone to bed, I felt good about the success of our lesson on reverence. Our children had truly learned something that night! But then a thought came as if someone had hit me over the head with a sledgehammer: The children had learned, but what about me? Did I know the meaning of the word reverence?

I thought about my past behavior. How many times had I whispered during church meetings and classes? How many times had I worked on talks or read during meetings? How many times had I interrupted others when they were speaking? Upon examining my own actions, I found that I had also been late for church and appointments, dozed off in meetings, and not looked at teachers or speakers when they were speaking to me. I seldom expressed appreciation to the teacher, the speaker, or others for a job well done. And occasionally I stood out in the hall during Sunday School class, visiting with people I saw only at church.

Together, Wendy and I looked up the word *reverence*. The dictionary defined it as "a feeling of profound respect often mingled with awe and affection." I began to see that a feeling of deep respect means much more than just not talking in church meetings. Leaving Cheerios on the chapel floor is irreverent, just as is allowing a child to run unsupervised through the halls. There are many little things I had never even thought of as having to do with reverence. I needed to work on being more reverent as much as my children did!

Since that day, our family has learned to enjoy our meetings and glean more from them than we ever have before.[3]

Remember that teaching is far more than just telling children what they should be doing. We must actually live the principles we are trying to teach if those teachings are to sink deep into the hearts of those we are teaching. Elder Theodore M. Burton said, "The greater the teacher, the greater the pupil may become."[4] Our teaching must be totally consistent and must not change over time. Nothing is more confusing to a child than to have parents who teach one thing and do another; or to teach one thing one day and differently the next. As President Spencer W. Kimball pointed out, "It would be a poor lighthouse that gave off a different signal to guide every ship entering a harbor."[5] Children need consistent and unchanging signals from their "lighthouse" parents.

To train up a child so thoroughly that he will not depart from it when he is old will take effort and determination. Following are a few thoughts that may help in this effort.

Children Need Both Parents' Influence

In many homes, the teaching of children is mostly left to their mothers. This trend requires change. When both parents become involved in the training, it increases the chances that the youth will accept what is taught. I saw the subtle power that a father can have I served as a bishop. I often visited the opening exercises of Primary, and one day I noticed the Blazer boys were acting irreverently while practicing for a musical program in the chapel. James was especially animated. As the boys stood to sing a lively song, he tried to entertain the other boys in his class with his antics. I then noticed something that this young Blazer failed to see. His father, one of my counselors, had walked in at the back of the chapel and quietly watched his young son put on a spirited show. The father immediately walked up and stood in the aisle right beside his young son. At first James failed to notice his father. He continued clowning around until he turned to his right and saw his father standing right beside him. The father didn't speak a word to his son, yet the change in his son's behavior was dramatic. He straightened up, looked at the chorister, and began to sing appropriately. It was a powerful example to me—the influence a loving father can have in the lives of his children. Both mothers and fathers are needed in the home to teach important values and to guide their children. Elder H. Burke Peterson said, "A boy needs a father who will correct him when necessary, but beyond that, one who will love him and like him, and accept him regardless of his performance. . . . It takes quite a dad to look beyond the actions of boyhood and see the potential of manhood—and even more important, for him to get a glimpse of eternity."[6]

Unfortunately, there are far too many homes where the father's influence is not being felt as it should be. Long hours at work, along with heavy church responsibilities, often make it difficult for fathers to be fully involved in teaching their children. Some media researchers believe that by the time a child is eight years old, they will have spent more time watching television than they will spend in an entire lifetime talking to their fathers. We must change this!

Let the Church Assist Us in Teaching

One of the great blessings of living in this day is to have the Church help us teach our children. A sister was asked if she was raised in church. She replied, "No, I was raised *by* the Church." While the Church is a supplement to the family, its influence cannot be overstated. President James E. Faust said, "This Church does not necessarily attract great people but more often makes ordinary people great."[7] We must take advantage of the tremendous power that comes from fully immersing our families in its wonderful programs.

I have been amazed through the years with how much the Church can help in teaching my family. Imagine a church that is already teaching a three-year-old how to speak in public and providing opportunities to practice. This is an organization that furnishes programs and activities for every age group. We must take full advantage of the opportunity, however, by participating when and where we are supposed to with a good attitude.

Teach with Enthusiasm

Have you ever thought about why the world is so appealing to some of our youth?

One reason is that parents and teachers of youth do not make the truth of the gospel exciting. You often hear youth make comments that family home evening or church meetings are boring. I am not trying to be rude, critical, or judgmental, but sometimes the youth are stating the truth. Sometimes we do make the truth seem boring! I've noticed that far too many speakers spend half their time telling us how they are not a good speaker or how they didn't really have time to prepare. How many times have you heard something like, "As I was preparing this talk this morning . . ."?

A few years ago, my wife and I had the opportunity to visit the Whitney Store in Kirtland, Ohio. Our guide was Sister Vera, a young full-time missionary and an amazing teacher. Her description of the events that occurred there made me feel so blessed to be a part of this wonderful work. She took us to the room where the revelation on the Word of Wisdom was received and then bore a powerful testimony of the truth of this work. We then sang "Praise to the Man." The spirit was so strong and the experience so memorable that I know I will never forget our time there.

We then went to the Morley Farm and instantly loved the Burrells who were serving as senior missionaries. Elder Burrell described the events there as if he had participated in the events himself. This is where Joseph Smith received the great 1833 revelation about the gospel filling North and South America. The Burrells' great love of the work helped us appreciate our great heritage even more because they bore powerful testimony.

Next, we traveled to the John Johnson farm where section 76 of the Doctrine and Covenants was received. I was so excited to be there—I just knew this special place would be the pinnacle of our visit. Again, a senior missionary couple served as our guides. The sister never said a word while the brother took us on the tour. He showed us some slides and briefly ran through some of the events that happened there. This kind brother explained the events of Section 76 as if he were describing a trip to the dentist. We, along with others in our group, were disappointed with the lack of enthusiasm in his presentation, especially after witnessing such fervor at the other historical sites. His demeanor made it seem like he was on a mission because someone called him to go and he just did it. He never in any way bore testimony of what he was explaining.

As I pondered what happened that day, I imagined these missionaries in their role as parents. Even though Sister Vera was only twenty-two years old, I could see her being an enthusiastic mother with children who love the gospel with all their heart. I'm sure the man who took us around the John Johnson farm was already a father. I just hope he was more excited about the gospel in his home than when he was telling us about it.

I have heard people, almost out of breath with excitement, describe the latest blockbuster movie that they'd seen. It goes something like this: "Did you see _____ Wow, the special effects were unbelievable and the acting was superb. You have got to see it! I'm going to see it again. It was *that* good. I'm going to buy it the day it comes out on DVD. "

When I was young, we had a cure-all medicine when we got sick called castor oil. Many parents believed this medicine would cure any ailment. I think one of the reasons it worked so well was that we would pretend we felt better just so we wouldn't have to take it. Sometimes I think we often take the castor oil approach to the gospel. "Okay kids, I know the scriptures are boring, but we are going to read them if it kills us, because they are good for us. Now, get in here and act interested." How is it that the greatest truths of the ages would be considered boring? The gospel is the most exciting aspect of our lives. When we are teaching it, we should be excited about our subject.

Use Objects to Teach

While at BYU, I took a youth leadership class from a man by the name of Rulon Skinner. One day, he placed a beautiful cake on the desk in front of the class. We were discussing how we present ourselves in public and the importance of looking and acting our best. The teacher made the point that it matters how things are presented because others make judgments about us and who we represent based on how we present ourselves. About ten minutes before class was over, he commented that his wife had made a cake for our class. Since it was almost lunchtime, I was very excited about that. He then asked how many people wanted a piece of cake. Almost every hand in the class immediately shot up. He took a paper plate, spoon, and napkin to all who raised their hands. Next, he picked up the beautiful cake and walked to the nearest student. I noticed that the cake had not been sliced and the teacher did not appear to have a knife with him. Suddenly, he thrust his hand directly into the cake and brought up a mangled glob. He then squeezed it a little and plopped it down on the girl's plate. She was obviously disgusted with the mess on her plate. He proceeded to do the same thing to all the students who raised their hands. Of course, not one of us made any effort to eat the cake on our plates. We wondered why he would ruin such a beautiful cake when we were so hungry. He then went back to the front of the room, took a towel, out and cleaned his hands off slowly. He looked at us and said, "You see, it does matter how things are presented!" That powerful message was given nearly thirty-five years ago. It left an impression upon me that I will never forget.

Teach Them to Think

Someone once said, "One of the greatest strengths of a good teacher is the ability to provoke people to think." Bishops have a responsibility to conduct an annual tithing settlement for ward members. Several times, while serving in this calling, I observed faithful parents who were shocked to discover that their working teenage children had paid little or no tithes and offerings for the year. On more than one occasion, I was asked to teach these children the importance of paying their tithing.

How could I teach them to think about what they were doing? I wrote down the problem at the top of a piece of paper in my planner and prayed for the answer. I have found that teaching children to think is one of the greatest things I could ever do as a teacher. Finally, the following illustration came to me. I began by asking the youth how much tithing they owed if they earned ten dollars. Of course, they looked at me as if I was insulting their intelligence, then answered, "One dollar." I then said, "Now let's imagine you got paid ten dollars for work in one dollar bills. You know you should pay your tithing, but you don't have a gray envelope with you, so you promise yourself that you'll only spend nine of your pay. One day you put the ten one dollar bills in your pocket and go to the mall to buy a new t-shirt. It is a very hot day, and you are very thirsty. As you walk into the mall, you see the t-shirt you've been wanting in store A. The price is exactly nine dollars including tax. This is perfect! You can buy the shirt and still pay tithing. After you purchase the shirt, you walk out of the mall and pass a sign that says, 'Special—32 oz. Orange Julius, $1.00.' You can't believe your good luck—that's the cheapest you have ever seen them. You reach into your pocket for the money, but it hits you that all you have left is your tithing. What would you do?" Almost every teenager answered the same way: "I would probably buy the drink and then pay two dollars on the next ten dollars I made." This is the major problem for our youth, isn't it? Because the next pay period, there is always something else to buy, and you owe three dollars on your next ten. Before long it begins to look as if tithing is thirty percent instead of ten percent, and the youth feel overwhelmed.

Then I gave them a different scenario. Let's suppose that you get paid ten dollars. This time, you take the gray envelope you brought home from church and put one dollar in it to give to the bishop. You feel great, knowing that you are contributing to the worldwide Church by helping build new chapels and temples that dot the earth. And then there is the quiet satisfaction of knowing that you are helping with the electricity, phone, library materials, activities, and all the other things that tithing helps pay for locally. However, you still need a t-shirt at the mall. You put your nine dollars in your pocket, go into store A, and see just the t-shirt you want for nine dollars. You start to pay for it, but then you hesitate and decide to go to a few more stores. To your surprise you see the exact t-shirt you saw in store A for only eight dollars in store B. You pull out eight dollars and walk out with your new shirt. It is a very hot day, and you are very thirsty. As you are walking out, you see that there is a thirty-two ounce Orange Julius on sale for one dollar. You reach into your pocket, pull out the dollar, and buy the drink. Now you have paid your tithing, bought your t-shirt, and bought your big drink. How were you able to buy the drink and still pay your tithing? It took the youth a moment to figure out where the extra dollar came from, but soon they figured out that all they did was find a better deal on the t-shirt. I explain that the owner of store A will probably have to buy a somewhat smaller Mercedes because he didn't make as much profit on us, but that's okay. We are not worried about people getting rich. We are worried about taking the gospel to the world. Tithing doesn't *really* cost anything at all if we just look for 10 percent better deals throughout life.

Many youth seem to be able to relate to this example because truth is logical. It just makes sense. If we can help our children to be thinkers, they will be well on their way to gaining a testimony of the truth.

Teach Them to Pray

Even when parents are consistent in teaching their children truth, they may not always understand or even agree with the principles they are taught in their home. Children need to be repeatedly taught to go to Heavenly Father in prayer if they question the standards taught. Many have wondered if Nephi ever doubted the wisdom of leaving Jerusalem as did Laman and Lemuel. I think the answer is yes. However, he handled his doubt differently. Instead of rebelling, he turned to prayer for confirmation. He states, "And it came to pass that I, Nephi, being exceedingly young, nevertheless being large in stature, and also having great desires to know of the mysteries of God, wherefore, I did cry unto the Lord; and behold he did visit me, and did *soften my heart* that I did believe all the words which had been spoken by my father; wherefore, I did not rebel against him like unto my brothers" (1 Nephi 2:16).

Our goal as parents is to teach our children correct principles. Occasionally, they may have doubts about the rules. If they are taught to take the same approach that Nephi did, they will learn obedience. When they leave home, they will be able to make wise decisions that will keep them clean and pure. Unhappiness springs largely from non-observance of the Lord's commandments. The home is the best place to teach obedience that leads to this happiness and protection. As President Boyd K. Packer pointed out, "Obedience is a powerful spiritual medicine. It comes close to being a cure-all."[8]

Notes

1   John Taylor, "The Organization of the Church," *Millennial Star*, November 15, 1851, 339.
2   Joseph F. Smith, in Conference Report, April 1910, 6.
3   Randal A. Wright, "Our Family's Reverence Lesson," *Ensign*, August 1986, 43–44.
4   Theodore M. Burton, in Conference Report, April 1961, 128.
5   Spencer W. Kimball, in Conference Report, April 1976, 7.
6   H. Burke Peterson, "Prepare the Heart of Your Son," *Ensign*, November 1982, 44.
7   James E. Faust, "Five Loaves and Two Fishes," *Ensign*, May 1994, 45.
8   Boyd K. Packer, "Balm of Gilead," *Ensign*, November 1977, 60.

UNDERAGE
DATING

MISTAKE: Permission for children to date before age sixteen.

"I wasn't supposed to date until I was sixteen, but when I was fourteen, I was voted one of the school princesses and allowed to go on a date. I think my mom cared more about me being popular with my friends than about underage dating. This proved to be very unwise."

Every active Latter-day Saint has heard the Prophet's counsel on waiting to date until age sixteen. Yet, many of the youth in the Church are going directly against this counsel. Maybe one of the reasons for this lack of obedience is confusion in defining what a date actually is. What is your definition of a date? I remember asking a group of institute students to define the word *date* after reading the following quote by President Spencer W. Kimball. "In order to avoid difficulty and possible temptation, I suggest again the following standard. Any dating *or pairing off* in social contacts should be postponed until at least the age of sixteen or older."[1]

Seldom have I seen so many differences of opinion to such a simple question.

I would describe these responses and the discussion they generated as bordering on chaos. We had about as many opinions as we did students that day, all defending their views. No one seemed to agree with each other on the definition of a date. Every time a student tried to offer his definition, someone would disagree. I told these college students it is very hard to follow the prophet's counsel when no one seems to know what a date is. One beautiful college freshman said she felt as if any time two people paired off, they were on a date. A prominent Church leader's son said, "That is not a date! That is just pairing off. A date is when you pre-arrange to go somewhere with a member of the opposite sex and then go and pick them up." Of course, that was followed by, "What about . . . and how about? . . . " Most of the responses reflected views taught or accepted in their own homes. Several times I thought I could hear the parents speaking through their children. To further add to the confusion, I gave them some true-life scenarios to see if that would help them agree upon what a date is. Since that time, I've presented the following examples multiple times to youth and parents across the Church. The results are without exception the same—mass confusion and disagreement. As you read the following true illustrations, ask yourself if these young people are on dates. All of these youth are from completely active LDS families.

- A twelve-year-old boy named Brad and a twelve-year-old girl named Melissa really liked each other as best friends. Following a growing tradition of elementary school students going with someone to the homecoming game, Brad and Melissa both rode with their own parents to the football stadium. Outside the gates the parents and twelve-year-olds met. Melissa (or parents) had bought Brad a small flower. His mother helped him pin it to his shirt. Brad (or parents) bought Melissa a big mum corsage with ribbons running down to the ground. After her mother pinned the corsage on her, the young couple went into the student section together to enjoy the game. After the game they met their parents at the gate and went home separately. Were Brad and Melissa on a date?
- Rebecca, a thirteen-year-old LDS girl from a prominent family, was invited to attend a formal junior high banquet and dance with a fourteen-year-old nonmember boy named Derek. She asked her parents for permission to go with him. They said "no" since their family rule stated she couldn't date nonmembers nor date until she was sixteen. After much discussion, however, her parents told her she could go and meet the young man at the event— as a friend. Rebecca explained the situation to Derek, and he

agreed to the arrangement. When they met before the banquet, he presented her with a beautiful corsage, and she pinned a boutonniere on his tuxedo. They sat together the entire night and danced together exclusively. They also had their picture taken together. Was Rebecca on a date?

- The mother of a fifteen-year-old girl named Susan was totally impressed with an eighteen-year-old boy named John who was getting ready to leave on his mission. Susan's mother invited John over to their home on many occasions before he left. Susan and John were left alone on the sofa in the living room on several occasions so they could get better acquainted. John was also invited by her mother to go out to eat with her and Susan several times before he left. Was Susan dating at age fifteen?

- Ed, a fifteen-year-old boy, and Laurie, a fourteen-year-old-girl, really liked each other. Ed wanted to invite Laurie to go with him on a family activity to another city. They would be leaving about three in the afternoon and returning home that night about midnight. Knowing that Laurie was too young to date, Ed had his parents invite her to go. Laurie asked her parents if she could go with Ed and his parents to the event. After a short discussion, they agreed to let her go since she would be going with his parents. They traveled to the event and then dropped Laurie off at the appointed time. Was this young couple on a date?

In all four cases, these young people had parental approval. A statement by President Spencer W. Kimball seems to apply to these situations. "This too-young dating is not uncommon and is often done with parental approval. Yet it is near criminal to subject a tender child to the temptations of maturity."[2]

When these four real-life examples were presented to my institute students, the majority did not think any of these young couples were on dates. Since that time, I have given the examples to many youth groups, and the response is always the same. The majority do not think they are dating. With the last example, I add one extra piece of information. Eddie told me personally that on the way home that night, while his mother and dad were talking in the front seat of the Suburban, he and Laurie were in the back seat making out. After sharing this added detail, I ask the youth again how many think they were on a date. A large number of youth will change their minds and raise their hands in agreement that it was a date after all. I then ask someone who changes their mind why they did so. Without fail, they reply that because they were making out that made it a date. To this I say, "So what you are saying is that if there is making out involved then it is a date, but if there is not, then it isn't a date." Of course they say, "No, that is not what I mean." You can see the look of confusion when they are pushed to define what a date is. The bottom line is that many youth, and obviously some of their parents, can't seem to define what a date is.

Dating is often loosely defined. I have seen fifteen-year-old LDS youth walking through neighborhoods holding hands with parent approval since they aren't on a date. We have young children dropped off as couples at the movies, bowling alleys, swimming pools, and school dances with everyone's assurance that it is not a date. Since that institute class, I have come to the conclusion that the word *date* means whatever the person involved wants it to mean. In fact, I think it has lost any kind of real meaning. I have also learned over the years that none of our active LDS youth *ever* date before age sixteen. Not even one! At least they say it is not a date no matter what they do. How can we possibly follow the prophet regarding dating if we can't even agree on what a date is? And how is it that we have young LDS girls getting pregnant every year who have never been on a date? A date need not necessarily be the formal process of a boy calling a girl, asking her to go somewhere, and picking her up at her home. There are formal dates and casual dates. Both are dates regardless of what we decide to call them.

One freshman girl at the institute class that day expressed her feelings about the definition of a date by saying, "I think what the prophet is telling us is that we should not be pairing off one-on-one with anyone before age sixteen." Although many strongly disagreed with her, I personally think she had given us the exact meaning and the intent of our prophet's counsel. Consider a phrase that is used three times in a section of the *Young Women's Handbook* relating to this topic. "Group social activities should be provided as alternatives to early dating or to activities that encourage teenagers to *pair off*. . . Some youth who do *pair off* exclusively in their early teens are emotionally and socially immature. That is one reason why the church counsels youth to date only after age sixteen and even then not to *pair off* exclusively with one partner."[3]

Why not throw the old traditional word *date* out the window since we can't seem to define it anyway and use *pairing off* in its place. That way we can more easily see through the four examples given above and the hundreds of other situations we could present. Just ask one question: "Are the young boy and girl paired off?" If the answer is yes, then they are on a date.

Some may ask why waiting until age sixteen to date is so important. Most of us have heard comments, such as, "My daughter is very mature for her age." I don't know all the reasons why our youth have been counseled to wait until they are age sixteen, but I am aware of a few very important reasons. Look closely at the following quote and see if you can find three good reasons to wait. "Do not date until you are at least 16 years old. Dating before then can lead to immorality, limit the number of other young people you meet, and deprive you of experiences that will help you choose an eternal partner."[4]

I have discovered over the years that as prophets give counsel, their words can usually be confirmed by research. For example, two Utah family researchers conducted a five-year federally funded study on teenage pregnancy. Terrance D. Olson, professor of family sciences at BYU, and Brent C. Miller of Utah State University researched the moral practices of 2,200 teenagers in New Mexico, Arizona, Utah, and California.

The message in their findings is unmistakable. The earlier youth enter the dating years, the more likely they will be immoral. The optimal time to start dating is age sixteen.

Percent of Youth Having Sexual Relations by High School Graduation
Dating Age; % Having Sex

12; 91%
13; 56%
14; 53%
15; 40%
16; 20% [5]

Some may be comforted by the fact that this study included large numbers of those who were not members of the Church. However,

Bruce H. Monson, another LDS researcher, found that "Over 80 percent of those who reported dating before age sixteen had become sexually involved enough to require a bishop's court held in order for them to repent."[6]

Over the years, I have had the opportunity to work with many outstanding young people. Some stick out more than others in my memory. One youth I remember well is Monica. She played the piano, was a straight A student in high school, and never missed a day of early-morning seminary in four years. She was also very pretty. After graduating from high school, she went away to college, but eventually came back and married a returned missionary from her home area. Shortly after her marriage, she spoke to the young men and young women at a youth standards night. She was the perfect one to speak on that occasion since she had maintained such high standards during her teenage years.

Monica related that as a young girl she made a vow that she would follow the prophets. This is not an easy thing to do when it applies to dating in our very permissive society. She said before she turned sixteen, she was asked out on dates multiple times. She had an easy way out because she could tell them she could not date until age sixteen. The biggest event during her eighth grade year was the end-of-the-year banquet, a formal dinner/dance. Monica was one of only a few girls who attended this special event without a date. Even some of the LDS girls met their "friends" at the banquet, exchanged corsages and boutonnieres, then spent the evening exclusively with each other. It was a very hard night for Monica.

When she turned sixteen, she discovered a problem she had not fully anticipated. Although the phone continued to ring, most of the young men on the other line were not members of the Church and did not have the high moral standards she was seeking. She took a stand and decided to follow the prophets, even though she lived where there were few members and attended a large, predominately nonmember high school.

With time, the phone quit ringing, and the young girl who had decided to follow the prophets' guidelines wound up with very few dates. However, during that time she was able to work on goals such as sewing, cooking, getting good grades, reading the scriptures, and obtaining her Young Womanhood Recognition. She was also one of the high school beauties and an officer for the dance team. Monica did well enough in high school to receive a scholarship to Brigham Young University. After a year, she met a young, good-looking returned missionary. They courted and then began a new life together after their marriage in the temple.

She next told the youth that as she knelt across the altar of the temple, she thought of the eighth-grade banquet and how hard that night was as she looked at the other LDS girls with their "friends." Then came her powerful point. She said, "I want to tell all of you here that when I knelt across the altar at the temple, and looked into the eyes of a worthy priesthood holder and heard 'married for time and eternity,' I knew it was all worth it!"

Following the prophet may seem hard at times, but the rewards in the future are well worth it. Going against the prophet may bring temporary pleasure, but it always brings long-term consequences.

Challenge

We live in a fast-paced world. We have fast food, one-hour photo, instant messaging, Quick Lube, and Jiffy Mart. We watch thirty-minute TV programs that solve complex problems in minutes. Our society plays on the natural-man tendency to be impatient. If we are not very careful, we might allow that same philosophy to enter our children's lives when it comes to dating. It truly is okay to let kids be kids. Pairing off with a member of the opposite sex is something that should wait until the appropriate time. This is especially true since they are being placed in the dangerous situation of potentially losing that which is "most dear and precious above all things, which is chastity and virtue" (Moroni 9:9).

Many parents hesitate to set any dating standards for their children, yet the dangers of not doing so are great. While doing family research, we asked high school students how many dating rules their parents had and how those related to the students' willingness to have premarital sexual relations. Some of the questions follow: Do your parents set an age at which you begin dating? Do your parents require you to double date? Do your parents not allow you to steady date during the high school years? Do your parents set a curfew for you? Do your parents restrict who you are allowed to date? See the following results:

Percent Willing to Have Premarital Sex Based on Number of Dating Rules

Five rules; 33%
Four rules; 43%
Three/two rules; 60%
One rule; 62%
No rules; 75% [7]

The results are clear. The more rules youth have, the less likely they will be to have premarital sex. One of these rules to strictly enforce is the age at which dating begins.

I suggest that you take the time to discuss the meaning of the word *date* with your spouse and family members. Once you have agreed upon a definition that you feel best coincides with the prophet's intent, then take a stand and don't back down. Elder Robert D. Hales has observed, "Sometimes we are afraid of our children—afraid to counsel with them for fear of offending them."[8]

Notes

1 Spencer W. Kimball, "President Kimball Speaks Out on Morality," *Ensign*, November 1980, 96.

2 Spencer W. Kimball, *The Miracle of Forgiveness* (Salt Lake City, UT: Deseret Book, 1969), 223.

3 *Young Women Handbook*, (Salt Lake City, UT: The Church of Jesus Christ of Latter-day Saints, 1988), 20.

4 *For the Strength of Youth*, (Salt Lake City, UT: The Church of Jesus Christ of Latter-day Saints, 2001), 24.

5 *Church News*, September 10, 1988, 16.

6 Unpublished research in author's possession.

7 Unpublished research in author's possession.

8 Robert D. Hales, "With All the Feeling of a Tender Parent: A Message of Hope to Families," *Ensign*, May 2004, 90.

STEADY
DATING

MISTAKE: Allowing children to steady date during the teen years.

"I feel my parents' mistakes were to be too trusting of what teenagers who were taught the gospel would do when placed in tempting situations. Going steady was my downfall. For an LDS youth to fall they must be broken down first. Going steady provides that break down. It starts off innocently but then you rationalize that you really care for the person so showing that physically is OK I don't see how anyone can go steady for over a few months without making mistakes. The temptation is just too strong."

When my nephew Joseph was eight-years-old, he and his large Texas family visited us while we were living in Utah. He was known to have on occasion irritated his sisters and girl cousins. One day during their visit, we went to a water park in Provo for a family activity. As we arrived at the water park, Joseph's older brother, Cory, came up with a little payback plan for his little brother. He made Joseph watch the high school and college kids coming off the tallest chute ride called Sky Breaker. Cory explained how much fun these riders were having. Cory then began pressuring his brother to ride down the chute. Of course, Joseph was afraid to do it—it was a multi-story ride. But before long, all his brothers and cousins were pressuring him to do it. Still, he refused. Finally, Cory found a motivation that helped Joseph give in—the promise of a big box of candy if he would go down the ride.

With a lot of trepidation, Joseph walked with his older brother toward the stairs leading up to the ride. It was apparent that he really did not want to go; however, the candy proved to be too tempting. Of course, everyone below was cheering him on. Someone yelled for him to be sure and spread his legs coming down so he wouldn't go too fast. We watched as Cory negotiated with the high school lifeguard over the height and age regulations. Finally, the guard let him pass, to his siblings' and cousins' delight. I'll never forget the look of absolute terror on Joseph's face when he shot out of the air, about two feet above the chute. He came down at a very high rate of speed, his legs spread wide apart. He seemed to be clawing at the side with his hands, trying to dig in with his feet to slow down, but it didn't help. I have to admit I thought it was funny, knowing the irritation he'd been to all the girls. Hearing him scream a little didn't take away from the fun we were all having at his expense. When he hit the water, he had trouble finding the bottom. One of his older brothers, while laughing uncontrollably, saw his predicament and pulled him out. Once Joseph was out of the water, he walked by us and appeared to be crying. You could tell that he was very upset. Thinking back on that experience now, I realize that there are age and height regulations on those rides for a reason. They are probably not nearly as fun for an eight-year-old as they are for a college student. The ride is probably also a little dangerous for those who can't swim well. However, in this example, Joseph came through fine and was happy again when he got his big box of candy.

Joseph and the rest of us can learn a few valuable lessons from this experience. I have learned through this experience and many others that, in general, when people are pressuring you to do something, it is usually not a good thing. We can also learn that what is fun and appropriate for one age group is not necessarily appropriate and fun for another. These lessons can also be applied to dating practices. What may be totally appropriate for young single adults may not be proper for YM/YW. Is going steady one of those dating practices in society this lesson applies to?

Pressure in Schools

One of my friends studied peer pressure at the middle school level for his dissertation. He found that the number one pressure among junior high students he surveyed was to have a steady boyfriend or girlfriend. Of course, this social pattern is not just in junior high school, but is even stronger during high school grades. Even elementary school children feel the pressure to pair off. This practice has crept into the Church, and many of our youth are involved, even though we have been repeatedly warned of its danger. In one of my son's missionary districts, five of the other nine missionaries had girlfriends who were waiting for them, indicating they were going steady prior to their missions.

Many Get Excited

It is not just young people who get excited about steady relationships; often the whole family encourages it. Perhaps you may have heard comments like these from LDS parents:

"His little girlfriend . . ."
"They are so cute together."
"She is waiting on her missionary."
"She is so good for him."
"He is like another one of our children."

So what's the big deal about steady dating in the teen years, if huge numbers are doing it and many are excited about it? After all, don't many of our youth appear happy when they start going steady? Maybe the problem is that this happiness is usually very short-lived. Unlike courting young single adult couples who are encouraged to marry when they find a compatible mate, steady dating teenagers must remain in limbo for years to come. They can't choose to marry because they are still far too young. No responsible parent would encourage two sixteen-year-olds to get married. And yet, many are fine with their teenagers acting as if they are married, as long as they come home at night and sleep in their own beds. President Spencer W. Kimball commented on this trend of early steady dating, "To speed up the physical process of maturity by early steady dating is like forcing a rose from a bud or eating fruit before it is ripe. . . . Those parents who permit or encourage early social activities are unwittingly begging for sorrows and heartbreaks."[1]

Most of these relationships involving LDS youth start off innocently. With time however, young couples begin to spend more and more time together. Then in all too many cases, those around them notice a countenance change. Soon parents who were so excited about little Junior having a girlfriend try to figure out what is wrong with him. Oftentimes inappropriate behavior has entered the picture because, given enough time, going steady typically leads to immorality.

Reasons Teenagers Should Not Go Steady

In reality, there is nothing cute about children going steady during the high school years. At this age they should be thinking about schoolwork, developing talents, and Eagle Scout and Young Women awards. Many are thinking of love and planning possible future marriages. We're losing many of our brightest stars to this worldly social practice. For those who may wonder why LDS youth should not go steady, the following brief list may be helpful.

Prophets Have Repeatedly Counseled against It

Every prophet in modern times has strongly warned parents and youth about the dangers of steady dating during the teen years. When parents allow their children to steady date, they are going directly against counsel from the prophets. The following are just a few of these warnings:

President Spencer W. Kimball: "A vicious, destructive, social pattern of early steady dating must be changed. . . . It is my considered feeling, having had some experience in interviewing youth, that the change of this one pattern of social activities of our youth would immediately eliminate a majority of the sins of our young folks."[2]

President Ezra Taft Benson: "Avoid steady dating with a young man prior to the time of his mission. . . . If your relationship with him is more casual, then he can make that decision to serve more easily and also can concentrate his full energies on his missionary work instead of the girlfriend back home."[3]

President Howard W. Hunter: "Youth are cautioned against steady dating. . . . I am sure you will agree that it is not a good idea for a young man and a young woman to begin steady dating until they have arrived at the marriageable age."[4]

President Gordon B. Hinckley: "Steady dating at an early age leads so often to tragedy. Studies have shown that the longer a boy and girl date one another, the more likely they are to get into trouble. It is better . . . to date a variety of companions until you are ready to marry."[5]

Social Opportunities Lessened

Youth need exposure and interaction with a variety of people to make friends and to develop social skills. Going steady limits this needed exposure. Many youth who have steady relationships claim it's because of the increase in their social activities. In reality, the opposite often occurs. Instead of having more social activities and fun, most youth who steady date find themselves participating less. This results because the steady partner does not want their partner to go anywhere socially without them. Young couples become tied down and restricted. As one girl said, "Instead of going steady, I wound up staying home steady because of his jealousy." Even when these couples do attend social activities together, there's often little involvement with others.

President Spencer W. Kimball commented, "Dating and especially steady dating in the early teens is most hazardous. It distorts the whole picture of life. It deprives the youth of worthwhile and rich experiences; it limits friendships; it reduces the acquaintance which can be so valuable in selecting a partner for time and eternity."[6]

Family Life Disrupted

When youth go steady, family life is often disrupted. With frequent visits to each other's homes, many family activities and rituals are interrupted. Homework may be neglected and chores not completed.

When they are not together, steady couples are continuously on the phone or instant messaging. Some become almost obsessed with each other. Of course, when a partner fails to make contact, anxiety can escalate. Because of doubt and worry about why they haven't called, many teens become cranky and irritable with family members until the awaited call.

Teenagers who are going steady will spend less and less meaningful time with their own families. Family activities that were once treasured are now frequently avoided. Steady-dating teens, no matter how exciting or exotic the destination, usually dread family vacations. Even when teens do consent to go, they frequently make other family members miserable with constant complaints and the desire to go home. Turmoil in the family is usually not far behind. Some, of course, find reasons why they can't go on family activities and trips, thus putting themselves in an even more dangerous situation.

Insecurity Usually Results

Another reason young couples give to justify going steady is the security it provides. In reality, it is usually just the opposite. Courting during the teen years is filled with doubts. Insecurity would be a better way to describe these relationships. Constant worry often plagues both individuals. They ask themselves, "What if he doesn't call?" or "What if she breaks up with me?" or "Why is she looking at him?" or "Is she prettier than I am?" Teens are usually too young to handle the strong emotions they feel when steady dating.

Life becomes an emotional roller coaster for those involved. Moods and attitudes depend upon day-to-day happenings. Insecurity actually increases in many relationships. Of course, this insecurity is usually justified since most all teen relationships eventually end. These break-ups lead to hurt feelings, damaged self-esteem, and even depression in one or both youth involved. One teenage girl said, "I cried every day for a month after he broke up with me." The experience can actually be quite similar to a divorce, with many of the same emotions erupting.

Others may feel pressure to stay in a relationship. They may want to break off the steady relationship and date other people, but worry about hurting the other person. These immature relationships may take on the characteristics of an addiction. They repeatedly try to break-up, but fail, and then get back together over and over. Fragile emotions are easily damaged when such strong feelings are involved. Insecurity is often the result.

Immorality Increases

Youth who have been taught the gospel of Jesus Christ are usually hard to break down morally. They would seldom be involved in inappropriate behavior with someone they only casually date. Many parents assume that same holds true for those who steady date because they are such good kids and, after all, they have been taught gospel principles. Elder Larry R. Lawrence warned of this danger. He said: "Parents can prevent a lot of heartache by teaching their children to postpone romantic relationships until the time comes when they are ready for marriage. Prematurely pairing off with a boyfriend or girl-friend is dangerous. Becoming a 'couple' creates emotional intimacy, which too often leads to physical intimacy. Satan knows this sequence and uses it to his advantage. He will do whatever he can to keep young men from serving missions and to prevent temple marriages."[7]

There are three things usually needed to break down a good kid's resistance. First, time together, resulting in familiarity with each other; second, exclusive commitment to each other; and third, feeling of love for each other. With time, going steady often provides all of three of these elements.

Once these things are in place, couples want to express their love and commitment to one another. There are many ways a couple can do this. One way is to verbally express their feelings by saying, "I like you" or "I love you." Another way, and much more powerful than the verbal expression, is to physically show how they feel. For example, hugging someone says, "You are my friend." Holding hands says, "I really like you a lot." Kissing says "I have strong feelings for you." Sexual intimacy says, "I love you, and I am committed to you and only you forever." At least that is what these things mean to a well-trained LDS teenager. Some in our society have discovered they can lie about these things for selfish purposes, and others still believe the actions will keep their meaning. If the adversary is going to capture our youth morally, it is more likely to happen when very strong feelings exist between couples. The path to disaster starts when those feelings are expressed in a physi-cal way.

A sister talked to me at BYU Education Week and told me about her sixteen-year-old daughter who was going steady with a seventeen-year-old young man. They had been together for a couple of years. She had asked her daughter how much she cared for her boyfriend, to which the young woman exclaimed, "Mom, I love him so much I would die for him!" It appeared that the mother was very touched by her daughter's love for this young man. As I listened to this mother, I couldn't help but think how much danger this young couple was in. A very blunt warning from President Spencer W. Kimball came to mind. He said, "Mother, where were you when she was dating steady at fourteen? Were you off to work or were you just asleep? Or were you trying to have another young romance for yourself, by proxy? Where were you when your little girl started dating?"[8]

We have a term in our society for children who are in danger. We call them "at risk." When teenagers go steady, they are definitely in the *at risk* category for becoming immoral. Some youth admit steady dating becomes a license for increased sexual intimacy. One young girl expressed it this way, "You get to feel married, and that's dangerous!"

Bruce H. Monson surveyed high school students for his doctoral dissertation and found that 31 percent reported having a current boyfriend or girlfriend. Of those going steady, 94 percent had been involved in making out (or kissing passionately), and more than half of them had transgressed some form of the law of chastity.[9] President Gordon B. Hinckley said, "Steady dating at an early age leads so often to tragedy. Studies have shown that the longer a boy and girl date one another, the more likely they are to get into trouble."[10]

Pressure from friends can be incredibly influential in the lives of our children. However, when that pressure comes from someone they believe they love, it may be very difficult to resist. Our role as parents is to see that our children are not placed in these dangerous positions.

Notes

1   Edward L. Kimball, ed., *Teachings of Spencer W. Kimball* (Salt Lake City, UT: Deseret Book, 1982), 289.

2   Edward L. Kimball, ed., *Teachings of Spencer W. Kimball* (Salt Lake City, UT: Deseret Book, 1982), 287–88.

3   Ezra Taft Benson, "To the Young Women of the Church," *Ensign*, November 1986, 82–83.

4   Clyde J. Williams, ed., *The Teachings of Howard W. Hunter* (Salt Lake City, UT: Deseret Book, 1997), 124.

5   Gordon B. Hinckley, "A Prophet's Counsel and Prayer for Youth," *New Era*, January 2001, 13.

6   Spencer W. Kimball, "President Kimball Speaks Out on Morality," *Ensign*, November 1980, 96.

7   Larry R. Lawrence, "Courageous Parenting," *Ensign*, November 2010, 99.

8   Spencer W. Kimball, *The Miracle of Forgiveness* (Salt Lake City, UT: Deseret Book, 1969), 223.

9   Unpublished research in author's possession.

10 Gordon B. Hinckley, "A Prophet's Counsel and Prayer for Youth," *New Era*, January 2001, 13.

INTIMACY

MISTAKE: Failure to teach family members the importance and proper role of intimacy.

"My parents never mentioned the word sex *in our home and never taught me one thing about it. Even when I was preparing for marriage, they never mentioned it once. I have talked with lots of roommates and many of them have expressed the same concern. I don't know where LDS parents expect their children to get correct information. I was forced to decipher on my own between what popular culture teaches and the Church doctrine regarding issues of morality. Luckily, I escaped some of the dangerous pitfalls. However, many of my close friends (and brothers and sisters) did not."*

Several summers ago while visiting cousins in Utah, it was suggested that we drive up to eastern Idaho for the weekend to visit other relatives. After looking at our time schedule and other options, we finally decided not to make the trip. As we watched the news the next evening, we were very thankful we'd made that decision. The Teton Dam broke that day, destroying millions of dollars in property and causing untold misery in the very area we would have visited.

Functioning the way they are intended, dams bring needed water to the farms below. Crops receive the required water and grow to maturity. These crops are then sold at the market, bringing nourishment to all who partake. However, when the Teton Dam collapsed, a huge wall of water came down, destroying everything in its path. Dams are a lot like the sexual drives humans have been given. When used as God intended, they enable love to grow and flourish. But if used at the wrong time, these same drives can destroy and bring misery to those involved.

The youth today face sexual decisions and temptations that their ancestors and parents never had to deal with. The average youth today sees more sexual stimuli per year than his grandparents saw in a lifetime. Our society bombards them with the vicious lie that immorality is attractive and without consequences. Henry Bowman said, "When all is said and done, there is nothing gained from pre-marital adventure except immediate pleasure, and that at tremendous risk and exorbitant cost. No really intelligent person will burn a cathedral to fry an egg, even to satisfy a ravenous appetite."[1]

Are we countering this influence by teaching the beauty of chastity? Can we really expect young people to say "no" to premarital sex if the benefits of virtue and the consequences of immorality are never even introduced to them? How many youth will fall before parents wake up and fulfill their responsibilities to teach righteous sex education in the home? Our children *will* get a sex education. The only concern is where they will obtain their information. We must teach the need for chastity before society and peers instill permissive sexual values in the minds of our children.

Teach Chastity

It is our responsibility as parents to teach our children about chastity and the consequences of immorality. Youth must be taught that sexual relations are so beautiful and so special that they are worth waiting for. A loving Heavenly Father has chosen sacred intimacy as the way of bringing his spirit children into the world. He is the creator. It is his plan. No true saint would view proper sexual intimacy between a married couple as something base. If mortals were stripped of their desire for intimacy, the human race would very quickly die out and God's purposes would be defeated. The main purpose of earth life is that husbands and wives "be one flesh, and all this that the earth might answer the end of its creation" (D&C 49:16). Since God is the author of this plan, he sets the rules for its use. The rules are that sexual intimacy is appropriate only within the bonds of marriage. As parents, it is our duty to teach this.

President Ezra Taft Benson taught, "The home is the teaching situation [for sex education]. Every father should talk to his son, every mother to her daughter. Then it would leave them totally without excuse should they ignore the counsel they have received."[2]

When to Begin

Parents should not wait for their children to ask all the questions regarding morality. There are things a child should know at each stage in life. It is our responsibility to provide this teaching. A *Church News* editorial states the Church's position on this subject.

> When their playmates tempt them, when they see similar temptation on the screen and in books and magazines, too many of these children, as yet undeveloped mentally and spiritually, say to themselves, "Why not?"
>
> They need to be told why not. They need to be told by their parents why not. They need to be told by older brothers and sisters who are sensible the why not of such conduct.
>
> So parents: Whether you think they need it or not, you in the privacy of your own home—you in your confidential talks with your children—TEACH CHASTITY.
>
> Some youngsters, in their early teens especially, even from the best of families, when under the pressure of their peers may yield. Parents owe it to their children to build fortifications against such conduct, and let them know the seriousness of it.[3]

The Lord's counsel, through His latter-day prophets, is for parents to teach virtue in the home and teach it early in our children's lives. The topic of intimacy may be more difficult to discuss if our children are older when the subject is first approached. President Spencer W. Kimball taught this same principle, "Our children must be taught from infancy that sex outside of proper marriage is an abomination in the eyes of the Lord and that boys and girls must keep themselves clean and unspotted from the world and free from all sexual impurity. They must learn that there must never be sexual improprieties of any kind in the premarriage days and that every boy and girl should bring to the marriage altar a clean body and an unpolluted mind."[4]

Seriousness of Sex Outside of Marriage

Gospel truths do not change over the years. Chastity and virtue have not suddenly become important. These are eternal standards. President Gordon B. Hinckley said, "Shun immorality. It will blight your life if you indulge in it. It will destroy your self-respect. It will rob you of pleasant opportunities and make you unworthy of the companionship of lovely young women."[5]

How many parents actually understand how essential chastity and virtue are to happiness? Prophets and apostles, from Adam to our day, always considered morality more important than life itself. Moroni taught, "And after depriving them of that which was *most dear and precious above all things,* which is chastity and virtue . . ." (Moroni 9:9). Many youth fail to realize the seriousness of sex outside marriage. Perhaps even in the Church, there are those who have become complacent.

Sex Education in the Schools

The public school is not the place for youth to learn about the sacred nature of sex. In an environment that prohibits any show of religious belief, we cannot expect the school to teach youth the magnitude of the law of chastity. After many years of public sex education, teen pregnancies are astronomical and STDs are an epidemic among our youth. What we need is not more sex education in the schools. We need more abstinence education in the homes.

The First Presidency warned parents not to turn over their responsibility in this area. "We believe that serious hazards are involved in entrusting to the schools the teaching of this vital and important subject to our children. This responsibility cannot wisely be left to society, nor the schools; nor can the responsibility be shifted to the Church. It is the responsibility of parents to see that they fully perform their duty in this respect."[6] Yet in many cases this is not happening. Many parents choose to neglect this delicate topic and inadvertently turn it over to the schools, mistakenly feeling it would be easier for children to hear this information from a stranger.

The neglect of parents to teach sex education is glaring. In a survey conducted with American youth, we sought to determine the sources of high school students' first sexual information. The following sources were found and are ranked in order:

Source of First Sexual Information; %

Teachers; 10%
Parents; 20%
Media (TV, Movies); 21%
Peers/Siblings; 49%[7]

But something doesn't quite make sense. If friends are the number one source for youth receiving sexual information, where are these friends receiving it? In reality, youth have been bombarded with sexual facts since they were born, mainly from our sex-saturated culture. We also compared the students' sources of first sexual information with their willingness to have premarital sexual relations. The following was found.

Source of First Sexual Information; % Willing to Have Premarital Sex

Parents; 37%
Teachers; 61%
Peers/Siblings; 68%
Media (TV, Movies); 82%[8]

The message is very clear from these numbers. The best source of sexual information is from the parents, while the media proves to be the worst possible source. Also note that just because parents talk to their children about sex, it does not mean they teach them correct principles. In our study, we found that only 54 percent of parents of high school students actually taught them that sex outside of marriage was wrong. Another 24 percent of the youth said their parents taught them nothing about sex. Finally, 22 percent of these students had been taught by their parents to use birth control methods *if* they had sex outside of marriage.[9]

Even though it is much better to start from the cradle teaching virtue, it is never too late to start. Why do not more parents do not talk to their youth about sexuality if it is so important? Here are some common reasons for this neglect.

Too Embarrassed

The discussion of sex is difficult for many parents. Some fail to talk to their children because they feel uncomfortable and embarrassed. Unfortunately, children may pick up on their hesitancy and develop an improper attitude about sex.

I'm sure that the adversary loves parents who fail to teach their families about this crucial subject. He wants to do the teaching in this area through his emissaries. The forces of evil are not the least bit embarrassed or shy about teaching our children about sex. These loathsome teachings are spread with boldness in sex education classes, movie theaters, advertisements, television programming, and print.

Unhealthy Views

Some parents have an unhealthy view of sex themselves. If they do discuss sex with their children, the only messages they give are negative ones. A young man was heard to say, "All I ever hear about sex from parents and teachers is that it's sinful. Isn't there something positive that can be said?"

It is important that we impress upon these young minds the beautiful and eternal nature of their sexuality. As parents, we should always remember that our mortal bodies are given to us by a loving Heavenly Father for a divine purpose. President Gordon B. Hinckley said, "Let parents teach their children the sanctity of sex, that the gift of creating life is sacred, that the impulses that burn within us can be and must be disciplined and restrained if there is to be happiness and peace and goodness."[10]

When our Heavenly Father established the marriage bond, he also ordained the sexual union between husband and wife as the means by which they can express one of the highest forms of love. Through this love, he sends his spirit children to earth. We become partners with God himself in this most sacred process. Only outside the marriage covenant is the sexual union inappropriate. We should teach youth that it is honorable and sanctified within marriage.

Uninformed

During my wife's first pregnancy, we attended several childbirth classes. The instructor told us some of the questions she had encountered during her years teaching this class. One woman from a small town asked when her "belly button" would open up, so the baby could be delivered. The instructor, of course, thought she was kidding. Unfortunately, she was not. Her mother had given the young woman this silly notion years before and had never corrected it.

President Hugh B. Brown warned, "Many marriages have been wrecked on the dangerous rocks of ignorant and debased sex behavior, both before and after marriage. Gross ignorance on the part of newly-weds, on the subject of the proper place and functioning of sex, results in much unhappiness and many broken homes."[11]

Knowledge May Lead to Experimentation

An old saying states, "Keep them ignorant, and they won't get into trouble." In our day, if loving parents teach youth, the opposite appears to be true. Those who are uninformed or who have been given false or misleading sex information are more likely to get into trouble with sexual experimentation. Research indicates, "Discussion of sexuality in the home seems to be related to the postponement of sexual activity. . . . Specifically, as the number of sex topics discussed by parents increased, the likelihood for engaging in intercourse decreased."[12]

Too Late

Several years ago, a father told me he took his high school freshman on a little trip to teach his son about the facts of life. This father found he was several years too late for this talk. According to research, the average child in our day learns about sexuality at about nine and a half years old. If parents wait for the big "birds and bees" talk, the child may already know more than the parent about the subject—or at least they think they know more, which is equally as dangerous. Human intimacy is discussed so openly in today's society that youth cannot avoid hearing about it, even at very young ages. Most of what they hear will instruct them in the world's view of sexuality. The home is the place to teach the Lord's plan for this sacred power.

Teach Children to Be Chaste

Teaching morality requires a reverence for the subject, along with deep spirituality. President Boyd K. Packer states, "If there is one essential ingredient for the teaching of moral and spiritual values . . . it is to have the Spirit of the Lord with us as we teach."[13] Like the name of Deity, we should not discuss sexuality in a casual manner but rather at appropriate times with a prayerful attitude.

Sexual facts or anatomy lessons may be important, but not nearly important as the righteous teaching of chastity. We have been counseled to "be cautious to keep your own bodies and intimate sexual relations private. . . . They may feel threatened if a parent becomes too descriptive. Children usually learn subtly and cumulatively from ordinary daily contact. There is much good that comes from drawing a veil between the children and yourself regarding private, intimate life."[14]

Steps Leading to Immorality

Scientists know that there is a simple formula that produces fire: fuel + heat + oxygen = fire. Family experts also know some simple formulas that can equal immorality. The Commitment Formula says steady dating + single dating + time = immorality. The Physical Formula says handholding + kissing + necking + petting = immorality. It is essential to teach that some of the steps leading up to full sexual relations are, in themselves, grave sins.

Modesty

Over the past few decades, much of the fashion in our society has declined in modesty. Immodesty is paraded constantly before our family's eyes. It has become the norm for the world, and many of our own youth are tempted to follow these worldly fashions. Some families fail to establish rules and guidelines regarding dress and grooming. Youth leaders are subsequently forced to fight the battle at Church-sponsored activities. Immodesty often starts when children are young and becomes more extreme as they become teenagers. For many, the seeds of immorality are planted early in life because of immodesty in dress.

Research has demonstrated over the years that the way we dress actually affects our behavior. If a person dresses like a Latter-day Saint, he or she will be more likely to act like a Saint. Of course, the opposite is also true. Those who feel they are the most sexually and socially attractive report the highest levels of sexual permissiveness. In other words, those who dress to emphasize their sexual side often find themselves involved in behavior that matches their clothing. President Kimball warns, "I am positive that the clothes we wear can be a tremendous factor in the gradual breakdown of our love of virtue, our steadfastness in chastity."[15] And in our day Sister Elaine Dalton said, "Virtue encompasses modesty—in thought, language, dress, and demeanor. And modesty is the foundation stone of chastity."[16]

Handholding

Once youth begin to pair off, handholding is very common even in casual relationships. Though handholding alone can be very innocent, it can signal the beginning of a physical relationship. It is usually the first of many steps in the path leading to sexual relations. The first time you hold the hand of a person, you say to that person, "I like you!" A stronger bond forms at that point, but it soon loses its thrill, and a person is tempted to ask, "What's next?"

Kissing

Kissing usually comes after handholding and affectionate hugs. President Kimball remarks,

> Kissing has been prostituted and has degenerated to develop and express lust instead of affection, honor, and admiration. To kiss in casual dating is asking for trouble. What do kisses mean when given out like pretzels and robbed of sacredness? . . . [Doing so is] an abomination and stirs passions to the eventual loss of virtue. Even if timely courtship justifies the kiss it should be a clean, decent, sexless one.[17]

Young people should be taught that kissing is sacred. It should be saved for the proper time, place, and the right person. Almost without fail, the passion that eventually leads to immorality began with inappropriate kissing. Once youth begin kissing, they usually enjoy the pleasure it brings and want to continue. Kissing is not something to toy around with, no matter what the world teaches. It can progress to more serious or immoral behavior and is similar to playing Russian roulette with morality. When kissing has lost its glamour, the tendency is to ask, "What's next?"

Necking

The next step down the path toward immorality is necking. This is an improper relationship and considered a sin by the prophets. Many parents have been confused about the definition of necking. Is it just kissing? Is it fondling? President Spencer W. Kimball helped explain this with these words, "Instead of remaining in the field of simple expressions of affection, some have turned themselves loose to fondling, often called 'necking,' with its intimate contacts and its passionate kissing."[18]

Petting

Light petting is defined as touching, handling, or fondling the body of a member of the opposite sex above the waist. Heavy petting is touching, handling, or fondling the body or private parts of a member of the opposite sex below the waist.

Imagine yourself for a moment craving a banana split after a hard day. You go to the freezer and take out your favorite flavor of ice cream. You then open the refrigerator and take out bananas, pineapple topping, chocolate syrup, whipped topping, cherries, and nuts to build an enormous banana split. After you scoop a heaping portion onto our spoon and bring it to your mouth, you remember that you are on a diet. What would you do at this point? This is similar to the situation our youth find themselves in when they become involved in handholding, kissing, necking, and petting. As they approach the final steps, they remember they were told to be on a diet, avoiding sexual relations before marriage. It takes extreme willpower to back away from the last step in the chain.

When something loses its glamour, we search for more. With each step, the tendency is to ask, "What's next?" Once the relationship has gone to the petting stage, it is easy to let down the final defense and jump to the final step. President Gordon B. Hinckley said, "Petting is simply a step on the road to sexual transgression or immorality. In fact, it is transgression. It is the seeking of physical satisfaction through the invited or forced involvement of another. By the standards of the Church it is unholy, unrighteous, and evil. . . . Petting frequently leads to the most serious kind of immorality. . . . It has done so with thousands."[19]

Fornication

Once a relationship reaches the final stage, a grievous sin has been committed. The fire has been ignited, and it is unnatural to halt the process. Fornication is sexual intercourse between two unmarried people. Sex before marriage is a damning sin. How serious is this sin? Alma said to his errant son Corianton, "Know ye not, my son, that these things are an abomination in the sight of the Lord; yea, most abominable above all sins save it be the shedding of innocent blood or denying the Holy Ghost?" (Alma 39:5).

It is important to remember that immorality does not usually happen overnight. President Spencer W. Kimball declared,

> Immorality does not begin in adultery or perversion. It begins with little indiscretions like sex thoughts, sex discussions, passionate kissing, petting, and such, growing with every exercise. The small indiscretion seems powerless compared to the sturdy body, the strong mind, the sweet spirit of youth who give way to the first temptation. But soon the strong has become weak, the master the slave, spiritual growth curtailed. But if the first unrighteous act is never given root, the tree will grow to beautiful maturity, and the youthful life will grow toward God, our Father.[20]

Teach Children the Rewards of Virtue

When we avoid the consequence of breaking God's moral law, we enjoy peace of conscience, greater family trust, and the influence of the Holy Ghost. We experience the joy of offering our companion the priceless gift of purity. President N. Eldon Tanner comments on the great rewards of virtue, "What a beautiful and glorious thing it is for a young couple to be able to face each other over the altar in the temple of God, knowing they have kept themselves clean and pure, that they are building their own home on a foundation of mutual trust and respect."[21]

Our world teaches that problems can be solved almost instantly. It takes merely fifteen to thirty seconds to resolve any problem on a TV commercial. Relationships are fully developed during the course of a sixty-minute program. We are accustomed to everything occurring in a very short time span. We must teach youth that despite what the world teaches, the importance and value of waiting for intimacy until marriage is inestimable.

An elderly sister spoke to a seminary class I once taught. She told of a Christmas long ago when she was a small girl, where the gifts were wrapped and kept in her parents' bedroom. One night her parents went out and left her and her sister at home. The last thing they told the girls was not to go into their bedroom. But the temptation was too great for this youngster. She told her sister, "Let's just look in the door." That was the first step. Then it was, "Let's just shake the box. . . . Let's just peek inside. . . . Oh my, a doll! . . . Let's just play with it for a little while." After the girls had played dolls for a while, they wrapped the presents back up. They felt very guilty and worried that their parents would discover what they had done. I'll never forget what she said at the end of the story: "You know, Christmas just wasn't very fun that year!"

I have since thought how closely that story relates to our Heavenly Father's plan for human intimacy. If our children will be patient and wait until the proper time, they will be able to receive beautiful presents, free from guilt and worry. If not, then they can be consumed by desire. Elder Neal A. Maxwell said,

> Those who mock the traditional moral values should heed this lesson of history from the Durants: "A youth boiling with hormones will wonder why he should not give full freedom to his sexual desires; and if he is unchecked by custom, morals, or laws, he may ruin his life before he matures sufficiently to understand that sex is a river of fire that must be banked and cooled by a hundred restraints if it is not to consume both the individual and the group."[22]

Notes

1 Henry A. Bowman, cited by Hugh B. Brown in "Purity is Power," Brigham Young University Speeches, Sept. 30, 1962), 10–11.

2 Ezra Taft Benson, in Conference Report, 1974, 4.

3 Editorial, *Church News*, October 21, 1978, 12.

4 Spencer W. Kimball, in Area Conference Report, August 1974, 10.

5 Gordon B. Hinckley, in Conference Report, October 1999, 71.

6 First Presidency, as quoted in "Policies and Procedures," *New Era*, November 1971, 47

7 Randal A. Wright, "Family, Religious, Peer and Media Influence on Adolescence Willingness to Have Premarital Sex" (PhD dissertation), Brigham Young University, 1995, 115.

8 Ibid.

9 Ibid.

10 Gordon B. Hinckley, *Teachings of Gordon B. Hinckley* (Salt Lake City, UT: Deseret Book, 1997), 49.

11 Hugh B. Brown, *You and Your Marriage* (Salt Lake City, UT: Publishers Press, 1960), 73.

12 Tommie J. Hamner and Pauline H. Turner, *Parenting in Contemporary Society* (Upper Saddle River, NJ: Prentice Hall, 1985), 78.

13 Boyd K. Packer, *Teach Ye Diligently* (Salt Lake City, UT: Deseret Book, 1975), 272.

14 *A Parent's Guide*, (Salt Lake City, UT: The Church of Jesus Christ of Latter-day Saints, 1985), 30.

15 Spencer W. Kimball, *Faith Precedes the Miracle* (Salt Lake City, UT: Deseret Book, 1972), 163, 168.

16 Elaine S. Dalton, "Stay on the Path," *Ensign*, May 2007, 112–13.

17 Spencer W. Kimball, "Chastity, Its Price Above Rubies," radio talk to youth, February 1960.

18 Spencer W. Kimball, "President Kimball Speaks Out on Morality," *Ensign*, November 1980, 95–96.

19 Gordon B. Hinckley, *Teachings of Gordon B. Hinckley* (Salt Lake City, UT: Deseret Book, 1997), 47.

20 Spencer W. Kimball, "President Kimball Speaks Out on Morality," *Ensign*, November 1980, 95–96.

21 N. Eldon Tanner, "The Glory of Cleanliness," *Ensign*, July 1975, 3.

22 Will and Ariel Durant, *The Lessons of History* (New York, NY: Simon & Schuster, 1968), 35–36.

COMMUNICATION

MISTAKE: Failure to keep communication lines open with children.

"I guess our problem was communication, communication, and communication. I often felt very alone with my problems and didn't have anyone to confide in. I think all us kids kept everything to ourselves and hid our struggles. We never felt like we could discuss anything with our parents, so we sought the information and advice from other sources."

M any years ago, I called my wife from work to give her a quick message. Our nine-year-old daughter, Naomi, answered the phone. I immediately asked to talk to her mom. Before obeying, she asked me two penetrating questions: "Why don't you ever want to talk to me?" I tried to defend myself by saying that I did want to talk to her, but was just in a big hurry. Her next question was, "Why are you always in a hurry?" I had no good answer for that question.

Why are we in such a hurry that we don't have time to stop and talk to our children? We need to spend more time in meaningful conversation with our children. Some feel that they don't have the skills to communicate effectively with their children, but President Thomas S. Monson stated, "The ability to communicate is not something we are born with. We have to learn it and earn it."[1]

The following is an excerpt from one of my journal entries while serving as a bishop. The entry illustrates a need our children have.

We got a new family into the ward two weeks ago—a father and his four little boys. One of the boys is named Isaac, and he participated in the primary program today. He is a cute little boy with thick glasses and a big cowlick. His parents had only been divorced a few weeks before they moved in. During the primary program I noticed that someone was singing very loudly. At first I couldn't tell who it was, but soon figured out that it was our new boy, Isaac. Before long, everyone in the audience had big smiles on their faces as they listened to this young boy sing at the top of his lungs. The longer the program went, the louder and more expressive he became. Soon the smiles turned to laughter, watching this young man giving it everything he had. It was as if he had the solo part and the rest of the primary was his backup singers. Sitting on the stand, I could see his red-faced father in the very back of the chapel. After the program, Isaac's dad came onto the stage. I wondered what he would say to his son. When he got to his son, I heard him say, "Isaac, why were you singing so loud?" He replied, "Dad you were sitting at the back of the church, and I wanted you to hear me sing!" A huge grin came over the father, and he hugged his son. I think this young man expressed what many of our children desperately want—and that is to be heard.

Through the years, several surveys and research projects have been undertaken to determine the communication patterns in teenagers' homes. In a survey conducted during my graduate degree, I asked a large group of teenagers if they felt close enough to their parents, while growing up, to talk to them openly. The vast majority said they could not. Many felt that they would be judged, get a lecture, or be rejected if their parents were taken into their confidence.

How often were you able to talk openly with your parents growing up?

Father; Mother
Never 25%; 11%
Rarely 27%; 15%
Usually 32%; 34%
Always 16%; 40%[2]

What a sad commentary that only sixteen percent of high school students felt they could always talk to their fathers openly, and only forty percent with their mothers. An even more alarming finding in the survey was that only eleven percent of all high school respondents felt they could always talk openly with both their mothers and fathers. If youth cannot communicate with their parents, in many cases, they turn to their peers to confide their feelings and ask questions without criticism. Another study found that "fathers spend around eight minutes a day talking to their children, while working mothers spend around eleven minutes. Even stay-at-home mothers do not talk to their children for more than thirty minutes a day."[3] Youth are going to go to someone, somewhere, to be listened to, and we should see that we are that someone and our home is that somewhere.

The Consequence of Sin

When communication lines are down, serious consequences always occur. President Spencer W. Kimball points out one tremendous cost of failure to communicate. He said, "Sin comes when communication lines are down—it always does, sooner or later."[4] There are many sins associated with this failure to communicate, but perhaps the most frightening is shared by Elder Robert L. Backman, who said, "As I interview young men who have broken God's moral law, I ask myself how many of them could have been spared that soul-shattering experience if they had had open communication and consistent moral teaching from their fathers."[5] We found that 86 percent of high school youth who felt they could not talk with either their mother or their father would be willing to have premarital sexual relations.[6]

There are multiple reasons for communication problems between parents and their children. One reason that youth and parents have a hard time communicating is because of their past history. Perhaps there have been altercations in the past that have damaged relationships and led to feelings of resentment. President Gordon B. Hinckley said, "Love is the very essence of family life. Why is it that the children we love become so frequently the targets of our harsh words? . . . 'There is beauty all around,' only when there's love at home."[7] We should speak with the same words of kindness to our children as we would when speaking to our best friends. Some would never think of talking to friends the way they talk to their own children.

Perhaps some have become so busy that good communication

never really occurs with their children. President Kimball, who was very direct and bold, asked these penetrating questions of parents who may have fallen into this trap:

> Mothers, are you so busy with social life, [with projects], with clubs, with working out of the home, or with housework, that you have not time to sit down and talk to your little girls and tell them the things they should know when they are nine, and ten, and eleven, and older? Can you be frank and loving to them so that they in turn can be frank in giving you their confidences?
>
> And you fathers, are you so busy making a living, playing golf, bowling, hunting, that you do not have time to talk to your boys and hold them close to you and win their confidence? Or do you brush them off, so that they dare not come and talk about these things with you?[8]

Communication means to impart, to convey, to make known. It involves an interchange of thoughts, opinions, facts, and feelings. Too often conversations between parents and youth are not communication at all, but one-way directions or commands. Passing by a messy bedroom and yelling, "How many times have I told you to clean your room?" is not an interchange of thoughts. Youth need to know that their parents will carefully listen to them. If we, as parents, respond with a "go away, don't bother me now" attitude, they will go elsewhere or they will quit giving important messages.

Inattentive parents give children one of the greatest insults of all—that of acting as if the person does not exist. Many may not even be aware they are sending the "go away" signals to family members. As powerful as verbal language is, body language can be as forceful in getting a message across. Elder Lionel Kendrick said, "Our communications reflect in our countenance. Therefore, we must be careful not only what we communicate, but also how we do so. Souls can be strengthened or shattered by the message and the manner in which we communicate."[9]

There is much we tell our youth by body posture, eye contact (or lack thereof), tone of voice, and expressions. Without saying a word, people will know we are interested in what they say and that we want to listen, or that we'd rather be doing something else. How many times have you observed someone looking at their watch or taking steps backwards as they talk? Their message is "I need to be going."

A wise man by the name of Epictetus observed, "Nature has given man one tongue, but two ears, that we may hear from others twice as much as we speak." Hearing is not the problem most of us have. It is estimated we hear a thousand times more words than we read and spend almost as much time hearing messages as we do reading, writing, and speaking combined. You would think with all this practice that all of us would be great listeners. Few people, however, master the art of effective listening.

One of the most frequent complaints from children today is their parents simply do not listen to their ideas, accept their opinions as relevant, or try to understand their feelings and points of view. An old Indian proverb says, "Listen or thy tongue will keep thee deaf." Failure to listen with understanding and proper attention is one of the biggest roadblocks to communication. Most of us have experienced times when we felt no one was listening. Few things are more frustrating and humiliating than to be talking to someone and know that they are not listening to you. Youth whose parents do not know how to effectively listen would have similar feelings as Lord Chesterfield: "I would rather be in company with a dead man, than with an absent one; for if the dead man gives me no pleasure, at least he shows me no contempt; whereas, the absent man, silently indeed, but very plainly, tells me that he does not think me worth his attention."[10] Perhaps the psalmist was describing these parents when he wrote, "They have ears, but they hear not" (Psalm 135:17).

Inattentive parents are a contributing factor of sexually active youth. Young people are crying out for attention from their parents. If we, as parents, fail to listen to our children, they will seek peers who will. We must spend quality time with our children, before friends and society begin to pressure them. Respect for a person often begins with listening to them. If a person feels that they are being listened to, they feel respected. This helps boost self-image and helps protect them from worldly influences.

Our family's happiness is closely related to our ability to effectively hear family members as they communicate their thoughts, desires, wishes, and feelings. Listening is not a passive exercise, but a concentrated effort.

Be Willing to Listen

Children have a need to be heard and the freedom to express their thoughts and feelings. Nikki Alley's experience reflects this need:

> I teach the four-year-old Primary class and have a little boy in my class who volunteers every week to say the prayer. Last week, he thanked Heavenly Father for not letting us talk to strangers, then he thanked Him for the alphabet, and proceeded to bless the letters A, B, C, through Z, then he thanked Heavenly Father for numbers and blessed the numbers 1–20, then he thanked Him for colors and blessed 10 different colors. I wondered if I should stop him. I didn't mind the prayer's length, but I worried about his classmates getting impatient. When I looked around the other children had their eyes closed and were listening intently, so I just let him keep going. I was glad I did because he finished by saying, "And thank you for Sister Alley because she doesn't make me stop praying like my mom does."[11]

Always Answer Questions

Many years ago, Elder Richard L. Evans said something that had a great impact on me.

> And one of our urgent opportunities is to respond to a child when he earnestly asks—remembering that they don't always ask, that they aren't always teachable, that they won't always listen. And often we have to take them on their terms, at their times, and not always on our terms, and at our times. But if we respond to them with sincere attention and sincere concern, they will likely continue to come to us and ask. And if they find they can trust us with their trivial questions, they may later trust us with the more weighty ones.[12]

When children are small, they constantly ask questions and tell parents to come see. How we handle them at this young age may well determine our future relationship with the child. We must be willing to listen to them when they are ready to talk. We should respectively try to answer every question, no matter how trivial or silly it may seem. If we don't have the answer, we should try to find it. This practice takes time, patience, and sacrifice but will pay off and be a great protection for our children when they feel comfortable asking sensitive questions. It is not a coincidence that speech is widely used as a treatment by social workers, psychiatrists, counselors, and other family specialists in helping solve personal and family problems. We can provide opportunities for our children to communicate in our own homes and enjoy the love and security that follows. Children want the attention now, and if we don't give it, they may quit asking. When they become teenagers, they may not come to us for counsel and friendship.

Avoid Judgment

One of the major barriers that prevent people from communicating deeply with others is the fear of a negative reaction and judgment of the listener. Many words portray the tendency to judge and criticize. Some include ridicule, condemn, harsh judgment, threaten, lecture, analyze, disagree, warn, order, preach, withdraw, blame, mock, putdown, insult, sarcasm, silence, pouting, rubbing-in, destructive teasing, and laughing at mistakes. Isn't it interesting how many ways there are to judge and put people down? Maybe James realized this when he said, "If any man among you seem to be religious, and bridleth not his tongue, but deceiveth his own heart, this man's religion is vain" (James 1:26).

Only when there is assurance of understanding and complete lack of judgment will youth feel safe to let down their guard and really communicate. Let's think back on the conversations we have had with our family during the past week. Were there times when our words, expressions, or the tone of our voice were used to embarrass, accuse, or belittle? How did it make our children feel? Elder Marvin J. Ashton, in speaking of good family communication, gave this counsel: "Try to be understanding and not critical. Don't display shock, alarm, or disgust with others' comments or observations. Don't react violently. Work within the framework of a person's free agency. Convey the bright and optimistic approach. There is hope. There is a way back. There is a possibility for better understanding."[13]

Plan Talk Time

We all have the same number of hours in a day, therefore we must plan time to listen to our children. President Ezra Taft Benson counseled, "Take time to be a real friend to your children. Listen to your children, really listen. Talk with them, laugh and joke with them, sing with them, cry with them, hug them, honestly praise them. Yes, regularly spend unused one-one-one time with each child. Be a real friend to your children."[14]

One excellent way to spend time with your children is to interview them on a regular basis. This should be a friendly open discussion, sitting down to discuss their concerns, problems, and feelings. A good day could be the first Sunday of every month.

Keep Confidences

One of the quickest ways to lose someone's trust is to share their confidences with others. We need to let our children know that they can talk to us without any fear of our telling others. A person will usually not disclose their innermost feelings if they don't feel it will be kept confidential. When we build relationships on trust and understanding, a problem that has taken on mountainous proportions will often be brought back down to a molehill perspective.

Love Demonstrated

When there is effective communication in the home, strong bonds are developed. Elder William R. Bradford stated, "Within each of us there is an intense need to feel that we belong. This feeling of unity and togetherness comes through the warmth of a smile, a handshake, or a hug, through laughter and unspoken demonstrations of love. It comes in the quiet, reverent moments of soft conversation and in listening."[15]

The following experience was shared by a friend and former institute director:

> In the early 1970s, my Church Education assignment caused me to travel a great deal. In order to continue building relationships with my children, I would often take one of them with me in my travels. On one such occasion my six-year-old, Mike, and I traveled from Springfield, Missouri to Fort Smith, Arkansas. We talked about school and related topics as we drove along the interstate. I decided it would be a good time to teach my son about the creation of life. I pondered on the understanding he had about this sacred subject.
>
> I decided to test his knowledge and try to teach him some valuable

lessons of life. I said, "Mike, have you noticed there is a difference between boys and girls?" After thinking about it for a while, he said, "Yes, Dad. Girls are pretty and boys are ugly!" Though I was tempted to chuckle, I remained serious, and tended to somewhat agree with him. I asked if he realized what it meant for his mother to be pregnant. "Yes, Dad. It means she is going to have another baby!" I asked, "Well son, do you have any questions about that?" He thought for a moment then asked, "Does everything Mom eats go down and hit the baby on top of the head?" Again, I had to restrain my feelings to laugh. I explained that the baby was carried in a special place so that the food did not hit him in the head.

For the next 45 minutes, we had a most interesting talk as we traveled toward our destination. Finally, as the conversation waned, I told my son how much I had enjoyed our talk together. Then being desirous to recap this experience, I asked, "Mike, what did you learn from our discussion today?" I was anxious to hear him repeat some of the great knowledge I had imparted to him. He pondered for some time, then stood up in the seat of our old Volkswagen. He stepped over the console, put his arms around my neck and said, "I learned I love my Dad!"[16]

This experience demonstrates the truth of a principle taught by Elder Charles A. Didier, who said, "Language is of divine origin. Some may know this but do not realize its implications in their daily family life. Love at home starts with loving language."[17]

Notes

1 Thomas S. Monson, *Improvement Era*, February, 1969, 4.

2 Unpublished research in author's possession.

3 Puja Pednekar, "Parents Too Busy to Talk to Their Kids," *DNA*, April 25, 2012.

4 Spencer W. Kimball, in Conference Report, April 1972, 29.

5 Robert L. Backman, "What the Lord Requires of Fathers," *Ensign* September 1981, 8.

6 Unpublished research in author's possession.

7 Gordon B. Hinckley, "Let Love Be the Lodestar of Your Life," *Ensign*, May 1989, 67.

8 Spencer W. Kimball, *Miracle of Forgiveness* (Salt Lake City, UT: Deseret Book, 1969), 258.

9 L. Lionel Kendrick, "Christlike Communications," *Ensign*, November 1988, 23.

10 Lord Chesterfield, *Letters*, September 22, 1749.

11 Nikki Alley, "On the Bright Side," *Church News*, January 8, 2000, 2.

12 Richard L. Evans, Thoughts for One Hundred Days, Vol. 5 (Salt Lake City, UT: Publishers Press, 1970), 114–15.

13 Marvin J. Ashton, "Family Communications," *Ensign*, May 1976, 52.

14 Ezra Taft Benson, "Parents' Fireside," Salt Lake City, UT, February 22, 1987.

15 William R. Bradford, "Selfless Service," *Ensign*, November 1987, 75.

16 Personal correspondence in author's possession.

17 Charles A. Didier, in Conference Report, October 1975, 36.

SELF-WORTH

MISTAKE: Failure to build a positive self-image in their children.

"Life has a way of battering your self-image. It would be helpful to come home and be built back up by your parents. Unfortunately, that never happened in our family. We never seemed to do anything good enough to get our parents' approval. Even if we did do it good enough, we never heard about it. It would have been nice to hear that we were doing a good job."

When I was in the ninth grade, I wanted badly to be a basketball player. Every day after school, I went to the outdoor basketball court near the church and practiced for several hours. After a great deal of work, I found myself becoming better each day, and I actually became a legend in my own mind. By the time basketball season started and our ward began to practice together as a team, I felt very confident that I was going to be the star player. Our coach (who had never played basketball before) had watched me enough to know that I was the best player on the team. Before our first game, he gave us what I thought was a great pep talk. He said, "Okay, guys, if you want to win this game, you are going to have to give the ball to Randal and let him shoot. If he misses, get the rebound, pass it back to him, and let him shoot again." I thought to myself, "This coach is a genius." I was excited to show off my superior basketball ability.

Our ward (Williamson) was out in the country, and our players didn't have as much money as the members in the city ward (Beaumont) we were going to play. Their entire team had matching uniforms and nice Converse All-Star basketball shoes. None of our players had basketball shorts or jerseys, and only two starters even had basketball shoes. Two other players went barefoot, and I wore my scuffed-up Sunday shoes, which I also wore Monday through Saturday. As we began warming up before the game, the opposing coach complained to the officials that my hard-soled shoes were scuffing up the gym floor. After some discussion, I became the third member of our starting lineup playing barefoot.

When the game started, I excitedly followed the coach's advice. On offensive plays, I dribbled the ball down the court and shot every time I got near the basket. If my teammates got a rebound, they passed the ball back to me, and I shot again. I was also excited because there was a young lady in the stands I really wanted to impress. What better way to do this than for her to see I was the star of the team. As the game progressed, I continued shooting the ball over and over again. I heard one of my teammates' fathers screaming at me, "Pass the ball off!" but I ignored him, assuming he was jealous, and followed my coach's pregame instructions to shoot every time I touched the ball. I decided his son was given the same opportunity to practice each day, and it certainly was not my fault he had failed to do so. Into the second quarter, I discovered I had a problem. Not used to going without shoes, my feet formed huge, painful blisters. Finally, with about two minutes left in the game, the pain became so intense, I had no choice but to ask the coach to take me out. The first time my replacement got the ball, he made a jump shot and scored two points. The crowd roared with excitement. The final score that day was Beaumont 52, Williamson 2. My replacement scored the only points for our team.

Needless to say, I was humiliated by my off day. With my self-esteem very low, I dreaded going to church the next day and having to face those who witnessed or heard about the game. I wished one of my parents had attended the game to offer some encouraging words to build me back up.

Of course, these confidence-killing experiences continue for all of us throughout life. During my first year in college, I had another serious blow to my self-esteem. English was an especially painful experience for me. My professor was merciless with his red pen on everything

I turned in. It was as if he needed to show me how smart *he* really was. He never had one positive thing to say about my writing. Looking back on this experience, I admit my writing was probably not the best. My dad grew up in an alcoholic home in a Louisiana logging camp and only finished the sixth grade. My mom grew up in rural Alabama and dropped out of school in the eighth grade; because of the death of her mother, she had to care for her younger siblings. So in my home, it wasn't as if we read the *Encyclopedia Britannica* every night for story time like perhaps my smart professor's family did. From my perspective, I was happy I'd even been accepted to college. I guess it helped that it was a college with an open admission policy. I took his class to learn how to be a better writer not to be ripped to shreds on every paper I turned in. This teacher did far more to hurt my writing skills than he ever did to help improve them. I can relate to a statement by Elder H. Burke Peterson, who said, "Criticism is a destroyer of self-worth and esteem."[1]

After my freshman year, I was drafted into the US Army and had no choice but to put college on hold. I did nothing to improve my English skills during those two years. Upon returning, I attended a local college and then transferred to Brigham Young University. Although dreading the thought, I enrolled in another English class. My teacher was Dean Rigby, and I will never forget what he did for me. He talked to us from the first day as if we were great budding writers whom he was privileged to teach. He had us write a paper every week during the semester. Even though he was a very kind man, I was still terrified until I got my first paper back. I was shocked to see that it did not have one negative comment on it. Had I really gotten that much better at writing?

The next week he did the same thing. This instructor made me feel good with his encouraging comments in the margins. I actually found myself enjoying writing the third paper. The results were the same—nothing but positive comments. The fourth week was the same. The fifth week was just a little different. He still pointed out things he liked about the paper, but then he added a couple of constructive comments, such as, "You may want to check your use of . . . in this sentence." He never said I was doing it wrong; but offered a few things to think about. I greatly appreciated his feedback. This process continued for the next three weeks. During the third month and for the rest of the semester, he became more direct and specific on how I could improve my writing. His method of teaching totally changed not only my attitude toward writing, but also my self-esteem.

As I look back, I realize that my freshman English professor was not a teacher at all. He was a writing critic. Expecting me to already know how to write before I came to his class, he ripped me apart because I was not at the stage he demanded. Dean Rigby was an English teacher in every sense of the word. He built up his students and helped them believe in themselves.

Criticism kills motivation and desire in students and children. Teachers should teach and build. As parents, we are appointed to be teachers to our children, not their critics. "Wherefore, be faithful; stand in the office which I have appointed unto you; succor the weak, lift the hands which hang down, and strengthen the feeble knees" (D&C 81:5).

When your children's self-image takes a hit, it would help them for you to say, "Just because you had a bad day or a bad class doesn't make you a bad person or a failure." Unfortunately, it is often from those in our own family that our self-esteem gets damaged most. Too often criticism, nagging, ridicule, teasing, and mocking come from a sibling or even a parent. Often, family members remind us that our ears or our noses are just a little bigger than they should be. Many times it is family members who are first to laugh at us when we make a mistake or say something that wasn't well thought out. When this happens, we often feel discouraged about ourselves. We forget that self-depreciation is a sin and that we will never rise higher than the confidence we have in ourselves. How can we be truly happy if our self-worth is not what it should be?

Studies show that a child's feeling of self-worth has an influence on his behavior. Those with poor self-concepts are more likely to engage in risky or immoral behaviors. A child's self-esteem is learned, particularly when he hears others compare him in a negative or positive way. We should remember the counsel of President James E. Faust, who said, "One of the root social problems of our day concerns the lack of self-esteem."[2]

When trying to build your children's feelings of self-worth, there is always a temptation to follow the world's formula: start at an early age to seek popularity for your children, because a child's popularity will determine his self-worth. Put them in pageants and contests starting at about age four. Make sure the hefty entry fees guarantee your children large trophies for their participation. The more trophies they have in their rooms, the better they will feel about themselves. Allow them to start calling, emailing, and texting members of the opposite sex at age nine or ten and going steady about age eleven. Buy them the most expensive clothes the mall offers. Make sure they won't need to wear the same clothes twice in a month. When they turn sixteen, it is very important to buy them an expensive new sports car. Of course, they will need the freedom to come and go as they please with whomever they choose to be with. They then should be ensured a place with the most popular kids at their schools. That will give them high self-esteem. That is exactly what marketing departments would have you believe.

Unfortunately, the world's view of self-esteem usually has little to do with feelings of self-worth and everything to do with vanity. Using the world's formula for developing high self-esteem usually makes us feel even worse about ourselves. President Spencer W. Kimball stated, "The Lord's way builds individual self-esteem and develops and heals the dignity of the individual, whereas the world's way depresses the individual's view of himself and causes deep resentment."[3]

Teach Youth Who They Really Are

What can we do to build our children's feelings of self-worth? One of the most effective ways is to constantly teach our children who they really are. President Hugh B. Brown said, "If one has a vivid sense of his own divinity, he will not easily be persuaded to deprave his mind, debauch his body, or sell his freedom for temporary gain."[4]

Without the true knowledge that they are literally children of God, children may reach out for anything to help them feel better about themselves, including immorality. Sexual relations allow teens to feel attractive and worthy of another, if only for a very short period of time. Those who seek to build self-image through immorality and sin, however, soon find out how cruel the adversary's lies can be. Instead of building self-worth, sin destroys any they did have, leaving victims feeling inferior, exploited, and unloved. Those involved often quit caring about themselves, playing right into the enemy's hands. With a low self-image, they spend their lives looking for something or someone to tell them they are special.

Our children must know they are of infinite worth and that they are on the Lord's errand. President Ezra Taft Benson quoted Wilford Woodruff who said, "The Lord has chosen a small number of choice spirits of sons and daughters out of all the creations of God, who are to inherit this earth; and this company of choice spirits have been kept in the spirit world for six thousand years to come forth in the last days to stand in the flesh in this last dispensation of the fullness of times, to organize the kingdom of God upon the earth, to build it up and to defend it and to receive the eternal and everlasting priesthood [of God]."[5] This message should be ever present in our minds and one that our children hear over and over again throughout their lives.

Make Them Feel Special

While teaching a seminary in-service lesson, I asked the class to think of their favorite teacher—one who built them up and gave them confidence in themselves. Most struggled to come up with even one name. Finally, Yolanda, a convert, told us about her second grade teacher, a Catholic nun in the private school she attended. Yolanda said she decided she wanted to be a nun. I asked what the teacher did to make such an impression upon her. She said that the teacher pulled up her robes and slid down the slide with them. I was a little surprised and asked, "So, the reason she was your favorite teacher is because she would slide down the slide with you?" She responded, "No, that wasn't the real reason. I guess, she just made me feel special." Here was a compassionate teacher who knew how to build the feelings of worth in her students. President Brigham Young said, "Let us have compassion upon each other, and let the strong tenderly nurse the weak into strength, and let those who can see guide the blind until they can see the way for themselves."[6]

Another sister said her parents were her favorite teachers and they did the same thing the nun had done. She continues, "They often complimented me in front of their friends and associates. I also knew that others thought highly of me because when outsiders gave compliments, my parents always remembered to tell me about them. That

262

built my feeling of self-worth and worked well as a deterrent to the times when I thought I might do something I shouldn't." Elder Neal A. Maxwell said, "We can add to each other's storehouse of self-esteem by giving deserved, specific commendation more often, remembering, too, that those who are breathless from going the second mile need deserved praise just as the fallen need to be lifted up."[7]

Maybe one of the reasons that many have low self-esteem is that so few make the effort to make others feel special. How are you, as a parent, doing in this area? Do you make your children feel special? I have frequently pondered this statement I heard in college: "Children don't care what you do for them. They care how you make them feel." Most couldn't care less if you bought expensive clothes or a car if you do not make them feel special.

Build Others

As a bishop, I became concerned when I learned the priests were in charge of the skit for our ward campout. That evening as Jeff came out leading our daughter, Naomi, with a towel over her head, I knew that my concern was well-founded. Jeff declared, "What we have here is the world's ugliest woman. If anyone can look at her for ten seconds, we'll give you ten dollars. Who would like to try?" A couple of hands went up. These people had obviously been involved in the skit's preparation. The first person came up and slightly lifted the towel. Then with a shocked look on his face, he yelled loudly, "She's too ugly! I can't look at her!" He quickly ran away. Jeff then commented, "This woman is so ugly, we'll give someone fifty dollars to look at her for ten seconds." Another previously arranged volunteer was called out of the audience. The towel was again raised, and the boy made the expected screech of how ugly she was and ran away.

I knew we should have put adults in charge of the skits. Then Jeff cried out, "This woman is so ugly, we will give anyone one-hundred dollars if they can look at her for 10 seconds." Jeff called on one of my counselors in the bishopric, Brother Penrod, to look under the towel. I could tell, as he slowly walked toward the front, he was *not* an informed part of the skit and that he wasn't sure what was expected of him. However, he was a good sport and wanted to help make the priest's skit successful. Just like the two participants before him, he slightly lifted the towel and was about to yell, when our daughter screamed at the top of her lungs, "He's too ugly!" As she ran off, Brother Penrod was left with a puzzled expression and the towel in his hands. Of course, the ward members thought all of this was hilarious. Brother Penrod took it all in stride, and the campout continued.

After the program ended, the priests and Laurels gathered around, commenting on how they had tricked Brother Penrod. Naomi noticed one of the eleven-year-old girls in our ward standing close by, as if she wanted to talk. This young girl had a severe speech problem. When Naomi approached, the little girl said, "You not u-u-gly, you pritty!" Obviously misunderstanding the skit, she was there to build Naomi up and make her feel better about herself because she thought other ward members had made fun of her. She probably knew what it felt like to be the source of ridicule and didn't want anyone else to go through the same experience. We need to be aware of those in our own households who may be struggling with their self-worth and build them up as this young girl did.

Help Them Develop Talents

When my friend Phil and his family were moving from their home, a worker from the moving company asked his wife, "Who is this guy?" In the boxes the mover was carrying were art supplies, woodcarving tools, books written in Greek, and many other items that indicated a wide variety of interests and talents. "How can one man have so many talents?" the mover asked. Phil's wife explained that her husband had a tradition that began in his family growing up. At the beginning of every year since his teenage years, he picked a hobby or talent to work on. During the next twelve months, he concentrated on this talent, becoming very proficient. When the year was over, he picked up a new one, although he did not let his previously developed talents die. He continued to develop them when he could. Do you realize how many talents he has now after years of continuing this tradition? Once I heard him perform a beautiful and very difficult piano piece. Although he had never taken piano lessons before, he didn't let that hinder his progress. This was one of the talents he worked on for the year.

What a powerful idea! In twenty years, a person could develop twenty different talents. While not everyone needs to be proficient in a new talent every year, people do need opportunities and encouragement to develop their talents. Wise parents will expose their children to a variety of activities and urge them to pursue those they seem to have an aptitude for.

Encouraging children to develop their talents is an important way to build self-worth. It doesn't seem to matter what the area of competence is, as long as it is a worthy endeavor. Proficiency adds to the feeling of value. Elder Joe J. Christensen stated, "Every child should be helped to develop some skill or talent by which he or she can experience success and thus build self-esteem."[8]

While searching the scriptures and Church history, I have been impressed with the men and women who had the self-image and determination to stand up to the pressures of the world. They all developed their talents. I am especially impressed with Nephi and his willingness to stand up and face challenges, no matter what the opposition. He was probably able to go and do what the Lord commanded because he had developed a high self-esteem gained through his many talents. Not only did he personally refine the ore and make metal plates on which he wrote, but he also knew the Hebrew and Egyptian languages and reformed the Egyptian for recording on the plates (1 Nephi 1:2). He made a bow of wood when his steel bow broke (1 Nephi 16:23). He was a skilled hunter who did "slay wild beasts" (1 Nephi 16:31). He fashioned metal tools to build a ship of exceedingly fine workmanship (1 Nephi 17:16). He established a city, built a temple, and taught his people to build buildings and to work with gold, silver, brass, copper, iron, steel, and wood. He made weapons for the defense of his people, using the sword of Laban for a guide (2 Nephi 5:14). Nephi obviously worked hard to develop his talents.

Many of the great Book of Mormon leaders possessed similar talents and skills, including those who finally closed out the record. Moroni passed the knowledge of these great men to Joseph Smith. He became a modern-day Nephi who did whatever the Lord commanded him to do without complaint. He kept records, was a military leader, mayor, city builder, scriptorian, linguist, translator, temple builder, Church president, colonizer, public speaker, and great leader. The Lord wants us to develop our talents, use them to build the kingdom, and feel good about ourselves in the process. President Brigham Young said,

"Every man and woman who has talent and hides it will be called a slothful servant. Improve day by day upon the capital you have. In proportion as we are capacitated to receive, so it is our duty to do."[9]

Get On the Lord's Side

However, it was not just the developing of talents that helped these great leaders have feelings of self-worth. They realized the most powerful builder of self-esteem comes when we are on the Lord's side. Elder Hartman Rector Jr. said, "When I'm on the Lord's side, keeping the basic commandments, I feel good about me, I esteem myself as a worthy child of God, and I find I am very positive."[10]

Helping our children get on the Lord's side will be the greatest thing we can possibly do to build the self-worth they need to fight their individual battles. Elder W. Don Ladd said, "The most important thing we can do—young or old—is develop a personal relationship with Jesus Christ. If we do, we will always be comfortable with ourselves. Any questions of self-esteem and self-worth will diminish, and we will have a quiet confidence that will see us through any trial."[11]

Notes

1   H. Burke Peterson, "Preparing the Heart," *Ensign*, May 1990, 83.

2   James E. Faust , in Conference Report, April 1981, 8.

3   Spencer W. Kimball, in Conference Report, April 1976, 124.

4   Hugh B. Brown, in Conference Report, October 1969, 106.

5   Wilford Woodruff, "Our Lineage," *Utah Genealogical Society Handbook*, 1933, Lesson 1, 4.

6   Brigham Young, "The Kingdom of God," *Journal of Discourses*, 10:213, June 14, 1863

7   Neal A. Maxwell, in Conference Report, October 1976, 16.

8   Joe J. Christensen, in Conference Report, October 1993, 14.

9   Brigham Young, "Influence of God's Spirit Upon Mankind," *Journal of Discourses*, 7:7, July 3, 1859.

10   Hartman Rector Jr., in Conference Report, April 1979, 41.

11   W. Don Ladd, in Conference Report, October 1994, 37.

SPIRITUAL
EXPERIENCES

MISTAKE: Failure to take full advantage of inspired Church-sponsored programs.

"I feel like our family did not take our religion seriously. It seemed like we were members in name only. We never had regular family home evenings, scripture study or prayers together. I wonder sometimes how our lives would have been different if my parents would have made those things a priority."

My brother Jack and his wife have eleven children, and they raised them in a neighborhood with many other children. Years ago, a ten-year-old boy named Chuckie lived close by. He was what our society would call a latchkey kid. While his mother worked, he watched TV, played video games, or roamed the neighborhood looking for someone to play with and ways to occupy his time alone. He was not provided with many opportunities to have consistent parental teaching nor exposure to spiritual experiences. Most families in the neighborhood tried to include him and treat him with kindness.

There were obvious times, however, when families needed to be alone. One Monday night, Jack told Chuckie they needed to have family home evening together as a family. The little boy got the message and began to walk in the direction of his own home. Jack could hear Chuckie's voice as he walked away. He said, "Come on, boy, let's go have family home dog." When I heard about this experience, I thought, "If this little boy doesn't have some spiritual training, he is going to go to the dogs!" When Chuckie reached adulthood, he struggled greatly. When children are not blessed with spiritual training and experiences, they struggle to fight off the worldly temptations we all face. There are many ways to provide our families with spiritual experiences to help keep them safe in these troubling times. Let's briefly discuss a few of these.

Family Home Evening

The prophets have repeatedly appealed to parents to hold meaningful family home evenings. President Spencer W. Kimball said we should "turn off the TV and radio, leave the telephone unanswered, cancel all calls or appointments, and spend a warm, homey evening together."[1]

Too many fail to follow this counsel for various reasons and, therefore, miss tremendous promised blessings. One Monday night, a friend went to his mother's home to check on her. She was an old widow at the time and in very bad health. When he walked in, he was surprised to find her alone at the kitchen table reading from the family home evening manual. He asked, "Mother, what are you doing?" She replied, "I am having family home evening." Surprised, he said, "You can't hold family home evenings by yourself." Her answer has stayed with me over the years. She said, "Who am I to question the Lord?"

President Harold B. Lee made one of the greatest promises ever given to families when he said, "If you will have your family home evenings and teach your children in the home, the promise has been made that there won't be one in a hundred that will ever go astray."[2] In a time when we are losing hundreds of thousands of our youth to the world, perhaps it is time we took advantage of this wonderful promise.

Elder Dallin H. Oaks stated, "It is a striking fact that the family home evening is the ideal time to accomplish almost every type of family togetherness. It is the ideal place for the family to pray together, learn together, counsel together, play together, and even work together. Most of us recognize this, but I wonder how many of us are really using the Family Home Evening to its full potential."[3]

Family Prayer

Close your eyes for a moment and think back on how often your parents gathered the family together for meaningful prayers. One day, your own children will reflect back on how prayer was used in your home. What will they say? Many of our best families in the Church do not have consistent family prayer and miss out on a tremendous power that is available. In the study of effective Mormon families, only 29 percent said that they always had daily prayers.[4] If 71 percent of our best families do not always have daily prayers, you would think that other families pray together even less.

Perhaps the neglect of this commandment is one of the reasons we are losing family members to the world. President Heber J. Grant said, "The Lord has called upon us to pray with our families and in secret, that we may not forget God. If we neglect this, we lose the inspiration and power from heaven; we become indifferent, lose our testimony, and go down into darkness."[5]

A few years ago, I attended a fast and testimony meeting where Tammy bore her testimony about the importance of family prayer. She had grown up in a less active family and married outside the church. Later, she became activated and her husband ultimately joined the Church. She was sealed to her husband and children eight days before bearing this inspiring testimony. In closing, she shared an experience from their family home evening the week they were sealed. Their topic that week was temples and the eternal nature of families who are sealed together and remain faithful. Their five-year-old daughter, Brittney, had several questions about the temple and being a forever family. At the close of the evening, Brittney was asked to offer the closing prayer. Her mother recounted that Brittney bowed her head and asked, "Heavenly Father, is it true? Can we really be a family forever?" After she had said those words, the room became totally silent. After a very long pause, her parents wondered if she had gone to sleep. Peeking at her, they saw she still had her head bowed and seemed to be thinking of what to say next, so they remained silent and patiently waited. Several minutes passed, and still Brittney said nothing. Finally, she opened her eyes, looked up at her parents, and said, "It's true. We really can be a family forever. Heavenly Father talked to me and told me we could." I'll never forget the warm feeling that came over me when I contemplated the eternal truth that families really can be together forever and the power that comes to a family when they pray together. This family learned firsthand that Heavenly Father really does answer prayers of faith for those willing to wait patiently for the answer.

No wonder Elder John H. Groberg said, "I appeal with all the fervor of my soul to every family in the Church, every family in the nation, every family in the world, to organize your priorities so that God is first in your lives and to show this by having regular family prayer. There may be extenuating circumstances occasionally; but as a rule, we should have family prayer every morning and every evening."[6]

Temple Attendance

Recently, I attended a gospel doctrine class where we discussed the importance of temple work. The teacher asked how we could help our families gain a stronger testimony of temple work. After several comments, I suggested we take family temple trips where every family member over age twelve visited the temple regularly to do baptisms for our own kindred dead. I commented that we often wait on the ward to provide these opportunities and miss out on the spiritual experiences that can come to our family members by doing this as a family. The teacher, the parent of two teenagers, looked shocked and said, "You mean that parents and children over twelve can go to the temple and do baptisms for their own family names?" This father thought the only time youth could attend the temple was during the twice-a-year ward YM/YW temple trips.

Early convert Benjamin Franklin Cummings recorded, "Concerning the work for the dead, (Joseph) said that in the resurrection those who had been worked for, would fall at the feet of those who had done their work, kiss their feet, embrace their knees and manifest the most exquisite gratitude."[7]

A Beehive girl in our Utah ward named Jessica went to the temple every Saturday with her family to do baptisms for deceased family members. One day in testimony meeting this young girl stood and shared a profound insight. She said, "When I am in the temple I feel like I never want to do anything wrong in my life." I can't think of many places where a young lady and her family can go to produce this kind of blessing.

President Gordon B. Hinckley made a wonderful promise to those who regularly attend the temple. He said, "If there were more temple work done in the Church, there would be less of selfishness, less of contention, less of demeaning others. The whole Church would increasingly be lifted to greater heights of spirituality, love for one another, and obedience to the commandments of God."[8]

Church History Sites

Abraham is a figure revered by Muslims, Jews, and Christians alike as a righteous prophet. He lived over four thousand years ago. His story is found in the Bible as well as the Quran (the Muslim holy book). Muslims believe Abraham escorted one of his wives, Hagar, and their son Ishmael to a barren area in Arabia and left them there, trusting that God would care for them. The area grew first into a small settlement and then into the city of Makkah, or modern day Mecca, in Saudi Arabia. To commemorate the trials of Abraham and his family in Makkah, including Abraham's willingness to sacrifice his son in response to God's command, modern-day Muslims from all over the world make a pilgrimage to the sacred city at least once in their lifetime. Before arriving in the holy city, Muslims remove their worldly clothes and dress in humble, all white attire. They believe that white clothes are symbolic of human equality and unity before God. Obviously, this once-in-a-lifetime pilgrimage has a tremendous effect on those who participate. Is it a coincidence that very few Muslims ever leave the faith?

Perhaps we could learn lessons about holding onto our families from the faithful of Islam. I have always been amazed at how few of our members take advantage of the tremendous spiritual experiences available at our sacred Church history sites in the East. Although most have been to Temple Square in Salt Lake City, few seem to have been to Kirtland, Adam-ondi-Ahman, Nauvoo, the Carthage Jail, the Sacred Grove, Peter Whitmer Farm, John Johnson Farm, and the Hill Cumorah. By not taking trips to these sacred sites, we miss out on tremendous spiritual experiences that help build testimonies.

A few years ago, after carefully saving our money, our entire family took a trip to the eastern United States. We went to an amusement park in Pennsylvania, a Broadway show in New York City, the museums and monuments of Washington D.C., the Joseph Smith birthplace in Vermont, and all of the major Church history sites in the East. The trip included camping, nightly games, lots of laughter, and pleasant memories. As we were coming home, my wife and I asked our two youngest daughters what their favorite part of the trip was. One said the Sacred Grove, and the other said the Washington D.C. Temple. There we were able to do baptisms for the dead with the two girls while everyone else went through an endowment session. Isn't it interesting that neither Broadway nor an amusement park came to their mind? I then asked myself what my favorite experience of the trip was. I loved everything about the trip, but my most memorable experience was seeing a daughter-in-law kneeling in prayer in the Sacred Grove and then wiping tears from her eyes. That alone would have made it worth all the sacrifice and expense that the trip required.

Several years ago, Elder Hugh W. Pinnock accompanied President Gordon B. Hinckley on a tour of the major Church history sites. Speaking to the staff, cast, and crew of the Hill Cumorah Pageant, Elder Pinnock said, "You have helped to create memories that will never die. Your dedication and spirit of service will be felt by all who attend. Forty-five years ago, while I was still in high school, my parents brought their three children to visit the Church history sites. The memory of those experiences burns brightly today."[9]

Seminary and Institute

If I were to tell you there is a program that would almost guarantee that your children would remain morally clean, go on missions, marry in the temple, and remain faithful in the gospel, would you make sure they took advantage of it? There is just such a program. And while many in the Church do take advantage of it, far too many fail to realize the tremendous power of this program. We are speaking of the seminary and institute program! Look closely at the promises that President Spencer W. Kimball made concerning this program: "In my stake conference meetings with the bishoprics and stake presidencies and high councils, I have insisted that if they would see that the young people attended the seminaries and institutes, that you would almost guarantee their morality and worthiness, and that they would fill missions, marry in the temple, and live beautiful LDS lives."[10]

When I first read that statement, I decided to find out for myself if it was true. I started to follow the LDS kids in one high school in Texas over a ten-year span to determine if attending seminary and institute produced the promised blessings. There were 168 young men and young women who graduated during this ten-year period. Of the LDS boys who graduated from seminary, ninety-five percent went on missions and ninety-six percent who married actually did so in the temple. Of the LDS boys who did not graduate from seminary, only nine percent went on missions and only three percent who married, did so in the temple. Of the girls who were seminary graduates and married, sixty-eight percent were in the temple. For the non-seminary graduates, only seven percent of these girls who married, did so in the temple. Some may wonder why the girls who graduated from seminary had a much lower rate of temple marriage than the boys. I do not claim to know the answer, but I believe it has something to do with the boys having such close shepherding after high school from leaders preparing them for missions. One thing I did find, however, is that of the thirty-two percent of the girls who did not marry in the temple, not one was enrolled in institute at the time of their marriage. Remember President Kimball said that the guarantee only applied to those who attend the "seminaries *and institutes.*" In the first ten years that I have been with the institute program in Austin, Texas, we have had several hundred marriages among our students. During that time, ninety-eight percent of those who were taking institute classes at the time of their engagement married in the temple.

If you want to marry a basketball player, you should probably hang out at the gym. If you want to marry a swimmer, you should stay close to the pool. But where is the best place for LDS young single adults to meet their eternal companions? President Gordon B. Hinckley said, "Every college and university student should take advantage of the institute program. It is the best place in the world to find your eternal mate, and you will be grateful all your lives if you do."[11]

I know the Church Educational Program can bless the lives of those who participate. It has blessed my own family greatly. Four of my five children married spouses who were actively attending the institute where I teach when they were courting. The other couple met at BYU. However, there are many more blessings that are also associated with attending seminary and institute. Elder L. Tom Perry said, "I would like to add my testimony to that of our great prophet-leader. I know the power that comes from associations in the . . . institute programs.

It has enriched my life, and I know it will do the same for you. It will put a shield of protection around you to keep you free from the temptations and trials of the world. There is a great blessing in having a knowledge of the gospel. And I know of no better place for the young people of the Church to gain a special knowledge of sacred things than in the institute . . . programs of the Church."[12]

Church Youth Programs

Years ago, I heard a local priesthood leader express his opinion that youth conferences, stake dances, and programs like Especially for Youth were not needed because it was the family's role to provide activities for youth. I could hardly believe what I was hearing, and two thoughts occurred to me. First, there are some things that even families cannot provide; and second, his four beautiful daughters were going to be in danger because they were not socially involved with other youth in the stake. Who would they go with to prom, and so on? The girls are all married now, and much to this father's surprise, not one married in the temple, and three of the four married outside the Church. Why do you suppose the Church provides youth conferences, stake dances, and other youth activities? All of these things provide a safe environment for our youth to learn how to interact and have fun with those with similar beliefs.

Some optional programs for youth, like EFY, are provided by the Church Educational System as a supplement to the official Church youth programs. This program has had a huge impact on my own family. I have worked with the program for twenty years and can truthfully say that I have never seen anything provide such a spiritual boost in such a short period of time. My own children have attended EFY—most multiple times. Some members complain that this program costs money. Of course it does. It also costs money to have your children at home for a week. We have always made some of these optional activities a part of our family budget. It costs money for food, clothes, visits to dentists and doctors. It costs money for tuition, books, car insurance, and so on. Why not say that occasionally it costs money for our children to have spiritual experiences? Ask yourself how much the following experience is worth.

Chelsey had a chance to attend an Especially for Youth program in

Texas, and she took full advantage of the opportunity. Although she comes from a large family and money is tight, she worked hard to earn the money to go. Like others, she went to meet new friends and to have fun. But that wasn't her main reason for attending. She wanted to learn more about the Savior. Because she went with that intent, her desire was fulfilled. She wrote the following letter after the event:

> EFY was the best spiritual experience I've had in my whole life, other than the temple trips I've made. The classes were extremely inspirational. Each class seemed to help me with different problems I was having. I know what they mean about being at the right place at the right time. Things that I've been hearing all my life just seemed to make more sense when I heard them at EFY. For example, I heard, 'When ye have done it unto the least of these my brethren, ye have done it unto me' in one of the talks. For some reason it seemed to take on a different meaning. I've always thought it applied to service, but I realized that when we are mean to a person, it's like we're being mean to Christ. After I thought about it, it really made me want to be nicer, sweeter, and more compassionate toward people. While I was there, we got to watch two slide shows about Christ, and it had beautiful music playing with it. I don't guess I've ever realized how much Jesus really loves me as an individual until I saw these slide shows. It made me want to try harder to get back to him. It just gives me chills to think about him embracing me and saying, 'Well done, thou good and faithful servant.' I think that EFY helped me realize how much harder I need to work to be able to live with him again. I love my Savior with all my heart, and there's nothing I'd rather do than spend eternity with my family and with God in the celestial kingdom. The testimony meeting was really spiritual. It just seemed to pull us all closer together. EFY was one of the best experiences I've had in my whole life.[13]

This program has such a tremendous effect on the youth who attend that you can almost pick out the ones who have attended when you visit with the youth of a stake.

Youth Conference

Youth conferences can also have a powerful spiritual impact on our children. When I first met Adam, I misjudged him badly. I thought because of his stylish clothes and hairstyle, he was at the youth conference for all the wrong reasons. But I was wrong. Although he had come to the conference to have fun and meet new people, he had also come seeking a testimony. He sincerely wanted to learn. Because he was where he was supposed to be for the right reasons, he got the peace he sought. After one of the youth conference speakers had spoken on the life of Christ, this young man decided he must do as Joseph Smith had done. When he returned home from the conference, he prayed for divine guidance. He wrote a poem that described his experience and shared it with me.

> *Tonight I felt something I've never felt*
> *While at bedside on my knees I knelt*
> *To the Father, a silent prayer I dealt.*
> *My knees hit the floor, and the bed gave a squeak.*
> *The flesh was willing but the spirit was weak.*
> *In the silent night, I heard my mind speak:*
> *Our Father in heaven—Canst thou hear my prayer?*
> *Does my muffled cry pierce thy heavenly air?*
> *Canst thou lift me from my earthly care?*
>
> *Did thy son to the world of old descend?*
> *Has thy church been restored to the earth again?*
> *Is it true what they say? That's all—amen.*
> *Does God really exist? Would an answer come?*
> *Could my feeble prayer reach his mighty kingdom?*
> *Could an infidel receive revelation?*
> *In the silent night, I yawned and sighed,*
> *Then an answer came as a peaceful tide.*
> *My heart did swell and hours I cried.*
> *The confusion fled, and all my doubts died.*
> *I had prayed with faith as the scriptures had said.*
> *Oh, that feeling forever—that prayer in my head*
> *Our Father in Heaven—tonight by my bed.*[14]

Because Adam went to that youth conference, he was touched by the Spirit and was prompted to pray. Because of his prayer, he learned for himself that the gospel has been restored and of the existence of God, just as the scriptures had promised.

Attending inspiring Church-sponsored programs can be a great help in gaining and strengthening testimonies. The Church youth programs are tremendous supplements to the family in helping youth stay on the straight and narrow path. We just need to make sure that our children take advantage of these wonderful programs.

Notes

1   Spencer W. Kimball, *Faith Precedes the Miracle* (Salt Lake City, UT: Deseret Book, 1972), 111.

2   Harold B. Lee, BYU Sixth Stake Quarterly Conference, April 27, 1969.

3   Dallin H. Oaks, "Parental Leadership in the Family," *Ensign*, June 1985, 11.

4   William G. Dyer and Phillip R. Kunz, *Effective Mormon Families* (Salt Lake City, UT: Deseret Book, 1986), 12.

5   Heber J. Grant, *Gospel Standards* (Salt Lake City, UT: Deseret Book, 1941), 156.

6   John H. Groberg, in Conference Report, April 1982, 76.

7   Truman G. Madsen, *Joseph Smith the Prophet* (Salt Lake City, UT: Bookcraft, 1989), 99.

8   Gordon B. Hinckley, *Teachings of Gordon B. Hinckley* (Salt Lake City, UT: Deseret Book, 1997), 622.

9   "Church Leader Visits 5 States in 4 Days," *Church News*, July 20, 1996.

10   Edward L. Kimball, ed., *The Teachings of Spencer W. Kimball* (Salt Lake City, UT: Deseret Book, 1982), 528.

11   "Messages of Inspiration from President Hinckley," *Church News*, December 2, 1995, 5.

12   L. Tom Perry, in Conference Report, October 1997, 82.

13   Personal correspondence in author's possession.

14   Personal correspondence in author's possession.

WARNING
SIGNS

MISTAKE: Failure to recognize warning signs when youth are struggling.

"I guess looking back on it, my parents were just in denial thinking that none of their children would ever rebel. I can see now that I gave them every warning sign you can think of that I was struggling. My grades began to drop in school; I avoided the family like the plague and had no interest in anything spiritual. During all of this time my parents acted like everything was fine. Maybe they just didn't know what the warning signs were. Thank heaven they did remember to pray for me and I came back."

Several years ago, I spoke at a youth fireside about the influence of music. A few days later I received a letter from a young man named Ben who was in attendance. During the talk I referred to a specific hard rock group that I had done extensive research on during graduate school. In the letter, Ben told me that before the fireside he thought the group I had referred to was the greatest band in the world. He went on to say he had all their CDs and listened to them all the time, with their posters all over his room. He said that after the fireside, he went home and threw out the CDs and posters. I was shocked when he said in the last paragraph that he was eleven years old. I wondered why an eleven-year-old boy was allowed access to such heavy metal music and why his parents had not seen the warning signs of danger.

I wrote him back thanking him for his letter, encouraging him to stay strong and be very careful of the music he listened to. Several months later, his mother called me to talk about her son. She told me he had a very high IQ, but he had not been doing well in school. She said that since he had gotten away from the heavy metal music he was making straight A's in school. She cried some, and we had a meaningful conversation. I encouraged her to watch Ben for danger signs.

Three years later, I called to check on how the now fourteen-year-old Ben was doing. His mom was very discouraged and said he had gone back to the hard music the year before. She said that in one semester he had gone from straight As to straight Fs in school. Apparently a few months before I called, school officials had caught him buying "grass" from another boy on campus. They couldn't prosecute, though, because it turned out to be real grass (from a lawn) that had been dried to look like marijuana.

From the things his mother related, it was obvious Ben was in extreme danger. Elder David B. Haight said, "If any of you are walking in ice fields near open crevasses, do you see the warning signs? 'Danger—don't go near the edge'? Don't trifle with evil. You will lose. We pray that you will not display the somewhat arrogant attitude of some who say, 'I can handle it!' or 'Everyone else does it!' "[1]

The mother went on to say that her son had been dressing in all black since listening to the hard music and that he had painted his bedroom totally black. With each new comment, a warning sign flashed! I feared that the parents were going to lose this boy if they didn't do something quickly. Then, I was told that he had spray painted the word "anarchy" on his bedroom wall. Then, she said that she walked into his bedroom as he was carving the word "anarchy" in his leg with a knife. At that point, they admitted him into a drug rehab center, where he was housed when I called. The family was at a total loss as to how to help their son.

I have tried to keep up with this family over the years. They are good people, and I know they have spent their entire life savings trying to obtain needed help for their son. I bring this experience up not to judge, but only to say that there were warning signs that this young man was in trouble long before he went to drug rehab. We will never know if things could possibly have been different had the parents been able to read these warning signs before Ben spiraled out of control.

We often hear about signs. For example, in the Church we hear about signs of the times. They are the events that will transpire before the Second Coming. In society, we hear about signs, such as the seven warning signs of cancer. The dictionary has multiple definitions for the word *signs*, but here we define it as something that gives evidence of a future event.

With youth, warning signs can alert parents of impending trouble. However, it is very difficult for parents to know all the warning signs, but experts in certain fields can help. Social scientists and law enforcement officials who study gangs can tell you which signs to watch for in children who might be involved. If your child is obsessed with a particular clothing color, prefers sagging pants or gang clothing, wears jewelry with distinguishing designs or wears it only on one side of the body, begins using hand signs with friends, is obsessed with gangster music or videos, consider these as warning signs. Experts in this field could walk into a school and point out those most likely to be involved in a gang because of the signs the experts have come to recognize.

Learn Youth Culture

Children are growing up in a very different world from that of their parents. It is a world full of temptation and peril. Parents must understand the culture in which children live and learn the warning signs of danger if they are to help protect them from evil influences. Who are the heroes of our children and why? What brands of clothing or jewelry do they want to buy and why? What types of music are they listening to and why? All of these details help reveal where they are spiritually and if there are signs of trouble.

As pointed out earlier, each school in America has certain groups or cliques. Walk into any lunchroom and you will see cliques sitting together. Most of these groups tend to exclude those not in the group and make fun of the other groups. In a Wisconsin study, middle school students were asked to draw a map of the lunchroom and show where the different cliques sat. Most of the lunchroom maps matched as the students identified where the preps, jocks, geeks, nerds, and skaters sat for lunch. This is a sad phenomenon because it destroys the unity that could exist. It is reminiscent of what happened in the Book of Mormon when the "people were divided one against another; and they did separate one from another into tribes" (3 Nephi 7:2).

Perhaps you are wondering why it is so important for parents to know that cliques exist in our schools. Within each of these cliques are expected behaviors and attitudes. Ask any high school student to tell you how an emo, goth, skater, or hick dresses. Now ask them what kind of music these groups listen to and what behaviors they engage in. They won't even have to think in order to answer your questions. They see it in living color every day.

Perhaps you are thinking that this is stereotyping and does not reflect reality. Then perhaps you should ask a high school student if a cowboy (hick) is more likely to drink beer, listen to country music, wear western clothes, drive a pickup truck, and have a smokeless tobacco ring than someone who listens to heavy metal.

If certain behaviors can be expected within certain groups, then we need to know which groups our children belong to. By taking the time to learn what our youth are involved in, we can recognize warning signs and know when intervention is needed.

One father of several teenagers told me with great pride that he didn't know one thing about the youth culture and that he thought it a waste of his time to inform himself about such nonsense. In today's permissive society, this father's lackadaisical attitude can be extremely dangerous. It may take some effort to become informed of the warning signs, but it could be the action that saves your child. If you catch cancer when the warning signs first appear, there is a much better chance of a cure. It is the same with the cancers of temptation that our children are exposed to.

Reading signs is always tricky, and we may misread the situation on occasion. I remember one day sitting at a red light next to a big passenger van with multiple windows. One of the guys sitting next to a window was drinking what appeared to be a soft drink. Our daughter Naomi, who was seven at the time, looked at the man and said, "Dad, look at that guy drinking a big ol' glass of marijuana!" Naomi didn't know how to read signs very well, so she misread the situation. If we do not do our homework about reading warning signs, we may not be able to discern when our youth are really headed for trouble.

Warning Signs

Recently, I surveyed a large number of LDS teachers who work with teenagers on a daily basis. I asked them to reply to a simple question: What are the warning signs that indicate a young person may be headed for trouble? While this list is by no means comprehensive, it may help us be aware of potential problems. The signs are listed in no particular order of importance.

- **Lethargy**—sleeping patterns change; stays up late, sleeps late with little motivation when awake
- **Heroes**—involvement with worldly heroes such as rock stars; a desire to attend their concerts, read about them, and have their posters on bedroom walls
- **Countenance Change**—a change in their countenance; seems to reflect gloom; refuses to look you in the eyes
- **Behavior Change**—an unexplained change in their normal behavior, such as extreme emotional mood swings
- **Being Disrespectful**—talks back and is disrespectful to parents, teachers, or leaders
- **Contentious**—exhibits a contentious attitude with frequent heated disagreements with family members
- **Irritability**—very easily irritated; overreacts to even mild criticism, especially from family members
- **Rejects Counsel**—resentful; rejects any kind of counsel or even feedback from parents, teachers, or Church leaders
- **Excessive Time with Media**—spends excessive time with music, television, movies, teen magazines, Internet, chat rooms, or video games
- **Excessive Phone Time**—excessive time spent on phone talking or text messaging friends; secretive phone calls
- **Style/Appearance**—overly concerned about appearance; a desire for the latest fashions; has obsession with appearance and weight
- **Unconcerned about Hygiene**—very careless or unconcerned about personal appearance and hygiene
- **Questions Church Teachings**—openly questions Church teachings, especially modesty, piercings, music, curfews, movies, or dating guidelines

- **Attitude toward Church**—not attentive; late or missing church; negative comments about how boring it is
- **Weak Relationship with Leaders**—poor relationships with and talks badly about their Church teachers and leaders
- **Sacred Becomes Casual**—a noticeable lack of appreciation for the sacred values that were once embraced
- **Family Religious Activities**—a lack of interest or even dislike for activities, such as family home evening, prayer and scripture study; often making derogatory comments
- **Friends More Important**—noticeable family disconnect; wants to spend all free time hanging out with friends
- **Breaking Family Rules**—frequently breaks established family rules, such as curfew or dating rules
- **Increased Seclusion**—a decline in participation in family activities; increased time spent secluded in their bedrooms when they are home
- **Dating Practices**—involved in going steady, underage dating, single dating, or dating those with different beliefs
- **Popularity Seeking**—overly concerned about popularity at school and peer approval
- **Preoccupation with Opposite Sex**—talking endlessly about members of the opposite sex
- **Change of Friends**—hangs out with friends with questionable standards; friends who are older than they are
- **Evasive, Vague, or Dishonest**—vague about or refuses to say where they have been, what they have been doing, or just outright dishonest about their activities
- **Question and Complain**—complains about almost everything; use phrases like "you are always trying to force me to . . ."
- **Risk Taker**—enjoys taking risks such as sneaking out with friends, skipping school, driving fast, drinking, smoking
- **Lack Self-Confidence**—a sudden loss of self-esteem and a lack of self-confidence in things they once excelled in
- **Changes at School**—a change at school, such as grades dropping, tardiness, truancy, or other disciplinary problems
- **Language Change**—uses street language or language that seems strange or that you are not familiar with
- **Loss of Interest**—exhibits a diminished interest in favorite activities, hobbies, sports, talents

- **Graffiti**—displays graffiti or strange drawings in their bedrooms or on items such as posters or books
- **Poor Attitude**—a general "I don't care" attitude about life in general

Of course, some of these warning signs may be exhibited and will turn out to be false signals or just growing pains. However, just as some of the cancer warning signs may turn out to be benign, it would be very unwise to ignore them. The more warning signs a child exhibits, the greater the chance that something truly is wrong.

To recognize the warning signs of our day, the Spirit must guide parents. President Hugh B. Brown said, "As with the road signs on the highway where you notice certain reflector signs which are visible only if the lights of your own car are shining upon them, so on life's highway there are many warning signs and signals, but the light of the Spirit must flash upon them else they may be invisible and therefore disregarded with serious consequences."[2]

Notes

1 David B. Haight, "Spiritual Crevasses," *Ensign*, November 1986, 36.

2 Hugh B. Brown, *The Abundant Life* (Salt Lake City, UT: Bookcraft, 1965), 228.

HOPE AND HELP FOR HURTING
PARENTS

After an Education Week class, I received the following note from a faithful mother of the Church. My heart went out to this good sister and all parents who have endured the pain that follows when a child rebels against God's commandments. For her, the counsel to prepare and prevent is past. Her family must learn to deal with the problem. She said, "My husband and I are active Church members. We love our kids, and we show it. We have regular family prayers and family home evenings, and we attend church together. Our problem is that our oldest daughter has chosen to be immoral. She still attends Church and appears perfectly whole to those who don't know, and no one knows except my husband and me and the Bishop. We are crushed, because she doesn't feel it is wrong because she is 'in love.' We have become aware of how rampant immorality has become within our ward and stake. But no one addresses the parents who are dying inside. What do we do?"[1]

Parents of rebellious children often think of themselves as failures. They deal with guilt and discouragement. They blame themselves for what occurred and let these feelings seriously disrupt their lives, when in fact they have done their best.

Some parents have made blatant errors in their personal lives, making almost every mistake discussed in this book, yet still have children who are on the right path. On the other hand, many righteous parents who love the Lord and do everything in their power to serve others live with the nightmare of wayward children. A great lesson can be learned from the inspired words of President Howard W. Hunter:

> A successful parent is one who has loved, one who has sacrificed, and one who has cared for, taught, and ministered to the needs of a child. If you have done all of these and your child is still wayward or troublesome or worldly, it could well be that you are, nevertheless, a successful parent. Perhaps there are children who have come into the world that would challenge any set of parents under any set of circumstances. Likewise, perhaps there are others who would bless the lives of, and be a joy to, almost any father or mother.[2]

We must remember that righteous children may have done what's right in any environment and rebellious children may have gone against God's commandments in any home. Regardless of why youth have gone astray, it is our duty to try to bring them back. Not only should we be helping our own youth, but we need to do everything in our power to help wayward youth of friends and neighbors. Sometimes a friend can have more influence than a family member. In the Book of Mormon, the prophet Alma realized at some point that he had little or no influence on his rebellious son Alma. There must have been many sleepless nights as he prayed for a miracle for his son. His prayers were answered, and the miracle turned out to be the appearance of an angel who convinced him of the error of his ways. Alma the Younger, of course, went on to become one of the greatest missionaries in world history. Perhaps you will be the angel to someone else's child who is struggling. Look around your ward and befriend a child who may have lost the way.

Over the years, inspired leaders have given inspiring words to those who have wayward children. These statements often bring comfort to the parents of those who are struggling. The following two are among my favorites:

President Boyd K. Packer: "Now parents, I desire to inspire you with hope. You who have heartache, you must never give up. No matter how dark it gets or no matter how far away or how far down your son or daughter has fallen, you must never give up. Never, never, never. . . . God bless you heartbroken parents.

There is no pain so piercing as that caused by the loss of a child, nor joy so exquisite as the joy at his redemption."[3]

Elder Orson F. Whitney: "You parents of the willful and the wayward! Don't give them up. Don't cast them off. They are not utterly lost. The Shepherd will find his sheep. They were his before they were yours—long before he entrusted them to your care; and you cannot begin to love them as he loves them. They have but strayed in ignorance from the Path of Right, [but] God is merciful to ignorance. Only the fullness of knowledge brings the fullness of accountability. Our Heavenly Father is far more merciful, infinitely more charitable, than even the best of his servants, and the Everlasting Gospel is mightier in power to save than our narrow finite minds can comprehend."[4]

During the summer of 1990, I was asked to direct a session of Especially for Youth in Williamsburg, Virginia, at the College of William and Mary. It was an incredible experience for me. Several times I asked myself why I was chosen to be over this great group of youth, since there were so many brethren more qualified. In attendance were youth from twenty-seven different states, many of whom were the only members of the Church in their high schools. I felt tremendous pressure to help make the week an unforgettable experience. I felt tremendous responsibility to invite the Spirit into the Thursday night fireside that I was assigned to present to the youth. The more I thought about it, the more apprehensive I became. On the day of the fireside, I asked one of the returned missionary counselors if he would give me a priesthood blessing. Although I had given hundreds of talks in the past, I had never before made such a request. During the blessing, he said something that I will never forget: "Many other brethren wanted to have this experience." I had realized this. He continued, "Many are as qualified as you, but the Lord wants you to do it." I can't tell you what that did to me. I was very humbled by these words. I still don't know why I had that privilege, but I am thankful I did.

Why do I mention that very personal experience? Because some of us wonder why we are called to be parents to the children we have. They could have been sent to a number of quality parents. Some may even be more qualified than we are. But the Lord wants us to have the children we have. He sent them to us for a reason. Our job is to teach them the gospel, love them, and live the gospel ourselves. If we will do that, the future looks bright no matter what we go through up until that time. During times of discouragement, remember the words of Elder Orson F. Whitney.

> The Prophet Joseph Smith declared—and he never taught more comforting doctrine—that the eternal sealings of faithful parents and the divine promises made to them for valiant service in the Cause of Truth, would save not only themselves, but likewise their posterity. Though some of the sheep may wander, the eye of the Shepherd is upon them, and sooner or later they will feel the tentacles of Divine Providence reaching out after them and drawing them back to the fold. Either in this life or the life to come, they will return. They will have to pay their debt to justice; they will suffer for their sins; and may tread a thorny path; but if it leads them at last, like the penitent Prodigal, to a loving and forgiving father's heart and home, the painful experience will not have been in vain. Pray for your careless and disobedient children; hold on to them with your faith. Hope on, trust on, till you see the salvation of God.[5]

Notes

1   Personal correspondence in author's possession.
2   Howard W. Hunter, in Conference Report, October 1983, 94.
3   Boyd K. Packer, in Conference Report, October 1970, 122.
4   Orson F. Whitney, in Conference Report, April 1929, 110.
5   Ibid.

INDEX